Professional Discourse

Continuum Discourse Series
Series Editor: Professor Ken Hyland, Institute of Education, University of London.

Discourse is one of the most significant concepts of contemporary thinking in the humanities and social sciences as it concerns the ways language mediates and shapes our interactions with each other and with the social, political and cultural formations of our society. The *Continuum Discourse Series* aims to capture the fast-developing interest in discourse to provide students, new and experienced teachers and researchers in applied linguistics, ELT and English language with an essential bookshelf. Each book deals with a core topic in discourse studies to give an in-depth, structured and readable introduction to an aspect of the way language in used in real life.

Other titles in the series (forthcoming):

Academic Discourse
Ken Hyland

Metadiscourse: Exploring Interaction in Writing
Ken Hyland

Using Corpora in Discourse Analysis
Paul Baker

Discourse Analysis: An Introduction
Brian Paltridge

Spoken Discourse: An Introduction
Helen de Silva Joyce and Diana Slade

Media Discourse
Joanna Thornborrow

School Discourse
Learning to Write across the Years of Schooling
Frances Christie and Beverly Derewianka

Professional Discourse
Britt-Louise Gunnarsson

Professional Discourse

Britt-Louise Gunnarsson

continuum

Continuum International Publishing Group
The Tower Building   80 Maiden Lane,
11 York Road   Suite 704
London SE1 7NX   New York NY 10038

British Library Cataloguing-in-Publication Data
A catalogue record for this book is available from the British Library.

ISBN: 978-0-8264-9213-5 (hardback)
       978-0-8264-9251-7 (paperback)

Library of Congress Cataloging-in-Publication Data
The Publisher has applied for CIP data.

Typeset by Newgen Imaging Systems Pvt Ltd, Chennai, India
Printed and bound in Great Britain by MPG Books, Cornwall

Contents

Acknowledgements

This book results from a long-lasting and great research interest of mine in professional discourse. Over the years I have explored text and talk in various professional contexts and carried out several studies, both at Stockholm University and Uppsala University. Students and colleagues have been involved in many of the research projects which I have directed at these universities. I have not space to enumerate all persons in these project teams nor to list all those scholars in different parts of the world with whom I have had inspiring conversation and correspondence. Throughout the book, however, their names will appear in the text and in references.

A few names, however, should be acknowledged on this page. First I would like to express my appreciation to Ken Hyland for inviting me to write this book in *Continuum Discourse Series*. I am also grateful to David Jones for correcting my English and to Marco Bianchi for helping me with the figures and tables. Finally, my thanks go to Elving Gunnarsson for his constructive comments on the book in draft form and for his constant support and encouragement.

Section 1

Introduction

This introductory section comprises three chapters. In Chapter 1, I set out to answer a number of questions related to the topic of 'professional discourse' and to this book in particular: Why is it important to analyse professional discourse? What is professional discourse? What distinguishes professional discourse from other types of discourse? What is the purpose of this book? How is the book organized? I distinguish six set of features which are more characteristic of professional than non-professional discourse, e.g. that professional discourse is formed in a socially ordered group, dependent on various societal framework systems and dynamically changing.

These more general ideas about the topic are developed in Chapter 2 with a description of my theory of the contextual construction and reconstruction of professional discourse. The construction of professional language is explored in relation to cognitive, social and societal dimensions and its continuous reconstruction in relation to different contextual layers: the situated frame, the environmental framework and four societal frameworks. This theoretical model offers deeper understanding of how – and why – professional discourse in different domains and for different purposes varies and changes. It is the basis of the contextual analysis of the empirical studies discussed in this book.

In Chapter 3, I present a multidimensional, textlinguistic methodology which explores the dynamic relationship between text and discourse. A central tenet developed throughout the book concerns the dual relationship between professional discourse and its contextual frameworks. This relationship entails a two-sided complexity, which means that discourse, i.e. professional text and talk, should also be analysed at different levels and in relation to different types of linguistic patterns. The multidimensional methodology, which examines texts at cognitive, pragmatic and macro-thematic levels, enables in-depth analysis of diachronic and synchronic variation and change. It has been applied to large corpora and in several studies, some of which will be discussed in this book.

1 Introducing the topic and the book

Why is it important to analyse professional discourse? What is professional discourse? What distinguishes professional discourse from other types of discourse? What is the purpose of this book? How is the book organized? In the first chapter of the book, I set out to answer these questions, thus introducing the reader to the topic 'professional discourse' and to this book in particular.

1.1 Why is it important to analyse professional discourse?

Professional discourse plays a great role in modern society. It lies at the heart of the business world and the state. It is discourse that enables the creation and maintenance of organizations and institutions as groups working for common goals. Discourse is also important in the development of an open and productive internal workplace climate and for the establishment of positive external relationships with those outside the group. Good contacts with clients and customers, owners and partners, mass media, government officials and politicians are of great importance for the survival of any professional group, and written and spoken discourse forms the core of a great deal of professional activity.

Written texts, spoken discourse and various forms of non-verbal communication have all played essential parts in the (historical) creation of professional practices, and they continuously contribute to the gradual reproduction and reshaping of these practices. Though the processes are as old as the professions, the interest in the understanding of the dynamics of professional discourse is quite new and growing among researchers as well as practitioners.

Probably due to the ongoing differentiation and specialization of professions, more and more people are becoming aware of the importance of effective communication between organizations and individuals in business and government. Not only do the old academic professions, such as lawyers and doctors, rely heavily on writing and speaking skills, but language has become one of the most important tools in most working-life contexts. Meetings, negotiations and conferences have become the cornerstones of contacts between professionals and between professionals and lay people. In the majority of cases, these spoken events are intertwined with, preceded and followed by writing practices, leading to an abundant production of memos, reports, contracts, proceedings, etc. The most recent technological advance has also created new forms of communication, leading to increased demands on the communicative competence of the individual. The internet is used to spread information to large reader groups and also for more individualized interaction. Emails, telephone calls, text messages are used for person-to-person contacts, in many cases with professionals attached to call or service centres remote from the organizations that employ them and from the individuals they communicate with. The ongoing globalization of professional life has also led to increased demands on language knowledge and language skills as well as cultural openness. Contacts over language and cultural borders are a common phenomenon in large organizations and institutions. Many people's professional activities consist of an intricate interaction between people and advanced technical equipment and systems. It is also frequent for professionals to need to use several different languages during a working day.

There is without doubt a growing demand among practitioners for increased knowledge about professional discourse in real life. Organizations and institutions have become aware of the importance of efficient and adequate communication, which means that they increasingly require specialized language and communication skills. We therefore find more and more cross-disciplinary programmes, courses, workshops and conferences that focus on problems related to discourse in the professions. For teachers and trainers this has of course also led to the demand for more knowledge about discourse in authentic working-life situations. General knowledge and skills no longer suffice to handle the complexity of discourse in a globalized working life.

The growing interest among practitioners is also reflected among researchers. During the last few decades, therefore, we find a steady increase in studies of specialized language and professional discourse. We also find a gradual shift in focus, from a mainly linguistic analysis of language variation to a multidisciplinary analysis of the dynamic and context dependent character of professional language and discourse. Discourse in real life occurs in situated professional events, which in turn take place in a complex set of contextual frameworks. In order to understand how professional discourse is created and recreated in real life, we must use a multidisciplinary approach to combine our linguistic analysis with knowledge from sociology, social constructivism, cognitive psychology, organization theory, and management and media studies.

Professional discourse has thus become an important area within applied linguistics. The study of discourse in authentic professional settings has made it necessary to further develop earlier theories and methodologies. The close relationship between discourse and context in professional settings, which means that professional discourse is situated and dynamic in a way that it is possible to explore, has led to new theoretical insights about language in general as well. Studies of professional discourse have therefore led to new knowledge about how professional life functions and also about how language works in different situations and contexts.

1.2 What is professional discourse?

The term *professional discourse* will be used in this book to cover text and talk – and the intertwinement of these modalities – in professional contexts and for professional purposes. This means that professional discourse includes written texts produced by professionals and intended for other professionals with the same or different expertise, for semi-professionals, i.e. learners, or for non-professionals, i.e. lay people. It also means that it includes talk involving at least one professional. Professional will here be used in a wide sense, e.g. as a synonym to 'paid-work related'. The term will thus cover both unskilled and skilled paid jobs, i.e. both cleaners and doctors who work in a hospital, both white and blue colour staff in a factory etc.

1.3 What distinguishes professional discourse from other types of discourse?

Let us look a little closer at what professional discourse is. Fully aware of the fact that it is impossible to draw a clear-cut borderline between professional discourse and other types of discourse, I will here distinguish a set of features which more characterize professional than non-professional discourse. The following features will be discussed: (1) *Expert discourse related to different domains*, (2) *Goal-oriented, situated discourse*, (3) *Conventionalized form of discourse*, (4) *Discourse in a socially ordered group*, (5) *Discourse dependent on various societal framework systems*, and (6) *Dynamically changing discourse*.

1.3.1 Expert discourse related to different domains

Professional discourse plays an important role in the construction of knowledge related to the domain, and the language and discourse used by professionals within a field reflect their expert knowledge

5

and skills and therefore distinguishes them from experts within other fields as well as from non-experts and learners.

The expert character of professional discourse distinguishes it from private discourse, which we gradually learn from the time we are born. Whether we come to learn English, German, French or Swedish depends on whether we grow up in England, Germany, France or Sweden. Private discourse belongs to everyone in a language community, while professional discourse is owned by the members of a specific group, a specific discourse community. If we choose a specialized education and working-life career we will be taught a particular expert language and discourse, which means that we will gradually be socialized into a particular professional community. Private discourse is mainly learnt unconsciously whereas professional discourse is taught to us as part of our professional or vocational training.

Professional activities entail domain-specific knowledge and skills which are created by – and reflected in – language and discourse. Terminology, text genres, conversation patterns vary from domain to domain. Interesting research questions are therefore how different professional languages have emerged, why they became different, and how and why they have changed over time.

1.3.2 Goal-oriented, situated discourse

Professional discourse is goal-oriented. From a pragmatic perspective, all types of discourse can be analysed in relation to 'goal'. For professional discourse, however, this goal-orientation is often explicit, not seldom specified in documents.

A professional environment (a working group/an organization/an institution) is held together by a set of common goals, often specified in documents, e.g. in annual reports, mission statements, goals and strategies booklets, contracts, instructions, etc. For different professions and trades we often find job descriptions and the like.

The explicit goals are often related to actions leading to concrete results. Hospitals are supposed to cure patients who are ill, which means that the doctor should examine the patient and prescribe medicine. Courts are supposed to see that justice is done, which means that the public prosecutor should question the accused, the judge should impose a penalty, etc.

Professional discourse is also to a large extent explicitly situated. Most professional discourse takes place in situations which are specified in terms of communicative event, participants and place. This does not mean that all professional discourse is related to one particular type of situation. It means instead that each group/organization/institution establishes a set of goal-oriented professional situations and these include who communicates with whom, how and where.

Professional discourse can occur in different types of communicative events involving different constellations of participants: single person communicative events (individual writing and reading), two-person events (face to face interaction, written dialogues: letter exchange, emails, chat) and group events (small group meetings, written group correspondence, collaborative writing, collaborative presentations, discussions, large group meetings, debates). It includes both communicative events in which all participants are in the same room as well as communication at a distance, via telephone, internet, video, mail, etc.

Of course, specialized, goal-oriented situated discourse can also, and not infrequently does, lead to asymmetries between the participants in the event: between experts and lay people, between experts and learners, between experts in different areas. Asymmetries have been analysed in many studies within applied linguistics, in particular asymmetries which cause comprehension problems, e.g. in communication between experts and lay people. In order to explore comprehension problems related to knowledge gaps, different types of data have been analysed, e.g. spoken interaction between doctors and patients in hospitals, interaction between judges and witnesses in courts, lay persons' reading and comprehension of legislative texts.

1.3.3 Conventionalized form of discourse

Another feature I wish to mention here relates to the conventionalized form of professional discourse. Practices established within a profession are created to attain professional goals in specific situations, which means that they become strongly conventionalized. The doctor-patient interaction, for instance, follows an established pattern: the doctor greets the patient, asks what is wrong with the patient, asks the patient to lie down for examination, etc.

The fact that professional discourse is conventionalized distinguishes one professional group from another; we do not expect a judge to use the same type of discourse as a salesperson. The conventionalized feature is also part of what distinguishes professional discourse from private discourse; we do not expect judges to talk in court in the same way as they do when they chat with their friends over a cup of coffee. The conventionalized form of professional discourse also makes it possible to teach students, and indeed also for students to learn, how to communicate in a professionally appropriate way: among other things, education at universities/colleges and training at work have the goals of socializing the students or trainees in a suitable communicative behaviour. We can talk about a professional communicative competence which entails being able to distinguish a professional from a non-professional through their spoken and written discourse.

1.3.4 Discourse in a socially ordered group

Professional discourse is often a part of a socially organized and structured set of activities within a workplace unit. The social order within the particular workplace is created and recreated in the various communicative situations, i.e. social patterns related to power, dominance, friendship and group feeling form a part of the communicative order at work. The social and communicative orders are thus intertwined.

Small group structures are established at different levels within an organization: there is a social group structure among those who are attached to the top level of the organization as well as among those who work on the factory floor. The various groups and structures are also interrelated and interdependent. The small, close-knit working group is related to other working groups and also dependent on the other levels within the organization, e.g. on the larger workplace, on the organization as a whole, on cooperation.

The social structure entails different problem areas related to the internal communicative structure and discourse flow. Within organizations, for instance, the top-level managers need to find an appropriate discourse for direction of the organization; middle managers need to find ways to lead and communicate with their working groups, and employees need to develop their communication skills to be able to obtain influence over what they do.

Much professional discourse is the result of collaboration between professionals within the working group, between professionals from different working groups and from different levels within an organization. Professional discourse is therefore to a large extent a collective responsibility and behind many products we find sustained, collective processes, e.g. the writing of an important document, the creation of advertisement campaign, the planning of a press conference, etc.

1.3.5 Discourse dependent on various societal framework systems

What also characterizes professional discourse is its dependence on various societal framework systems. I will here distinguish four framework systems: a legal-societal framework, a technical-economical framework, a socio-cultural framework and a linguistic framework.

Beginning with the *legal-political framework*, I will focus on the fact that specific genres are attached to specific professional activities in specific situations, which often also entails conventionalized discourse patterns. In some cases these patterns are a result of internal regulations, i.e. rules controlling discourse have been issued by a board attached to the profession, the organization, the workplace, etc. In many cases, however, these patterns emanate from external regulations. The local government, the state, the superstate impose laws and other types of regulations on professional activities and on professional discourse. We find, for instance, that many documents are produced as a result of such external regulations – annual reports, mission statements, contracts, anti-discrimination plans – and also many spoken events – annual general meetings, press information, hearings, etc.

Turning next to the *technical-economical framework*, I will claim that technology and technological advances are important for the dynamism within organizations of various kinds, as are the economy and economically driven changes. Professional life concerns the production of goods and services and finding markets for them. Product development, company mergers and workforce mobility create a framework which force organizations to develop a competitive and flexible structure, also in relation to communication.

The third framework, I wish to focus on is the *socio-cultural framework*. Cultural patterns, attitudes and social values are also essential aspects of communication in the professions. It is by means of discourse that socio-cultural frameworks are formed, at the same time as these frameworks are reconstructed over and over again in actual communication. Although we still find professional organizations which could be described as socially homogeneous and monocultural, social diversity and multiculturalism are more characteristic of organizations today. Furthermore, as many organizations wish to be distinguished by a specific culture and social ideas, professional discourse is often sustained in a complex socio-cultural framework system, where national and local frameworks are intertwined and interdependent.

The fourth framework which I claim is important for professional discourse is the *linguistic framework*. Every communicative event is also related to one or several languages. What characterizes professional discourse is the role played by the organization's language choice and language policy for work-related communication. There are indeed workplaces which are monolingual, i.e. where all employees can use their mother tongue at work. Throughout the world, however, we probably find more workplaces which are multilingual in terms of their workforce, where some employees cannot use their mother tongue at work and where some have little knowledge of the majority language at work. As large organizations often choose a global language as their corporate language, various linguistic frameworks are often intertwined in professional communicative events.

1.3.6   Dynamically changing discourse

The use of professional language and discourse is of ancient origin, stemming from the human need to adapt language to suit different types of activities. Consequently professionals have always created appropriate linguistic terminology, expressions and textual patterns to enable performance of the tasks assigned to them. From the point of view of our discussion here, what is relevant, however, is how and why professional discourses change from time to time.

Looking back a few hundred years we find that the language and discourse used by many professional groups have undergone changes in relation to purpose, content and language as well as to linguistic form and patterns. There have been variations in what knowledge is relevant and which skills are required for professionals within a domain over time. Changes are also related to the labour market so that some professional groups have become larger while others have dwindled or disappeared and some professional groups have enhanced the extent of their domain while others have given ground. Political changes are indeed also related to professional discourse. The establishment of new states and superstates often has consequences for professionals who even may have to use another language. Internationalization and globalization also affect professional discourse as do technological advances.

Borders between states and cultures are being eliminated in today's professional world, which means that questions like who owns and directs activities, who works in a particular organization, who is interested in the products and services offered, etc. find different answers from time to time. The organization and its communicative patterns have to be structured in a way that makes change possible and the employees have to be flexible and able to learn and relearn. The ongoing globalization and technologization of professional discourse means that the relationship between near and distant, and now and then, is transformed. New jobs and new professions are created and this raises the communication skills and flexibility required of the individual. The rapid changes are also reflected in instability and in the necessity to build up new forms of social organization.

10

In today's professional world we find an increasing number of global organizations which operate in different countries and which use different languages for their communication, with both customers and clients and with employees, partners and shareholders. Information about the organization, its products and services need to be presented in several languages and for audiences with different cultural affiliations so that organizations experience an increased need for translation, interpretation and parallel writing in different languages.

The ongoing globalization of the economy has also led to a global job market and increased workforce mobility. All over the world we find multilingual and multicultural workplaces. Many large, transnational organizations have chosen a cooperative language, not seldom English. English does not, however, work as a lingua franca in large parts of the world (in South America, the Middle East, Asia and Africa). It is also a fact that the use of English as a corporate language often creates a social divide between the top managers and the ordinary employees even in countries which teach English as the first foreign language. Multilinguality and multiculturality are thus issues that have to be handled by large organizations and institutions. They need to create policies on language and diversity issues in relation to the board, managers and employees.

1.4 What is the purpose of the book?

The purpose of the book *Professional Discourse* is to explore text and talk occurring in different environments in order to deepen our understanding of what professional discourse is, how it varies and why it changes. A central tenet elaborated in the different chapters of the book is the dual relationship between professional discourse and its contextual framework. This relationship is analysed as a two-sided complexity, i.e. as both a discourse-related and context-related complexity. As I will claim in this book, an in-depth analysis of variation and change should explore this two-sided complexity and also the dynamic character of professional discourse, how professional language and discourse is continuously contextually reconstructed.

The book gives a broad and multifaceted perspective on discourse in the professions, including law, business, medicine, science and the academic settings, technology and bureaucracy. The case studies presented are based on authentic texts and spoken data, collected within different environments and relating to different domains. The aim of each section is to offer theoretically grounded and systematically investigated answers to questions of relevance for advanced learners, practitioners and academic scholars. Each section will therefore include discussions of both theory and methodology to provide tools for applications and further studies.

In comparison to the majority of earlier studies on professional language and discourse, the studies presented in this book are totally innovative in their theoretically grounded and systematically undertaken analysis of authentic data (cf. overview in Gunnarsson, 2008). The theoretical basis of the case studies dealt with in this book derives from a range of disciplines: textlinguistics, pragmatics, genre studies, sociolinguistics, interactional sociolinguistics and sociology, psycholinguistics and cognitive psychology.

What all sections share, however, is the discussion of linguistic variables in relation to psychological, social and societal variables. Professional language and discourse are viewed as being constructed and reconstructed in relation to a system of contextual frameworks. As this book shows, we reach a deeper understanding of the emergence, development and constant change of professional discourse, if we discuss our findings in relation to contexts at different levels: the situated communicative event, the environmental framework (the workplace, the organization/the discipline) and the societal frameworks (the legal-political, the technical-economical, the socio-cultural and the linguistic frameworks).

Another factor common to the studies is that they all are based on detailed analysis of linguistic data. The book therefore develops and discusses applications of different methodologies: textlinguistic analysis of large corpora, concordance analysis, function-oriented text analysis, psycholinguistic experiments, ethnographic observations, interviews and discourse analysis.

Furthermore, several chapters focus on how and why professional discourse has changed over time and how it is likely to change in the future. One purpose of the book is thus to explore the dynamic and complex socio-historical reconstruction of professional discourse.

1.5 How is the book organized?

The book starts off with three introductory chapters. After this first chapter, the following two chapters present the main theoretical and methodological approaches of the book. In Chapter 2, I develop my theoretical model for contextual analysis of professional discourse. The construction of professional language is explored in relation to different dimensions – cognitive, social and societal – and its continuous reconstruction in relation to different contextual layers – the situated frame, the environmental framework and the four societal frameworks. This theoretical model is the basis of the contextual analysis in the various empirical studies discussed in this book. Chapter 3 presents a multidimensional, textlinguistic methodology. This methodology, which explores the dynamic relationship between text and discourse, has been applied to several large corpora. It examines texts at cognitive, pragmatic and macrothematic levels, thus making possible an in-depth analysis of diachronic and synchronic variation and change.

These introductory chapters are followed by four thematically organized sections on Scientific discourse, Legislative discourse, Workplace discourse and Discourse in large business organizations.

The section on 'Scientific discourse' comprises three chapters on the emergence and development of academic writing within different domains. Chapter 4 concerns the socio-historical construction of medical discourse. Medical articles from three centuries – the eighteenth, nineteenth and twentieth centuries – are analysed and discussed in relation to a pre-establishment stage, an establishing stage and a specialized stage. The multidimensional methodology is here used to analyse changes in text patterns at cognitive, pragmatic and macro-structural levels. The chapter also discusses changes in linguistic expressions of evaluation over time. In Chapter 5 my analysis concerns non-verbal representation in 90 scientific articles within technology, medicine and economics from 1730 to 1985. This chapter also concerns the construction of scientific discourse, in this case with a focus on graphic representation, formulas and tables. Chapter 6 views the development of the academic writing of economists from the perspective of internationalization and globalization. I analyse how textual patterns changed when what was originally a national journal of economics switched language from Swedish to English lingua franca and became an international journal with a global readership. My analysis focuses on the design of the journal, the general outline of its articles and the gradual changes in journal and article patterns. The development is discussed from the perspectives of the national scientific and linguistic communities.

The second thematically organized section is on 'Legislative discourse'. Legislative texts are used for a discussion of the goal-orientation and situatedness of professional discourse. I analyse the communicative processes attached to laws and their varied use from different perspectives: a function-oriented, or pragmatic, perspective, a psycholinguistic perspective and a sociolinguistic one. In Chapter 7, I present a theory of the functional comprehensibility of legislative texts and discuss the results of an experiment designed to test this theory. A model of law-text reading and comprehension is developed, which systematically analyses the context base of the law from the point of view of the citizen's use of the text. An alternative law-text was written based on this model. Reading and comprehension of laws relate to the more general issue of asymmetries between expert and lay discourse, and this experiment points to a way of improving legislative texts as well as other types of official documents. Chapter 8 explores the drafting of legislative texts from a combined cognitive-rhetorical and sociolinguistic perspective. Problems of law-text comprehensibility are here related to the legislative writing process. Using an ethnographic methodology I followed as an observer the drafting process of three pieces of consumer laws at different stages. My discussion of this study focuses on the stages of the writing process, the professional composition of the committees involved, the societal contextual frameworks and the readers targeted.

In the third thematically organized section, I deal with studies of 'Workplace discourse'. Professional discourse is discussed here in relation to the situated frame and the socially ordered working group. Chapter 9 elaborates and evaluates a sociolinguistic framework for the study of communication at work. The two concepts 'communicative community' and 'professional group' are introduced. In addition, the chapter includes a study of communication at a local government office. By means of a survey and in-depth interviews, I studied the organization of writing within the office, the interplay between speech and writing as well as collaboration. This study sheds new light on the social organization of writing within a small, monolingual workplace. In Chapter 10, my concern is the multilingual workplace. The complexity of workplace multilingualism is explored from a variety of perspectives, that of the professional group, the linguistic-cultural community and the individual employees. In addition to theories related to group formation, my theoretical approach also includes language dominance issues and interactional sociolinguistics. The empirical data focused on emanate from a research project which aimed to explore the daily work-related interaction at a public hospital and an international company in Sweden. An ethnographic methodology – comprising interviews, on site observations, recordings and text collection – was adopted for this project. Both workplaces are multilingual and multicultural in terms of their staff, and my discussion of results concerns the organizational structure of text and talk at work, workplace languages and the interaction of foreign language users at work. Asymmetries due to varied cultural and linguistic background will be dealt with.

The fourth thematically organized section analyses 'Discourse in large business organizations'. Chapter 11 explores the complex relationship between enterprise and discourse. Professional discourse is related to different contextual frameworks: the environmental framework and the various societal ones. A model of communication is presented which depicts the multilayered framework of texts within large organizations. With this model as a background, results from a research project on banks and structural engineering companies in Britain, Germany and Sweden are discussed. A series of interviews were conducted with managers and staff involved in writing and a large text corpus was collected and analysed. The first part of my analysis of the results concerns differences between the two sectors (banking and engineering), between organizations within one sector, and differences at national level. The second part presents an analysis of the construction of an 'organizational self' within the three banks. In the last part of the chapter I discuss how the simple sociolinguistic order found at small workplaces is intertwined in large organizations with various levels of other orders leading to a multifaceted and multilayered disorder. Societal frameworks at national and supranational levels influence discourse in large enterprises. Chapter 12 explores company websites from a diversity perspective, which means that I analyse the construction of an 'organizational self' from the perspective of the outsiders, i.e. the readers. Here my sociolinguistic framework is extended to include ideas about marginalization within sociology and political science. The reliance of modern companies on the internet for externally addressed information entails a complexity of a new kind while at the same time their policies and practices in relation to language and culture include or exclude readership groups. My analysis in this chapter concerns the customer-related and career-oriented websites maintained by five transnational companies. I explore these websites from a critical, sociolinguistic angle thus focusing on how the companies strike a balance between different concerns and values: local and global, economic and societal. One aim of this analysis is to grasp the company policies on diversity and multiculturality and the way they handle their corporate social responsibility.

In the concluding section, chapter 13, my focus is on the future, i.e. on professional discourse in the twenty-first century. I discuss the effects of technological advances and globalization in relation to different domains and environments. Furthermore, I dwell on workplace discourse in the 'new work order' and speculate about possible consequences for the individual employee. I also sketch some topics for future research. Finally, I sum up the main tenets of the book.

2 A theoretical model for contextual analysis of professional discourse

In this chapter, I develop a theoretical model for contextual analysis of professional discourse. This model will provide a basis for the empirical studies discussed in the different chapters/sections of this book. A consistent tenet in these discussions is that an in-depth understanding of what professional discourse is, how it varies and successively changes relates discourse to the contextual frames in which it occurs. I will claim that we need to use a multidisciplinary approach including cognitive, social and societal dimensions in our analysis.

In the first part of the chapter, I introduce my view on the roles which the three dimensions – the cognitive, social and societal – play in the construction of professional language and discourse. In the second part, I broaden my constructivist approach to include factors relating to the various contextual frames in which professional discourse is continuously reconstructed, i.e. a situated frame, an environmental framework and four societal frameworks. Lastly, I sum up my theory in a model of the reconstruction of professional discourse.

2.1 The construction of professional discourse

In every strand of human communication, discourse plays a role in the formation of a social and societal reality and identity. This is also true of the formation of the different professional and vocational cultures within working and public life. Historically, discourse has played a central role in the creation of different professions and it continues to do so in the development and maintenance of professional and institutional cultures and identities. Societal, social and cognitive factors all play important roles in the construction of professional cultures. Professionals try to create a space for their domain within society, to establish themselves in contact and competition with others within their group as well as with other groups. Their knowledge base and its linguistic forms are created in a societal and social framework.

The public sector, the academic world, and working life are continuously changing. New professions and trades appear, others disappear, and there is a continuous process among professionals to create and recreate their respective domains. Due to the specialization, technologization and professionalization of modern society, we have many more different kinds of professional language than a hundred years ago, and there are greater differences between the language varieties used for professional purposes by different expert groups. The tower of Babel metaphor has often been used to describe language situations, and it is most certainly an appropriate metaphor for professional language. Professionals have not finished building their tower of Babel; construction is always in progress. They are constantly changing their language and discourse as they try to make themselves both well-known and unique. In today's professional world, however, we also have to consider a language dominance dimension. Due to globalization and technological advances, the tower of Babel metaphor has come to include the choice of language as well. Professional discourse has come to be pursued in a second, third or fourth language in many contexts, as a result of the increased use of English lingua franca in professional life.

Written texts and spoken discourse therefore play and have always played an important role in forming the professions. Originally all professional communication was oral. Laws were drafted orally and memorized by lawmen, who could then quote them from memory in court. Medical advice and prescriptions were transferred through spoken discourse, and economic transactions were entered into and preserved orally. Gradually, written texts came into use and became the traditional form for more important purposes. Laws were written down, and so were contracts, and prescriptions were collected in pharmacopoeias. However, it is important to bear in mind that the written form represents a late stage in the history of professional discourse. It is only in recent centuries that writing has become widespread in professional practice. The functional divide between writing and talking, which has become part of our stereotype picture of the two media, has only developed gradually and, in terms of the history of humankind, quite recently (see Danet, 1997).

In modern society, written texts and spoken discourse have taken on new and more varied roles. New technology is leading to new ways of communicating, ways for which both the written-spoken dichotomy and the verbal-non-verbal dichotomy seem inappropriate. Distant communication is no longer only possible in writing, and spoken discourse can be preserved just as well as written texts. The new technologies are contributing to a change in the communicative situation in working life, among other things involving new and less distinct functions for written texts and spoken discourse, and for words and visual elements.

The written and spoken sides of communication are also difficult to keep apart in other respects. In modern society at least, the production of texts is largely a collective process, and one in which writing is intermingled with speaking to such an extent that it is difficult to know what role each medium plays. Behind a written document there is often a long process in which speech – meetings, discussions, comments – plays just as essential a role as the actual writing. In modern professional life, writing and talking are often strongly intertwined. Both media contribute to the form and content of the other, and gradually the functional distinction between oral and written discourse is disappearing, and both forms of communication are becoming equally important in the formation of professional cultures. What characterizes professional communication in the twenty-first century is also the extended use of computers, mobile phones, internet etc., thus encompassing new multimodal types of discourse.

To understand professional language and communication we must study it in its rich and varied totality. We must study the dynamic processes behind the construction of professional discourse. One relevant question is therefore what constitutes these processes, i.e. what dimensions have been involved in the construction of professional texts over time. In what follows I distinguish three dimensions – a cognitive, a societal and a social – which, I argue, must be considered if we are to acquire a holistic picture of the emergence and continuous re-creation of professional discourse.

2.1.1 Cognitive dimension

Every profession has a certain way of viewing reality, a certain way of highlighting different aspects of the surrounding world. Socialization into a profession means learning how to discern the relevant facts, how to view the relations between different factors. We are taught how to construct and use a grid or a lens to view reality in the professionally appropriate way. Written and spoken discourse helps us in this construction process. We use language to construct professional knowledge.[1] And if we consider a professional group as a whole, we see that its professional language has developed as a means of expressing this professional view of reality. Legal terminology, legal sentence structures, legal text patterns, and legal text and discourse content have developed as a means of dealing with reality in a way that suits the purposes of the law. Attitudes and norms are also built into the cognitive structure. The legal perspective entails attitudes and norms regarding what is legally acceptable, what is right and wrong, etc.

18

The knowledge base of one domain has a network of relations with other domains. The cognitive structure of a professional language thus reveals its dependence on and relationship to other knowledge domains and this knowledge-based network can vary over time. Metaphors, terminology, argumentation, and diagrams reveal the contribution of adjacent domains to the construction of professional knowledge. For example, many domains owe a debt to statistics, psychology, mathematics, sociology, physics, economics, politics and religion, and this debt can be seen in the language used.

The cognitive dimension is, of course, related to psychological processes within the individual members of a profession, e.g. to how they perceive and understand reality in professional communication.

2.1.2 Social dimension

Every professional group is also, like other social groups, formed by the establishment of an internal role structure, group identity, group attitudes and group norms. The need for a professional identity, for a professional 'we' feeling, for separation from the out-group, has, of course, played an important role in the construction of professional group discourse and constantly inspires people to adapt and be socialized into professional group behaviour. Socialization into a group also means establishing distance from people outside the group.

2.1.3 Societal dimension

Furthermore, every professional group stands in a certain relationship to the surrounding society: it exerts certain functions and is assigned a certain place within society. Its members play a role in relation to other actors in society, and the group they constitute acts in relation to other groups. They play – or do not play – a role in political life, within the business world, the education system, in relation to the press etc. And this cluster of societal functions is essential for discourse. It is via discourse that professional groups exert their societal function. If they are going to play a political role, they have to construct their communicative behaviour in a way that is appropriate for this purpose.

Relationships to texts and spoken discourse and to different genres are also important. Professionals adapt to established genres, but are also involved in forming new ones. The societal dimension is, of course, related to economic and political factors, to power and status patterns in society.

19

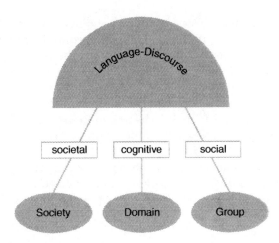

Figure 2.1 *Model of the construction of professional language and discourse (Adapted from Figure 1 in Gunnarsson, 1998: 25)*

2.1.4 Model of the construction of professional language and discourse

The three dimensions discussed above are strongly related to the emergence and continuous re-creation of language and discourse in the professions. Figure 2.1 illustrates the roles played by the three dimensions in the construction of professional language and discourse.

2.2 The contextual dependence of professional discourse

In order to understand the dynamic character of the reconstruction of professional discourse we must consider its contextual dependence, and also the complex interplay between different levels in this process. With a background in the three dimensions outlined above (in part 2.1), I will here continue with a discussion of the various contextual frameworks influencing professional discourse. I will then distinguish contextual frames at three levels: the *situated frame* at a micro level, the *environmental framework* at a macro level, and the *societal frameworks* at a supra level.

2.2.1 The situated frame

Professional discourse is situated and dynamic, which means that an analysis at micro level should focus on the dynamic character of the

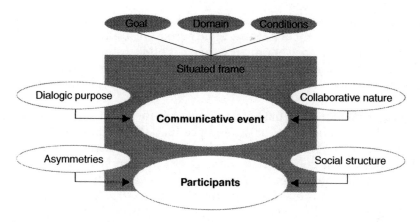

Figure 2.2 *The situated frame*

situated frame in which a *communicative event* involving one or several *participants* takes place (Figure 2.2).

As stated in the first chapter of this book, I use the term professional discourse to 'cover text and talk – and their intertwined relationship – in professional contexts and for professional purposes'. The *domain,* i.e. the professional context, and the *goal,* i.e. the professional purpose, are thus constitutive of a situated frame. The frame also varies with the *external conditions,* such as place, tools, time allotted etc.

Where the *communicative event* is concerned, our starting point is that such an event can involve both written and spoken discourse as well as their interplay. We should further note that a professional communicative event can involve one or several participants. A lawyer writing a text, a doctor tape-recording a medical report, an engineer reading an instruction and a secretary listening to a recorded report are therefore considered professional communicative events, even if these professionals are sitting alone in their offices. What is important for this classification is that the writing, recording, reading and listening, in these cases as well, have a *dialogic purpose,* i.e. the individually performed tasks are a beginning of – or part of – an exchange of texts and messages which form a dialogue. Although we find communicative events in professional contexts with individuals working alone, a characteristic feature of professional discourse is thus its dialogic nature.

Another feature, I wish to stress here, is the *collaborative nature* of professional activities. Many professional events are dyadic, i.e. they involve two participants, engaged in face to face interaction, telephone conversation or the exchange of written messages. Other professional events involve several participants, convened as temporary or more permanent groups. Small group meetings, written group correspondence, collaborative writing, collaborative presentations, discussions, large group meetings, and debates are examples of group events. Collaboration in group events is thus a common phenomenon in professional life.

This further means that professional activities often entail a shared, collective responsibility for the end-product – the document, the presentation, the report – and a possibility for group members to influence the process. The social dimensions of the collaborative work should therefore be included in the analysis of a communicative event. For a more permanent professional group, the *social structure of the group* and the relationships between the group members shape the situated frame of each event. In professional life we also often find communicative events which are linked by a common goal, thus forming a *communicative chain*. This means that each communicative event is not only directed towards the future but also part of a history involving earlier constellations of participants.

Another structural feature relates to possible *asymmetries* between the participants. In communicative events involving professionals with similar expertise, we are likely to find a fairly symmetric structure, while in many other events, differences in pre-knowledge, discourse strategies, attitudes and intentions will create an asymmetric structure. Communication between professionals in different positions or with different expertise can therefore be as asymmetric as communication between professionals and semi-professionals or lay people. Asymmetries, however, can also be due to external conditions. Place, time allotted and the assistance available can lead to asymmetries. If, for instance, we compare the situated frame for a participant who is given plenty of time and adequate auxiliary help to read and interpret a written report with the situated frame for another participant who is short of time and lacks help, we find considerable asymmetries, which indeed can result in differences in comprehension and interpretation.

To sum up, an analysis of the (re)construction of professional discourse at micro level should include cognitive and social dimensions and also take into account the particular conditions of the situation.

2.2.2 The environmental framework

An in-depth analysis of the reconstruction of professional discourse must also include the macro level, i.e. the environmental frameworks in which the communicative events, or chain of events, occur, and in which patterns for writing and talking at work are created. Text and talk in a small, close-knit working group with its particular social and communicative order therefore form part of traditions that evolve within an environmental structure, i.e. the small *working group* is included in a larger unit such as a *workplace*, which in its turn belongs to a *local branch* of a large *organization*. In many cases, we further find additional organizational levels, i.e. the organization belongs to a *corporation*, which in turn might belong to a net of *attached working partners*. Figure 2.3 illustrates the environmental framework of a working group that forms part of a large organization.

Although the number of levels varies from workplace to workplace and from organization to organization, a common denominator is the interdependence and interrelationship between various levels of the environmental framework. In one way or another, an environmental framework is held together by common goals, operative areas (domains) and markets. Further, a professional framework is attached to an organizational structure (involving hierarchies, clusters, group structure) and a certain social division of work (e.g. the relationship between qualified staff, skilled and semi-skilled workers, between seniors and learners, and between employer and employees). Some frameworks are also held together by explicit management ideas and attachment to social values. The environmental framework can thus be said to constrain the reconstruction of discourse at various levels. The social and communicative order of a small working group thus depends on the structure and ideas of the organization as a whole.

To sum up, an analysis of the (re)construction of professional discourse at macro level should include both a social and an organizational dimension. The analysis should then also consider how the

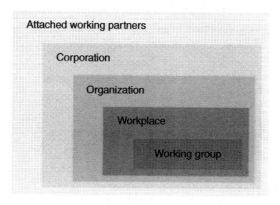

Figure 2.3 *The environmental framework*

interdependence and interrelationship between various levels of the environmental framework influence discourse.

2.2.3   The societal framework systems

A further characteristic of professional discourse is that to a large extent it is regulated and steered from the 'outside', i.e. from different societal frameworks, while at the same time it is an essential part of the construction of these frameworks. The relationship between professional discourse and societal frameworks is thus dual. My perspective below, however, will mainly deal with the way the societal frameworks constrain discourse. I will dwell on social and societal variables which are relevant for an analysis of professional text and talk. For the purpose of the studies presented in this book, I have chosen to distinguish four types of societal frameworks: a *legal-political framework*, a *technical-economical framework*, a *socio-cultural framework*, and a *linguistic framework*. These frameworks can be described at different levels: at *a local level* (e.g. the town or the region), at *a national level* (e.g. the country or the nation state) and at *a supranational level* (e.g. the union, the superstate, the international region). In various ways these frameworks, or rather framework systems, constrain text and talk in professional contexts.

Figure 2.4 illustrates the relationship between frameworks and levels. The four framework systems will be described in some more detail below.

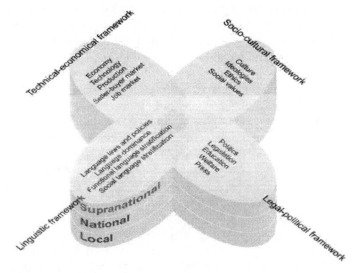

Figure 2.4 *The societal framework systems*

2.2.3.1   The legal-political framework

It is self-evident that professional discourse is constrained by the legal-political framework at local, national and supranational levels. *Politics* and legislative traditions are reflected in *legislation*, in laws and regulations which regulate professional discourse. The legal-political structures are also reflected in basic and higher *education*, *welfare* and the public ideology disseminated by the *press*. If we look more closely at professional documents, we find that a great number are produced in compliance with requirements from the local government, the state or the superstate, e.g. annual reports, contracts, protocols, environmental reports, mission statements, equal opportunity plans.

2.2.3.2   The technical-economical framework

Professional discourse is also strongly related to the technical-economical framework. *Economy* and *technology* are essential for the growth and development of professional activities and, indirectly, for the type and content of its discourse as well. Technological advances, economic growth and professional discourse are intertwined and interdependent at local, national and supranational levels. An organization depends on its *production* and also on its success in various markets: the *seller–buyer market* and also the *job market*.

Professional discourse plays an essential role as a tool for the creation and maintenance of an organization. It is by means of discourse that organizations and institutions manage to attract shareholders/owners, producers/working partners, customers/clients and future employees. It is therefore important for an organization to be visible and competitive in the various markets related to the technical-economical framework. Indirectly, this also means that an organization or institution needs to appear attractive and competitive in the eyes of politicians, journalists and the general public. Professional discourse therefore plays an essential role in providing a positive foundation for interaction with other professionals, semi-professionals and lay people.

2.2.3.3   The socio-cultural framework

Professional discourse is also constrained by the socio-cultural framework. Though vague as a concept, it is often relevant to distinguish between different *cultures* at different levels: local, national and supranational. At national level, for instance, we can find culturally

25

formed ideas as differences in views on collectivism versus remote power, self-assertiveness versus modesty, and competition versus solidarity and negotiation. The ethical codes adopted in a particular professional environment reflect, to a large extent, *ideologies* and *ethics* in the relevant socio-cultural framework. Ideologies related to citizen's rights, democracy and tolerance form the backbone of the societal ethical system and these are in turn reflected in the *social values* of professionals and of professional groups at various levels.

2.2.3.4 The linguistic framework

Professional discourse is indeed also dependent on the linguistic framework. The local language community, the national language community and the supranational or global language community establish and follow *language laws and policies* which directly or indirectly influence text and talk in the professions. Language choice and language practice in professional environments follow, to a large extent, the practice in the relevant discourse communities. Policies and practice on *language dominance* issues (local language versus global language; majority language versus minority language), *functional language stratification* (diglossia) and on *social language stratification* (elite and non-elite languages) formed within the various levels of the linguistic framework influence communicative events for professional purposes in terms of language choice and practice. The language knowledge of the participants in a professional encounter, whether professionals or non-professionals, reflects language politics and laws.

2.3 Model for the contextual reconstruction of professional discourse

Professional discourse is thus constructed and reconstructed in a complex interplay between different framework systems. As Figure 2.5 illustrates, professional discourse is reconstructed in a situated communicative event occurring within a working group which is a part of an environmental framework which operates at different levels: a local, a national and a supranational. At each of these levels professional discourse is also constrained and intertwined with different societal frameworks: a legal-political framework, a technical-economical framework, a socio-cultural framework and a linguistic framework.

Figure 2.5 *Model for the contextual reconstruction of professional discourse*

2.4 Conclusions

The theoretical model presented in this chapter will be used to ana-lyse the dual relationship between context and professional discourse. The model will be referred to in the discussions of the results of empirical studies of professional discourse in different domains and for different purposes. A purpose of these studies, which are based on authentic data, is to deepen our understanding of how, and also why, professional discourse varies and changes. The dual relationship between professional discourse and context is in turn related to a two-sided complexity. This means that we also need to find a tool for a micro analysis of professional discourse which grasps its contextual dependence. In the next chapter, I will introduce a multidimensional texlinguistic methodology which explores the dynamic relationship between text and context.

Note

1. Within the sociology of science tradition, many studies have analysed the role of texts in the establishment of scientific fact (e.g. Knorr-Cetina, 1981; Latour and

27

Woolgar, 1986 and Bazerman, 1988). A social constructivist approach in relation to written texts more generally is further found in Bazerman and Paradis (1991). In Gunnarsson et al. (1997), which examined both professional written communication and spoken interaction, the central theoretical issue is how language, written genres and spoken discourse are constructed as successive and continuous interplay between language and social realities.

3 Methodology to explore the dynamic relationship between text and context

In this chapter, I will present a multidimensional methodology the aim of which is to explore the dynamic relationship between text and context. The methodology, which examines texts at *cognitive, pragmatic* and *macrothematic* levels, enables in-depth analysis of diachronic and synchronic variation and change. As an introduction to the presentation of each aspect of the methodology, I will outline its theoretical background. For the cognitive aspect, which is an innovation, I will begin with a discussion of what a cognitive viewpoint can entail for text analysis. For the pragmatic and macrothematic aspects of the methodology, I will present earlier studies of relevance. The multidimensional methodology, which has been applied to several large text corpora, has also been used for contrastive comparisons, e.g. between English, German and Swedish.

The theoretical framework introduced in the previous chapter provides the basis for the methodology at cognitive level. This analysis makes it possible to analyse content more deeply than can normally be achieved by text linguistic methods. The contextual (re)construction of texts is related to an examination of the content of the text at a very abstract level. This is undertaken by assigning each element of information contained in the text to one of five *cognitive worlds: scientific, practical, object, private* and *external*, and within these to different content *aspects*. The content of the texts is further classified as *state-descriptive* or *action-descriptive*, as well as shifting to and from several (time-) *dimensions*. The cognitive worlds function much like the schemas and frames of cognitive psychology in that they serve to organize situation-bound knowledge and to provide a framework for the integration of new information.

The pragmatic and macrothematic aspects of the methodology also provide tools for an in-depth analysis of how contextual factors shape genre. Context, i.e. the situated frame in terms of goal, event and conditions, relates to genre conventions and textual patterns. The pragmatic method of analysis involves a categorization of the *illocution types* of the clauses, and a categorization of the *subsidiary function of the text parts* in the structure of the text as a whole. The macrothematic method of analysis involves a categorization of the texts according to the content structure into *superthemes* and further into *macrothemes*.

Originally, I developed this multidimensional methodology for an analysis of the diachronic and synchronic variation of scientific and popular science articles on economics, medicine and technology during three centuries, the eighteenth, nineteenth and twentieth centuries. Three hundred and sixty articles published in Swedish journals and periodicals during six periods from 1730 to 1985 are included in this corpus (Uppsala LSP corpus).[1] The methodology has also been found useful for contrastive analyses of large corpora, e.g. for an analysis of the variation between texts of different kinds written in English, German and Swedish and produced within banks, structural engineering firms, university departments of history and occupational medicine in Great Britain, Germany and Sweden in the 1990's (Uppsala contrastive corpus).[2] In another contrastive study, Fredrickson compared American and Swedish appeal court documents (1995).[3] The cognitive analysis has also been applied to a number of smaller corpora, which indeed show its broader relevance.

As several chapters of this book (4, 6 and 11) refer to results based on studies using this methodology, I here present the methodology in some detail and also sketch its theoretical basis. I begin with the cognitive analysis, then continue with the pragmatic analysis, and lastly with the macrothematic analysis.

3.1 Cognitive analysis

The innovation in the multidimensional methodology lies primarily in the cognitive analysis, which examines the content of the text at a very abstract level. As this aspect of the methodology is original, I have found it relevant to first outline what a cognitive viewpoint can entail for a text analysis. As mentioned above, the methodology at cognitive level is closely related to the theoretical framework introduced in the previous chapter. My outline in this chapter, however, will approach matters from the perspective of the author(s) and their collective formation of genre patterns.

3.1.1 Theoretical background

If written texts are viewed from a cognitive viewpoint, they can be seen as reflections of how the authors perceive matters. By studying the cognitive content of a text we should, therefore, be able to grasp how its author structures the world. This way of looking at things is, however, too simple, as a text undoubtedly also reflects how the author thinks matters should be presented, i.e. his or her conception of the contents required by the actual text type, or to put it another way the author's stored *cognitive genre frame*. However, the genre frame is in its turn formed as a reflection of the collective beliefs within the professional community. Genre developments thus reflect developments in the collective belief system, or in other words genres have developed as a means of expressing a professional view of reality (cf. Chapter 2).

A text reflects the beliefs and norms of the professional community to which the author belongs. The cognitive level of the text reflects how the author structures the knowledge he or she wants to present, or at least what the author believes is the accepted way of structuring this knowledge within the school or group to which he or she belongs. The text can thus be seen as the product of the author's adaptation to the requirements and his or her own unique way of structuring the subject matter.

Rather than an opposition between belief structure and cognitive genre frame, there exists a mutual correspondence. The cognitive structure the readers can discern in the texts they read influences their way of thinking so that texts are factors in the formation of a collective belief system. On the other hand, the way authors mentally structure reality is reflected in the texts they write, which means that we can study changes in the collective belief system of a group of people by studying the cognitive content of the texts they produce.

We must also consider that these collective belief systems are formed within society and within subgroups in this society. This means that the cognitive content of texts reflects the contextual framework in which the texts are produced. It also means that changes in the societal framework of a text genre are reflected in the genre patterns. Genre developments thus reflect developments in sections of society and in society as a whole.

As mentioned in the introductory part of this chapter, the cognitive analysis method was originally developed as a means to grasp how contextual factors shape scientific and popular science discourse during different periods. I have therefore found it relevant to also distinguish three frames: a *situated frame*, a *disciplinary framework* (cf. environmental framework), and a *societal framework*. Figure 3.1 gives an idea of the contextual framework for scientific writing within different disciplines.

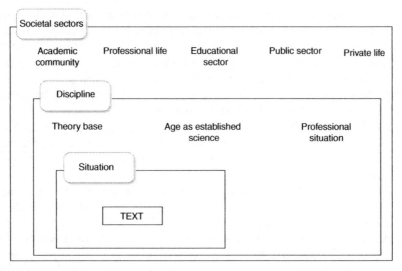

Figure 3.1 *Contextual frames shaping writing in the professions (Adapted from Figure 1 in Gunnarsson, 1992a: 208)*

The inner frame, regarding the actual production of the text, is more or less unique for each text. The production of the text can be seen as a communicative event, or a chain of communicative events. For genre-bound changes, however, the other two frames are the most important, the middle frame showing factors unique to each discipline and the outer showing factors common to discourse during a certain period.

Turning to the middle frame, my claim is that in many respects, each academic discipline has developed in its own specific way. Theory bases are unique to each discipline, and have certainly not been static in any discipline. Such changes in theory and in methodology can be assumed to be reflected in the related texts.

Disciplines differ in how long they have been established as sciences. Medicine, seen as a whole, is an old science. Technology and economics, on the other hand, are new and part of their evolution into established academic disciplines has taken place since the end of the nineteenth century. The process of becoming established can be seen as a change of worlds from a professional world of work with its rules to an academic world with its rules.

The professional situation is a third factor that is unique to each discipline. The role and status of the main professions in the three disciplines have changed. In 1980, doctors, engineers and economists had a high status in society and played important roles. The picture was, however, somewhat different in the eighteenth century and also at the beginning of the twentieth century, and these changes in the status and role of the professions are liable to be reflected in the texts.

Texts in each discipline can thus be assumed to follow their own specific courses of development due to their unique histories. In many respects, however, their development may be assumed to be the same, reflecting changes in society as a whole. As the outer frame shows (Figure 3.1), I have chosen to distinguish five sectors within the societal framework: *Academic community, professional life, educational sector, public sector* and *private life*. My claim is that these sectors are relevant for variation and change at cognitive text level.

3.1.2 Method for cognitive analysis

I will now continue with a presentation of the method for cognitive analysis. The aim of the methodology can be captured by the following questions: (1) How can we obtain a comparable picture of the content of texts on different subjects, in different languages and from different disciplines and periods? (2) How can we capture the changes that are relevant from a sociolinguistic point of view?

The aim of the cognitive analysis is thus to describe the content, i.e. the knowledge, presented in the text in a way that makes comparisons possible and relevant. The content in fact varies from discipline to discipline, from subject to subject, from text to text. At an abstract level it can, however, be said to vary with regard to five cognitive worlds: a *scientific world*, a *practical world*, an *object world*, a *private world* and an *external world*. These worlds can be related to the different sectors of society distinguished above (Figure 3.2).

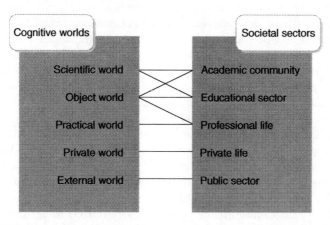

Figure 3.2 *Cognitive worlds and sectors of society (Adapted from Figure 3 in Gunnarsson, 1992a: 212)*

My world concept has similarities with the schema concept which we are familiar with from theories within cognitive psychology. There, schema is used to cover quite different types of storing, that of:

1. Specific, situational knowledge. Often the term script is used for situation-bound knowledge (e.g. Schank and Abelson, 1977) and the term domain-related knowledge for sector-bound knowledge (e.g. Spilich et al., 1979, Voss et al., 1980).
2. General knowledge, i.e. prototypical knowledge of a general kind – e.g., knowledge of text types, speech acts, personalities and so forth – that can be activated in different types of situation. The term frame is often used for this kind of knowledge (Bartlett, 1932, Thorndyke, 1977, Kintsch, 1978).
3. Global structuring, meaning that the individual sees reality as a whole from a certain perspective (Schutz and Luckmann, 1984).

My world concept has similarities with the schema concept, in the sense of specific and general knowledge. The five worlds – scientific, practical, object, private and external – are possible knowledge structures, which means that they form a background for idealized authors when they construct texts and for idealized readers when they try to build up a mental representation of the text they read. Reading as well as writing is thus seen as a text world production based on a common storage of cognitive and linguistic operations and using similar knowledge (e.g. van Dijk and Kintsch, 1983, Kucer, 1985).

This does not, however, mean that these worlds are equally available to all authors and all readers of professional texts. On the contrary, one of the purposes of analyzing texts by means of cognitive worlds is to describe the differences between authors belonging to different expert disciplines and specializing in different subjects, between authors from different periods and between authors with different pictures of their readers.

In the cognitive analysis, each item of information contained in a text is assigned to one of the five worlds. By means of the world analysis, we thus obtain an overall picture of the knowledge structure of a text. Figure 3.3 shows the five *cognitive worlds* and their related categories *aspect* and *dimension*. I have found it relevant to distinguish between two types of text content (text types): *state-descriptive* and *action-descriptive*. This distinction is not relevant for a categorization of the texts as a whole but rather of their constituent parts.

		Cause	Phenomenon	Process	Change
Scientific world	Theory	X	X	X	X
	Classification	X	X	X	X
	Experiment	X	X	X	X
Practical world	Work	X	X	X	X
	Interaction	X	X	X	X
Object world	Phenomenon	X	X	X	X
	Part focused	X	X	X	X
	Whole focused	X	X	X	X
Private world	Experience	X	X	X	X
	Personal situation	X	X	X	X
External world	Soc. econ. conditions	X	X	X	X
	Soc. econ. measures	X	X	X	X

Figure 3.3 *Cognitive worlds, aspects and dimensions: state-descriptive text parts (Adapted from Figure 6.2 in Gunnarsson, 1997a: 111)*

Within each world, I identify certain abstract categories that are common to different texts. On one level these categories relate to different aspects: within the scientific world to *theory, classification* and *experiment*; within the practical world to *work* and *interaction*; within the object world to *phenomenon, part focused* and *whole focused*; within the private world to *experience* and *personal situation*; within the external world to *conditions* and *measures* of social, economic and political kinds.

On another level, these categories relate to different (time) dimensions. For state-descriptive texts, these (time) dimensions are *cause, phenomenon, process* and *change*. For action-descriptive texts, they are *preventive measure/cause, phenomenon, measure/process* and *change/result*.

From this general, or invariant, description of the worlds and their subcategories, I will now turn to a more specified one. The worlds and categories also appear in variant forms. We can thus describe one text universe for the medical discipline, one for the technical discipline, one for the economic discipline, one for legal texts, one for business discourse etc. Figures 3.4a and 3.4b show the object world and its related categories for the medical discipline.

As mentioned above, the worlds and categories appear in variant forms for each discipline. In the medical discipline, the practical world becomes the hospital world and the object world becomes the disease world. As for the categories, cause becomes medical cause, object becomes disease, process becomes disease process and so on.

Figure 3.4a concerns elements of texts that are state-descriptive and Figure 3.4b those of texts that are action-descriptive. The (time)

		Cause	Phenomenon	Process	Change
	Phenomenon	medical cause	disease	disease process	medical change
Disease world	Part focused	cause of medical attack on organ	organ	process rel. to organ	change in organ
	Whole focused	earlier general condition	patient	process rel. to general condition	change in general condition

Figure 3.4a *Object world for the medical discipline. State-descriptive text parts (Adapted from Figure 5a in Gunnarsson, 1992a: 217)*

		Cause	Phenomenon	Process	Change/Result
	Phenomenon	prevention of disease	disease	treatment	result of treatment
Disease world	Part focused	prevention of disease rel. to organ	organ	treatment rel. to organ	result rel. to organ
	Whole focused	prevention of disease rel. to patient	patient	treatment rel. to general condition	result rel. to patient's general condition

Figure 3.4b *Object world for the medical discipline. Action-descriptive text parts (Adapted from Figure 5b in Gunnarsson, 1992a: 217)*

dimension is also present in these figures along the horizontal axis. In state-descriptive texts, disease is central within the disease world. The disease is preceded by medical cause (to the left in the schemata) and is followed in time by the disease process and the medical change (to the right). In action-descriptive texts (Figure 3.4b), the treatment is central within the disease world. Treatment is preceded by disease and by prevention of disease (to the left in the schema) and followed by the result of the treatment (to the right).

The vertical axis allows different aspects to be focused on. Disease is described with the focus on the phenomenon, the disease (at the top of the schema), on some part, an organ (in the middle) or on the whole, the patient (at the bottom). Treatment is described with the focus on the treatment as such (at the top of the schema), on treatment of an organ (in the middle) or on treatment of the patient (at the bottom).

To conclude this presentation of the cognitive methodology, I will show some examples of the categorization of the content. The relevant aspect is shown in brackets below each example.

Scientific world

(1)   Muscular palsy is a possible explanation, and this has been demonstrated up to six months after subcostal incisions.
(Aspect: Theory)

(2)   But pneumothorax is quite commonly regarded as a result of diagnostic or therapeutic measures or as a complication of complicated or advanced lung disease.
(Aspect: Classification)

(3)   During the period January 1977 until March 1978 29 patients were treated in 36 different cases of pneumothorax using the Heimlich valve (Table II).
(Aspect: Experiment)

Object world

(4)   Tuberculosis is an infectious disease which is caused by a living organism invisible to the naked eye, the tubercle bacillus, and which occurs not only in human beings, but also in animals.
(Aspect: Phenomenon)

Practical world

(5)   Insertion of the chest drain was preceded by premedication with pethidine and careful local anaesthesia.
(Aspect: Work)

Private world

(6) For the first few days after the insertion of the drain, many patients feel considerable pain.
(Aspect: Experience)

External world

(7) Introducing the simplified method of treatment proposed would result in significant savings.
(Aspect: Measures)

3.2 Pragmatic analysis

The second part of the methodology which I will present in this chapter analyses the texts at pragmatic level. For texts produced and used in the professions, goal-orientation, domain specificity and situatedness are constitutive features of the texts. As a theoretical background to the methodology I have developed, I will give a brief overview of the pragmatic field.

3.2.1 Theoretical background

In his *Foundations of the theory of signs* from 1938 Morris launched a semiotic theory in which he distinguished a semantic, a pragmatic and a syntactic level. When he used the term pragmatic for 'the relation of signs to their interpreters' (p. 30), he consciously connected his theory with the school of language philosophy called *pragmatism*. According to Peirce, one of the advocates of pragmatism, the meaning of a linguistic statement is the practical consequences which follow from the statement if this is true. 'To act is to act meaningfully' is a central idea within pragmatism, and, as Morris claimed, all our actions are goal-directed, which means that they can be described and explained fully, only if one can grasp the motives and purposes which lie behind them.

The cross-disciplinary character of pragmatics is also relevant for the methodology which I will describe below. The pragmatic analysis relates language practices to psychological, social and situational factors, thus also providing a basis for multidimensional understanding of linguistic actions. Pragmatic theory therefore has much in common with sociolinguistics, anthropology and ethnomethodology and is a useful tool for the analysis of both spoken and written discourse (cf. Levinson, 1983).

'Speech act theory' also developed within the philosophical tradition. In a series of famous lectures, Austin developed his ideas about *performatives*, which means that words, such as an utterance or a sentence, can perform an act if the situated frame is appropriate and in line with established convention (1976: 14–15). In his lectures, Austin further distinguishes three different senses or dimensions of the 'use of a sentence' or of 'the use of language': the locutionary act, e.g. the meaning, the illocutionary act, e.g. the conventional force of the utterance, and the perlocutionary act, e.g. what we bring about or achieve by saying something (p. 109). The illocutionary effect is achieved when an utterance/sentence is performed in a given context. The perlocutionary effect is related to non-verbal actions, which are performed as a consequence of the locutionary and illocutionary acts.

Searle (1969) developed Austin's ideas further, thus making it possible to apply them to authentic text and talk. One problem with Austin's theory was related to intention and effect. Austin stated that the illocutionary force is the successful achievement of the speaker's intentions. This, however, leads to difficulties for the analyst. How should one separate the speaker's intention from the effect? Instead Searle attaches the illocutionary force to the listener's interpretation of the utterance, or the reader's interpretation of the sentence.

Searle also distinguished some basic illocutions, under which all other illocutions could be categorized: Representatives, Directives, Commissives, Expressives, Declaratives. As many analysts have found, it is not always easy to assign one single force to an utterance in an authentic conversation or negotiation, where what is shown at a surface level, e.g. directly expressed, not infrequently differs from that which underlies it, e.g. indirectly meant. Spoken discourse is indeed a process where meaning is constructed successively and collectively. For the analysis of written discourse, however, I have found that *speech act theory* provides a useful tool to grasp the action orientation of the text at a micro level.

The conventional contract-bound character of discourse is also central for the ideas developed in Grice (1975). Grice, who was also a philosopher, proposed four conversational maxims that arise from the pragmatics of natural language and which were related to *quality, quantity, relation* and *manner*. The *contract* between speakers/authors and listeners/readers thus means that speakers/authors are assumed to follow certain maxims, i.e. to say or write what they believe is the truth (quality), make their contributions as informative as is required for the current purpose of the exchange (quantity), say what is relevant (relation) and express themselves in an orderly and clear way, avoiding obscurity and ambiguity (manner). Grice did not assume that all people should constantly follow these maxims. Instead they should be understood as describing the assumptions listeners and readers normally make about the way speakers will talk. If the overt surface meaning of a sentence, however, is not consistent with the

Gricean maxims although the circumstances lead us to think that the author/speaker is nonetheless obeying the cooperative principle, we tend to look for other meanings that could be implied by the sentence. In a communicative event when the speaker/author – either purposefully or unintentionally – flouts or violates the maxims, some other, hidden meaning might be implied. If someone (A) has suggested a game of tennis to a friend, who in turn just replies with 'It's raining', this short utterance is indeed a violation of the maxims of quality and quantity of spoken language. In the particular situated frame, however, the reasoning behind the utterance becomes clear to A, i.e. she understands the implied meaning.

A central idea in Grice's theory is the assumed *contract* between the participants in the communicative event. A similar contract lies behind the pragmatic approach, developed for instance in Rossipal (1978), which views all communication as *directly* or *indirectly action-directed*. The author or speaker is considered to have a main purpose in making the statement, and this main purpose can be traced to one or more parts of the text or sequence. This part of the text/sequence can be described as its *goal information*. The purpose of the other parts of the text is to help make readers cooperate, understand, agree to and know how to act in accordance with the author's goal. This later information is called *auxiliary information*. These categories and sub-categories will be referred to in 3.2.2.2., where I present the method for pragmatic analysis at macro level.

3.2.2 Method for pragmatic analysis

The pragmatic methodology described below is directed towards both the micro and the macro levels. The categorization of the *illocution types* of the clauses is directed towards the micro level of the text, while the categorization of the *subsidiary function of the text parts* is directed towards the macro level. The pragmatic analysis is therefore undertaken in two steps.

3.2.2.1 Micro analysis: illocutions

The first step of the pragmatic analysis has as its aim a micro analysis of professional texts and the method used is based on speech act theory, as this was developed by Searle (1969). Taking Searle's categories as a starting point (cf. above), I distinguish the following five main speech act types: *informative, explicative, expressive, argumentative* and *directive*. I further distinguished a sixth type, named *metacommunicative*. This type covers metacomments related to the text and comments on the disposition of the text. Under each of the other main types of illocutions a set of subcategories was distinguished.

Informative:	Describe
	Assume
Explicative:	Explain
	Clarify
	Compare
	Conclude
	Describe and explain
	Describe and clarify
Expressive:	Express involvement
	Question, doubt
	Disagree
	Agree
	Criticize negatively
Argumentative:	Maintain, claim
Directive:	Recommend
	Require
	Prohibit
	Permit
	Request
Metacommunicative:	Make metacommunicative comments
	Indicate text disposition
	Cite

Each macrosyntagm, or clause, of a text is categorized in relation to illocution. This categorization is based on the main verb of the clause, and in ambiguous cases also on surrounding adverbials.

3.2.2.2   Macro analysis: goal-directed structure

The second step of the pragmatic analysis is directed towards the macro level. Inspired by scholars who posited the action and goal-directed structure of communication (e.g. Rossipal, 1978), I developed a method

41

by which the subsidiary function of the text parts can be categorized in relation to the structure of the text as a whole. Written texts are seen as communicative events in which an author (or authors) addresses a reader (or readers) with an action-directed purpose. The author uses the text to get a message through to his or her readers, to make them act or think in a desired way. The author is considered to have a main purpose with his text, and this main purpose can be traced to one or more parts of the text.

The method for pragmatic analysis at macro level tries to grasp the subsidiary function of the text constituents in the structure of the text as a whole. In this analysis of pragmatic content, the smaller elements of the text are categorized in terms of their relationship to the main purpose, in terms of their role within the purpose structure of the text. A distinction is made between *goal information* and *auxiliary information* as shown below.

Goal information and auxiliary information

Categories	*Subcategories*
Goal information	Text goal
	Action goal
Auxiliary information aiming to secure reader's	
−cooperation	Marking of author's authority
	−Sender
	−Expert
	−Source
	Indication of addressee
	Indication of relevance of
	the message
−comprehension	Definition
	Categorization
	Summary
	Illustration
−conviction	Example
	Proof
−competence to act	Description of action

If relevant, the macrosyntagm, or clause, has been assigned to one or more of the categories and subcategories related to goal and auxiliary information. This means that some macrosyntagms are not assigned to any of these categories.

3.3 Macrothematic analysis

The third part of the methodology which will be presented in this chapter analyses the texts at macrothematic level. Professionals write and talk in accordance with the genre patterns which they have learnt and internalized as a part of their training and socializing into a community. These patterns organize the content, both at micro and macro levels, in ways which are relevant for the activities within the particular domain. For an analysis of how professional discourses vary and change over time, I have found it relevant to develop a methodology which grasps the content organization at macro level. As micro and macro levels are interdependent, I will include literature on both levels below.

3.3.1 Theoretical background

The content organization of spoken and written professional discourse – documents, meetings, negotiations, etc. – is to a great extent conventionalized. The progression of the information flow and the structure of argumentation and narration follow patterns which are formed within the particular professional community and internalized by the members of this community. Professionals write and talk in accordance with the genre patterns which they have learnt and internalized as a part of their training and socializing into a community. They have to learn how they should address their readers and listeners in a way that is both recognized as appropriate for the particular purpose and can be understood by the participants in the communicative event.

At a micro level, the information flow of texts has been described as an interchange between *themes* or *topics* (old information) and *rhemes* or *comments* (the new information). Czech textlinguists within the 'Prague school' related this information flow to a 'functional sentence perspective'. They claimed that each element of a sentence has a communicative function within the sentence as a whole. The various elements of the sentence contribute more or less new knowledge, which makes it possible to assign different information values to them (Daneš, 1970; also cf. Enkvist, 1974; Källgren, 1979).

Among the early textlinguists we also find scholars who endeavoured to develop a methodology for the description of the overall structure of a text – its *micro* and *macro structures* (van Dijk, 1977). In Kintsch and van Dijk (1978) textlinguistic and cognitive psychology theories are combined in a model which aims to grasp how a reader manages to create a mental representation of a text as whole, drawing on our stored knowledge of text patterns at macro level. The concepts of *schema, script* and *frame* (cf. 3.1.1), originally developed within artificial intelligence, turned out to have an explanatory force in relation to how we store knowledge of text patterns and text types and how they are used in writing and reading (Schank and Abelson, 1977; Thorndyke, 1977). By studying patients with brain injuries neurologists found how knowledge of wholes was stored in separate parts of the brain from knowledge of details (Lurija, 1976), findings which gave studies on holistic text patterns and text comprehensibility a cognitive basis.

Textlinguists interested in the macro structures of texts have also been influenced by narratologists who have tried to grasp the textual deep structures, e.g. Vladimir Propp, Roland Barthes and Algirdas Greimas. Other influential studies show how genuine popular narratives are steered by common patterns. When Labov and Waletzky (1967) interviewed poorly educated people they found the following common story structure: *orientation, complication, evaluation, resolution* and *coda*. Grimes and Glock (1970) also analysed popular narratives to reveal a similarity between these story patterns and literary prose. Another pattern found in narrative is the 'Problem-solution pattern'. In his book *On the Surface of Discourse*, Hoey (1983) distinguishes different general text patterns: a Problem Solution pattern, a Matching pattern, and a General-Particular pattern.

The aim of these theories developed within textlinguistics, cognitive psychology and narratology were to grasp universal linguistic patterns. For an analysis of professional discourse, however, it is necessary to find methods to grasp the more specific text features as well as those common to all texts. A relevant approach to the study of genre development emanates from a group of researchers in Birmingham, UK, in the 1980s.

In an article in 1981, Swales developed his famous CARS-model (CARS = Create A Research Space) for the description of the introductory parts of scientific articles. Swales analysed 48 articles from different academic disciplines, and found that the rhetorical structure of their introductions could be summarized in relation to four 'moves', which most often appeared in the texts in the following order:

CARS-model (Swales, 1981)

Move 1. Establishing the field
    a. showing centrality of the topic
    b. stating current knowledge of the topic
    c. ascribing key characteristics

Move 2. Summarizing previous research

Move 3. Preparing for present research
    a. indicating a gap
    b. question raising
    c. extending a finding

Move 4. Introducing present research
    a. stating the purpose
    b. describing present research

Other researchers have made a similar rhetorical analysis of other parts of the texts, e.g. discussion and result sections (Adams Smith, 1990; Peng, 1987; Dudley-Evans, 1986). Dudley-Evans (1989) thus found the following categories relevant for the analysis of discussion sections of scientific articles: background information, statement of result, (un)expected outcome, reference to previous research (comparison), explanation of a surprising or unsatisfactory result, deduction, hypothesis, reference to previous research (support), recommendation, justification. Huckin (1987), who made an attempt to apply Swales' four moves to the discussion section, found that there they appeared in reversed order:

Introduction	*Discussion*
4. Introducing present research	1. Statement of major results
3. Preparing for present research	2. Redescription of gap
2. Summarizing previous research	3. Selective literature review
1. Establishing the field	4. Implication for larger issues

The CARS-model has been used for a number of studies. It has been elaborated on since the 1980s by Swales himself (1990) and many others. In his extensive studies Bhatia (1993) has developed rhetorical analysis as a tool for the analysis of text of different kinds.

45

3.3.2 Method for macrothematic analysis

The methodology I present below is inspired by the moves analysis used by Swales and Dudley-Evans. In order to make it useful for the analysis of texts from different periods and from different genres (scientific and popular science), I have modified and expanded the Birmingham model. The most important differences are a distinction of a supertheme called *conclusion,* and of different macrothemes related to consequences and measures directed towards society.

This analysis of the content structuring comprises two steps. The first step involves a categorization of *supertheme.* Four superthemes were distinguished: *Introduction, Theme development, Discussion, and Conclusion.* The second step aims at a finer subcategorization of the content. For the Uppsala corpus of scientific and popular science articles from different periods (cf. Chapters 4 and 6), we found it useful to distinguish the following set of *macrothemes.* Although each macrotheme most often appears within one of the four superthemes, the two theme categorizations were made independently. Below, however, I have chosen to list the macrothemes in connection to the supertheme to which they are most often related.

Supertheme	Macrotheme
Introduction	Presentation of the area
	Problem/knowledge gap/ research question
	Relevance of the problem/area
	Research review/ research situation
	Current situation
	Earlier situation
	Purpose of the investigation/ the treatment/the experiment
Theme development	Phenomenon, e.g. disease, technology, economic situation
	Method
	Implementation
	Results

	Material
	Follow-up or extension
Discussion	Explanation/interpretation/analysis of results
	Validation, i.e. data presented as evidence for conclusions or hypotheses
	Deduction, i.e. conclusion or consequence of presented facts
	Recommendation of new investigation, treatment or method
	Summary of results
	Expected or unexpected outcome/ answer or no answer to questions
	Hypothesis
Conclusion	Future situation
	External, societal consequences
	Unsolved or future problems
	External measures, i.e. measures intended to have societal impact
	Problems related to external measures
	Justification of recommended investigation/treatment/measure
	Hypothesis of solution
	Suggestion for future measure/action

The macrothematic analysis of the corpus of scientific and popular science texts from different disciplines and periods presented above have included a categorization of each macrosyntagm, or clause, of the texts in terms of both supertheme and macrotheme. The variation and change in the content structuring of texts can thus be described through this analysis.

A superthematic categorization of the text parts can also be useful in providing a picture of the overall content structuring of the texts. As an example of how the linear progression of texts can be studied, I will present the method I used to analyse 90 scientific and popular science articles. Based on the results of the superthematic categorization of

47

Table 3.1 Superthematic structure in 90 articles (First published as Table 8.4 in Gunnarsson, 1993: 171)

Text	Linear structure	Text	Linear structure
Science		*Popular science*	
ES1	Φ · · · Φ · · Φ · · · Φ · · Φ · · ·	EP1	· · · Φ · · · · · Φ · Φ · · · · ·
ES2	Φ · · Φ · Φ · · Φ · · Φ ♦ Φ · · · · · · · ·	EP2	Φ · · Φ · · · · Φ · · Φ ♦ Φ · · · · · · · Φ · ·
ES3	Φ · · Φ · · · Φ · · · · · · Φ · · · Φ · · ·	EP3	Φ · · Φ · · Φ · · · Φ · · Φ · · ·
MS1	Φ · Φ · Φ · Φ · · ♦ · · · ·	MP1	Φ · · · · · · Φ · ♦ · · · ♦ ♦ Φ · · Φ · · · Φ · Φ ·
MS2	Φ · Φ · Φ · · · ♦ Φ · · Φ ·	MP2	Φ · Φ · · · ♦ ♦ · · Φ · · Φ · · · Φ · · ·
MS3	Φ · Φ · Φ · Φ · Φ · ·	MP3	Φ · Φ · · · · · · Φ · · Φ · ·
TS1	Φ · · Φ · Φ · · Φ · · Φ · · · · · Φ ·	TP1	Φ · Φ · Φ · · Φ · Φ · · · · · · ·
TS2	Φ · Φ · · · · Φ · · · Φ · Φ ·	TP2	Φ · Φ · Φ · Φ · Φ ·
TS3	Φ · · Φ · Φ · · Φ · Φ ·	TP3	Φ · Φ · Φ · Φ · Φ ·

Φ Introduction   · Theme cycle   ♦ Discussion cycle

Note: E – economic articles, M – medical articles, T – technical articles each article, I could describe its linear thematic progression in a way that made comparisons over time interesting. The four superthemes – Introduction, Theme development (T), Discussion (D) and Conclusion (C) were grouped together in three clusters or cycles: *introduction, theme cycle* and *discussion cycle. Theme cycle* here refers to a linear sequence starting with theme development and optionally followed by a discussion section and/or a conclusion section: the combinations TDC, TD, TC and T are each counted as one theme cycle. *Discussion cycle* refers to a linear sequence starting with the supertheme discussion and optionally followed by a conclusion section, the combinations DC and D are each counted as one discussion cycle.

Table 3.1 gives an exemplary picture of how such an analysis could be undertaken and how at an abstract level it could point to differences in the content structure of texts from different periods and in different disciplines.

A comparison of the structures of the economic articles – E at the top of the table – with those of the medical – M in the middle – and the technical – T at the bottom – shows that the economic articles are of a more theme repetitive kind, while the medical and technical articles are more straightforward in character and begin with an introduction followed by one or two theme cycles. If we look at the medical and technical articles, we will further find that this straight, simple structure is more characteristic of the later articles, period 3, than of those from periods 1 and 2. For medicine, we can also note that this linear structure characterizes science – left part of the table – rather than popular science – right part.

3.4 Conclusions

As mentioned earlier, this multidimensional methodology has been applied to several large text corpora: (1) to the 'Uppsala LSP corpus', which consists of 360 scientific and popular science articles published in Swedish journals and periodicals on economics, medicine and technology during three centuries; (2) to the 'Uppsala contrastive corpus', which consist of texts in English, German and Swedish, representing 14 different text types, produced within banks, structural engineering firms, university departments of history and occupational medicine in Great Britain, Germany and Sweden (in total 8,858 macrosyntagms); and (3) to Fredrickson's corpus, which includes all the documents from 24 court cases – 12 from an American court of appeal (Michigan) and 12 from a Swedish court of appeal (Svea hovrätt).

In these different studies, the texts were manually analysed in detail, coded and processed by computer according to statistical methods.

For the scientific and popular science articles, the various analyses were also integrated in a comprehensive textual description. As the macrothematic analysis was carried out concurrently with the cognitive and the pragmatic analyses, it was possible to relate the cognitive text structure and the pragmatic illocution pattern to the various superthemes. This meant that we attained a broad and multifaceted view of genre variation and change, also in relation to context.

The Uppsala research programme on the emergence and development of scientific writing has also focused on vocabulary and terminology. An extensive study of how the vocabulary used in texts from various areas of expertise has changed and varied over time was carried out on the basis of a quantitative analysis of the entire LSP corpus. The aim of this quantitative study has been to map diachronically the vocabulary in scientific and popular science texts in economics, medicine and technology from 1730 to 1985. All 360 articles included in the corpus have been computerized and computer processed in order to obtain frequency listings and concordances for the various text groups.

In different chapters of this book, I discuss results of analyses using the multidimensional text linguistic methodology presented above. Chapters 4 and 6, which both are included in the next section on 'Scientific discourse', discuss the results of the multidimensional text analysis. Chapter 4, which deals with the socio-historical construction of medical discourse, will also refer to the results of the quantitative analysis of the vocabulary of scientific texts.

In Chapter 11 included in the section on 'Discourse in large business organizations', the results of the application of multidimensional text analysis to texts produced in British, German and Swedish banks and structural engineering firms are discussed.

Notes

1. The 'Uppsala LSP corpus' was built up within two large research projects, which between 1986 and 1992 were funded by one of the major Swedish research foundations, namely HSFR. This Uppsala programme on scientific and popular scientific articles was undertaken at FUMS (Unit for Advanced Studies in Modern Swedish) at Uppsala University. The first, textlinguistic part of the programme, which studied articles from three periods of the twentieth century, was carried out within the research project 'LSP texts in the 20th century' and with a project team consisting of myself as director, Björn Melander, Harry Näslund and Björn Skolander. The second, vocabulary part, which studied articles from three centuries, 1730–1985, was carried out within the research project 'The emergence of languages for specific purposes'. The project team consisted of myself as director and Björn Skolander.

2. The 'Uppsala constrastive corpus' was built up within a research project entitled 'Texts in European writing communities'. This project, which was funded by Riksbankens jubileumsfond (a major Swedish research foundation) between 1994 and 1997, was undertaken at FUMS, Uppsala University, and involved an interdisciplinary team from three departments of this university: the Scandinavian, English and German departments. The project team consisted of myself as director, Bo Andersson, Ingegerd Bäcklund, Anna Levin, Ulf Norberg, Lena Norling, Eva Danielsson and Marie Sörlin.

3. Kirstin Fredrickson built up the Swedish part of her corpus during the 1991–92 academic year, when she was a guest doctoral student at FUMS, Uppsala University. In her doctoral dissertation in linguistics (Fredrickson, 1995), she compares appeal court documents from the Swedish Court of Appeal 'Svea Hovrätt' with documents from Michigan Court of Appeal.

Section 2
Scientific Discourse

This section, which comprises three chapters, explores the emergence and development of scientific discourse within medicine, technology and economics. Chapter 4, concerns the socio-historical construction of medical discourse. Medical articles from three centuries: the eighteenth, nineteenth and twentieth centuries, are analysed and discussed in relation to three different scientific stages: the pre-establishment stage, the establishing stage and the specialized stage. The multidimensional methodology which was presented in Chapter 3 is used to analyze changes in text patterns at cognitive, pragmatic and macro-structural levels. The analysis also deals with changes in linguistic expressions of evaluation over time. The theoretical basis for the study is the constructivist framework developed in Chapter 2.

In Chapter 5, my analysis deals with the non-verbal representation in 90 scientific articles within technology, medicine and economics from the same period, 1730–1985. This chapter also concerns the construction of scientific discourse, in this case with a focus on graphic representation, formulas and tables. The study compares article from the three fields in order to find out if and how they vary as to the role of the non-verbal representation. The changes found over time are also discussed in relation to an assumption about a possible connection between scientific thinking and communication.

Chapter 6 views the development of scientific writing within economics from the perspective of internationalization and globalization. I analyse how textual patterns changed when an originally national journal changed language from Swedish to English lingua franca and became an international journal with a global readership. My analysis focuses on the design of the journal, the general outline of its articles and the gradual changes in journal and article patterns. The development is discussed from the perspectives of the national scientific and linguistic communities.

4 The socio-historical construction of medical discourse

In this chapter I will sketch an exemplary picture of the emergence and development of medical written discourse. I will analyse and compare medical articles published in scientific journals during three centuries – the eighteenth, nineteenth and twentieth centuries – and discuss my results in relation to the varied contextual frameworks in which these texts were written. Socio-historical changes in relation to text patterns and linguistic expressions of evaluation will thus be related to different scientific stages: the pre-establishment stage, the establishing stage and the specialized stage.

My analysis in this chapter takes as its theoretical basis the constructivist approach developed in Chapter 2. In the first part of this chapter, I briefly recapitulate what a constructivist view entails for medical language at cognitive, social and societal layers. As an illustration of what scientific language was like at different periods, I cite in the second part selected excerpts from medical articles published in the eighteenth, nineteenth and twentieth centuries. In the third part, I return to the history of medical science and outline its development in relation to three scientific stages. Part 4 presents the study of scientificality in medical articles and discusses its results in relation to the content and content structuring of the texts (4.1), the formal organization of the texts (4.2) and the linguistic expressions of evaluations (4.3). In part 5, I return to the scientific stages and place the analysed articles on developmental axes. Part 6 includes my conclusions.

4.1 A constructivist approach to medical discourse

My claim in this chapter is that a constructivist approach[1] deepens our understanding of the historical development of medical language and communication in its rich and varied totality. Medical scientific discourse has emerged in a cooperative and competitive struggle among scientists to create the knowledge base of their field, to establish themselves in relation to other scientists and to other professional groups, and to gain influence and control over political and socio-economic means. In order to grasp the dynamic processes we should therefore include the cognitive as well as the social and societal layers in our analysis.

If we begin by considering the *cognitive layer*, we find that the medical profession has a certain way of viewing reality, a certain way of highlighting different aspects of the world around it. Socialization into the medical profession means learning how to discern the relevant facts, how to view the relationships between different factors. The medical practitioners and scientists are taught how to construct and use a grid or a lens to view reality in a professionally relevant way. Language, texts and spoken discourse help them in this construction process. They use language in the construction of medical knowledge. Medical terminology, medical text patterns, and medical text and discourse content have developed as a means of dealing with reality in a way that is appropriate for medical purposes.

Secondly, where the *social layer* is concerned, the medical group, like other social groups, is also formed by the establishment of an internal role structure, group identity, group attitudes and group norms. The use of medical scientific language during different periods is thus related to the type and level of the medical scientific community (the social group), its size, structure, degree of professionalization, degree of internationalization, degree and nature of mutual contacts, existence of publications, etc.

Thirdly, as regards the *macrosocial* or *societal layer*, the medical professional group also stands in a particular relationship to the society in which it operates: it exerts certain functions and is given a certain place within that society. The members of the medical profession play a role in relation to other actors in society, and the professional group acts in relation to other groups.

It is through language that medical professionals exert their societal function. If medical practitioners and scientists are going to play a role on the political scene, they have to construct their communicative behaviour in a way that serves that purpose. Their relationship to written texts and spoken discourse and to different genres is also important. The medical scientists adapt to established genres but are also involved in forming new genres, which means that the way in which language is used within medical science during different periods is linked with the relationship of the scientist and the scientific community to society in general. The societal layer is thus related to economic and political factors. It is related to power and status patterns in the particular society, e.g. the nation state, as well as on the global scene.

The cognitive, social and societal layers are strongly related to the emergence and continuous re-creation of professional language, and they are a part of the construction of professional language and discourse. Historically, language is constructed in relation to all these layers. The cognitive establishment of the field takes place at the same time as the professions are fighting for their place in society and to strengthen their group in relation to other groups.

4.2 Excerpts from medical articles from different periods

As an illustration of the emergence of the scientific use of language within medicine, I will cite selected excerpts from three medical articles. The excerpts have been selected to express the tendencies that were found more generally in the large medical corpus, comprising 60 articles, which will be analysed in this chapter. The articles cited below were written by Swedish scientists and published in the Swedish medical journal of the time. I present the excerpts in an English translation.

The first three excerpts are taken from an article from 1782 which was published in the Annals of the Swedish Academy of Sciences. The article deals with a method intended to cure tuberculosis, the so-called cowshed cure, which can be briefly described as requiring the patient to live and reside in a cowshed

Text 1[2]

(1)   Mr. *READ's* little Treatise on the Cowhouse Cure has attracted much attention from those suffering from tuberculosis in this Country since Dr. SCHÜTZERCRANTZ published and translated the work in Swedish in 1768. Many became curious and attempted this cure, and did so more often than not with blind trust that far exceeded those bounds to which common caution should have confined them: bounds that it would be harmful for a healthy person to transgress, let alone invalids.

(2)   In the month of September, the mistress moved into this room. By now the disease of tuberculosis had quite possessed her. [. . .] Her lack of breath was now so stifling that she had to spend both night and day sitting in her bed; and she was moreover afflicted with a permanent colicky diarrhoea and swollen legs. Dr. SCHÜTZERCRANTZ and Mr. *NATHORST* had, like me, given up every hope of her recovery.

This new accommodation seemed fairly strange to the sick lady to begin with. Unaccustomed to the noise of cattle, caused by the rubbing of their flanks and the contact of their horns with the mangers, for several nights she was unable to sleep, for as soon as she dozed off this clamour awoke her and that more often than not with some amazement. No less repugnant did it seem to her to eat in such a disagreeable room, with an open drain full of cattle dung. But she gradually accustomed herself to this new regime. She could see her husband's concern for her; she thought about her small children, of whom she was so fond; she contemplated her weak and decrepit condition; she could endure anything if only she could regain her health. I visited her daily as her physician; her husband and friends spent the best part of the day with her, and gradually she became used to this way of life, was merrier, undertook small chores, and hardly had a month passed before I fancied I could see clear signs of some recovery in the abatement of her diarrhoea and the improvement of her breathlessness, that she was able to do without a cushion or two to support her back to maintain her sitting position.

(3)   Moreover we know what exemplary effect a mild diet, of milk, vegetables, white meat etc., may have in improving the fluids. Today we have dissociated ourselves completely from the erroneous theories Doctors once embraced about the efficacy of Balsams on internal ulcers, they are scarcely used now externally, except in healthy wounds, as we could well do without them there too. /. . ./ In this form of consumption the cowshed cure can provide no visible gain, but rather worsens the condition with its irritating and softening qualities.

In his introduction (1), the author expresses explicit criticism, addressed directly to those beguiled into testing the method. This criticism is also aimed indirectly at those who introduced the method, Mr. Read and perhaps to some extent the translator, Mr. Schützercrantz. The author then goes on to describe three cases which he links to 'three personages of respectable rank, who, in each of their houses, made fitting arrangements in order to carry out this cure with every caution and with all seemliness that could be contrived'. The first case, excerpt (2), was that of the consumptive wife of a wealthy citizen in the southern part of Stockholm. What we can note is that the text very carefully describes observations of a single medical case. It provides a good deal of detail, also in relation to the individual patient and it contains dates. Another striking feature is of course its use of straightforward language. We can also note that there are no headings or references. Apart from the personal style and vivid description in excerpt (2), we can also observe that the author refers by name to two colleagues, 'Dr. SCHÜTZERCRANTZ and Mr. NATHORST', to corraborate his own judgement of the patient's condition. We can also note the subjective way in which the author describes his own assessment: 'before I fancied I could see clear signs of her recovery'. In the third excerpt (3), we can observe, among other things, the author's explicit and highly critical evaluation of previous medical theories: 'Today we have dissociated ourselves completely from the erroneous theories Doctors once embraced.'

The following three excerpts, (4) – (6), are taken from an article from 1842, which was published in the medical journal *Hygiea,* the predecessor of today's *Läkartidningen,* the Swedish medical journal. The article deals with asthma, or more specifically asthma thymicum. It discusses the research of other doctors and presents original findings.

Text 2[3]

(4) As this disease is still little known in this country, we have come to the conclusion that a more detailed description of its form is not superfluous, particularly in view of the fact that no such account exists in Swedish apart from the extract from *HIRSCH'S* thesis published in the Journal for Physicians and Pharmacists 1836, p. 261. Our intention will have been achieved if we can thereby also succeed in prompting among our own countrymen studies of this, in many respects, less widespread form of illness.

(5) The child awakes violently from sleep and emits a shrill squeaking noise, like the sound of inhalation during whooping-cough, but much shriller, higher and more superficial *(HIRSCH),* or even more like the sound caused by spasms of the bosom in hysterical women suffering from heart ailments. On closer examination one finds that this emanates from some obstruction to breathing; for the child becomes agitated, moves violently, and makes every effort to gasp in air, its face turns red, its eyes stare fixedly and immediately after the attack the patient has the appearance of terror and bursts briefly into tears.

(6) With regard to the *nature* and *essence* of the disease, on the whole two different opinions prevail. [. . .] But given the current state of the science it is, however, difficult to provide a satisfactory account of all the circumstances surrounding the disease. The increased size of the gland cannot here function mechanically by exerting pressure as notwithstanding that this pressure is continuous, during the first phases no sign of illness can be observed in the child between the paroxysms.

In his introduction (4), the author justifies his account by referring to the necessity of collecting information: 'Our intention will have been achieved if we can thereby also succeed in prompting among our own countrymen studies of this, in many respects, less widespread form of illness.' In excerpt (5), we can note that also in this article from 1842, the descriptions of the course taken by the illness are vivid. The perspective is, however, that of the watching doctor and not, as in the article from the eighteenth century, the patient. The author also refers to other colleagues, e.g. 'Hirsch'. The article on the whole contains a relatively extensive discussion of previous findings and the author identifies a large number of researchers and sources, and as excerpt (6) shows, the author does not merely list earlier findings uncritically but also adopts a standpoint to them.

Excerpts (7) – (10) are taken from a co-authored article published in 1980 in the Swedish medical journal *Läkartidningen*. The article deals with a method for the treatment of pneumothorax.

Text 3[4]

(7) The twofold aim of the treatment is both to re-expand the collapsed lung and also to prevent a relapse. What was recommended previously was a period of waiting for 4–6 weeks if there was no valvular pneumothorax (Becker, Müller 1970) or puncture with exsufflation (Schott, Viereck 1972). In recent years a more active attitude has been adopted with the introduction of chest drainage combined with continuous suction, known as the Bülau-drainage treatment (Becker, Müller 1970).

(8) *Materials and methods*
Between January 1977 and March 1978, 36 cases of pneumothorax, in 29 patients, were treated using a Heimlich valve (Table II).

The indications for the application of chest drainage were: 5–7 apical pneumothorax on a standing radiograph during expiration, or less severe, symptom-producing or persistent pneumothorax. All patients meeting these criteria were admitted to IVA.

(9) Removal of the Heimlich valve took place with the patient ambulant after drainage had been closed with the help of forceps for 4–6 hours and it had been determined that pneumothorax had not recurred with an X-ray.

(10) The combination of a short period of treatment with suction drainage and the Heimlich valve is a simple, reliable and effective treatment of various forms of uncomplicated pneumothorax. The treatment involves considerably less pressure on medical resources, mainly in Intensive Care Units. As fewer patients are confined to their beds for much of the treatment period, the method also involves a reduction of the total time spent in care.

In excerpt (7), we can observe how the accounts of the research of others have acquired their modern impersonal form, with attributions to articles in parentheses instead of explicit references to individual researchers. Here criticism is expressed implicitly: 'What was recommended previously'; 'In recent years a more active attitude has been adopted'. It is also veiled to a greater extent: 'The effect of the treatment on the function of the lungs seems to be fairly insignificant'. Excerpt (8) provides an example of how the authors can introduce their own research. Patients are viewed as quantifiable material. Methods are described using specialist terminology. There is an abundance of numbers and names of drugs and devices. We also find headings, tables and diagrams in the text. As excerpt (9) shows, the illnesses are described from the perspective of the physician, or more correctly of the researcher. Here experimental results are being analysed, not, as previously, cases being described. The article concludes with the adoption of an explicit stance on behalf of the method (10): 'a simple, reliable and effective treatment', 'involves considerably less pressure', 'the method also involves a reduction'. The author does not emerge here either, however, but the conclusion is presented as the logical deduction from the facts presented.

4.3 Stages in the development of medical science

All three articles cited above belong to the same genre, the medical scientific article genre. They were all written by medical scientists and for medical expert readers. Of more relevance for our discussion in this chapter is that the three articles were constructed in different contextual frames.

If we now turn to the history of medical science, we find that medical knowledge and practice took a great step forward in the seventeenth and in particular in the eighteenth century. However, it was only gradually that it developed into a science in the modern sense. Since the eighteenth century, all societies have undergone radical change. Changes have also taken place within the medical scientific community: (1) Medical knowledge has grown immensely; (2) Science in general and the philosophy of science have undergone changes. Statistics and empirical methods have developed. Positivism has become the only accepted view in many sciences; (3) The medical profession has gradually become increasingly established and recognized. Today, doctors are considered highly valuable professionals, and medical scientists and medical research are considered highly important to society; (4) The medical scientific community has become much larger. The number of doctors, medical scientists and students of medicine has increased, as has the number of medical journals and conferences.

Important changes have thus taken place relating to medical science, science in general, the medical profession and the medical scientific community. As the following discussion of results will show, language and discourse are essential elements in the construction of medical science, in profession-building and in the shaping of a medical scientific community. It will further show how academic genres play important roles in this process of construction – of scientific

61

knowledge, of the role of scientist in society, and in the growth and strengthening of the social network among scientists.

In this chapter, I will discuss changes involving language and text patterns in relation to three scientific stages: the pre-establishment stage, the establishing stage, and the specialized stage. For each layer – the cognitive, social and societal – the three stages can be summarized on a developmental axis:

Cognitive layer

Individual findings – Accumulation of findings – Integration into theory.

Social layer

Isolated researchers – Academic grouping – Advanced scientific community.

Macrosocial/societal layer

Scientists function within society – Scientists function within society and academic groupings – Scientists function within the scientific community.

4.4 Scientificality in medical articles from 1730 to 1985

The empirical results which will be referred to in this chapter are based on studies of Swedish medical language carried out at Uppsala University. The medical corpus which will be focused on here consists of 60 scientific articles: 10 from each of the 6 periods: I 1730–1799; II 1800–1849; III 1850–1880; IV 1895–1905; V 1935–1945; VI 1975–1985. All these articles come from scientific journals and deal with pulmonary diseases (30 articles) or skin diseases (30 articles).[5] The analysis has focused on different textlinguistic levels – the cognitive, the pragmatic, and the macrothematic – and also on vocabulary and terminology. For a detailed description of the methodology, see Chapter 3. My discussion below will be organized in the following way: in 4.4.1 I will focus on the content and content structuring of the texts, in 4.4.2. on the formal organization of the text, and in 4.4.3. on the linguistic expressions of evaluations.[6]

4.4.1 Content and content structuring of the texts

First, I will here relate the content and content structuring of medical articles to the stage reached by the domain of medical science, in terms of degree and type of scientificality, and also to the role of scientists in society.

As described in Chapter 3, the cognitive analysis examined the content of the text in relation to five *cognitive worlds*: a 'scientific world', a 'practical world', an 'object world', a 'private world' and an 'external world'. Within each of these, two or three *aspects* were discerned: within the scientific world 'theory', 'classification' and 'experiment', within the practical world 'work' and 'interaction', within the object world 'phenomenon-focused', 'part-focused' and 'whole-focused', within the private world 'experience' and 'conditions' and within the external world 'conditions' and 'measures'. The cognitive analysis also comprised an analysis of text content in relation to four time *dimensions*: 'cause', 'phenomenon', 'process' and 'result'.

Each proposition in the articles was categorized in relation to *world*, *aspect* and *dimension*. We could thus calculate the proportions of the total number of propositions representing each world, each aspect and each dimension in texts from different periods.

The analysis showed a very clear increase in the proportion of each text devoted to the scientific world, i.e. to the presentation of 'theory', 'classifications' and 'experiment' over the periods. On the other hand, there was a clear decline in the role of the external world in particular, i.e. in the proportions of texts dealing with 'conditions' and 'measures' of a political, economic and social nature. There was also an increase in the proportion of 'experiment/observation' within the scientific world and a drop in the proportion of 'measures' within the external world. The analysis further showed that the proportions of each text devoted to describing 'causes' and 'phenomena' have decreased over time, while the proportions devoted to 'processes' and 'results' have increased.

Another part of the analysis, as developed in Chapter 3, focused on the macrothematic structure. The content of the medical articles were then categorized in relation to the four *superthemes*: 'introduction', 'theme development', 'discussion' and 'conclusions'. This analysis revealed an increase in how much of each text is devoted to the superthemes 'introduction' and 'theme development' (i.e. to a description of materials, methods, results). The proportion devoted to 'discussion' and in particular to 'conclusions', on the other hand, had declined.

A third analysis, which aimed at a description of the pragmatic character of the texts, i.e. the types of *illocution* present, pointed to an increase as regards 'informative' and 'explicative' illocutions and a decrease in 'expressive', 'argumentative' and 'directive' illocutions.

To sum up, the changes in the content and content structuring of Swedish medical articles from 1730 to 1985 show the following tendencies: more 'scientific world' – less 'external world'; more 'experiment' – less social, political and economic 'measures'; more 'process' and 'results' – less 'cause' and 'phenomenon'; a larger proportion of 'theme development' – a smaller proportion of 'discussion' and 'conclusions'; more 'informative' and 'explicative' illocutions – fewer 'expressive' and 'directive' illocutions.

These findings relating to changes in the medical article genre point, for one thing, to a development in medical science. The knowledge structure of the texts appears to have changed to include more emphasis on experiment and on process and results. There is also a trend towards a genre of a more purely descriptive character, in which the main part of the text is devoted to developing the theme, i.e. to description of the experiment, observations etc. These are features which could be related to a positivist scientific ideal. All these results can be related to the cognitive layer of the construction of academic discourse.

These results reveal the role played by scientists in society. In terms of text content, the proportion devoted to the external world and external measures has decreased, as has the proportion devoted to conclusions and directives. Such results can be discussed in the light of the specialization and professionalization of society. Compared with earlier periods, scientists today are acting to a greater extent in a discourse community of their own. Science in general and medical science in particular is accepted and highly esteemed in modern society. Considerable funding is given to medical research. The role of large-scale experiments has increased.

The discourse changes can be related to this endeavour among medical scientists to become specialists with a profession of their own and their own exclusive domain to deal with. A high degree of scientificality in spoken and written discourse imparts prestige.

A more purely scientific genre has emerged. Scientist-writers have turned towards their own group, and the medical article genre has become a within-science genre. The popularization of medical findings is undertaken by others – by trained journalists. Scientists can write for their own group without having to bother about a growing gap between the lay public and the experts. The article genre has become more exclusively internal and less concerned with reaching out to other sectors of society.

These results can also be interpreted in the light of the interplay between the cognitive and societal layers. The role played by the medical profession in society interrelates with the presentation of scientific content.

4.4.2 Formal organization of the text

Secondly, I will relate the formal organization of the texts and their rhetorical patterns to the stage reached in the development of the medical scientific community. A robust scientific community reveals itself in firm genre conventions: in more homogeneous texts and also in explicit indications of group affiliation.

The number and types of headings in the Swedish modern articles vary over time. The use of section headings has increased dramatically. The type of heading has also changed. In the early periods, headings relate to the content of the article, while in modern articles they relate to its structure: Material, Methods, Results, Discussion, Conclusions. The modern headings thus structure the presentation in a general scientific way, which also reflects a more homogeneous organization of the texts.

An increasing homogeneity is also found in relation to the thematic article structure.[7] The articles from the period around 1980 (1975–1985) were clearly more homogeneous in terms of their linear text structure than earlier articles (cf. Chapter 3). Similarly, the introductions in articles from different periods revealed a gradually greater homogeneity. This homogeneity can also be seen in a contrastive perspective, i.e. the Swedish pattern has come to resemble that of the English scientific article, as this is described in Swales (1990).

Another finding relates to the information flow of the text. An analysis of the connection between content structure and graphical disposition in articles from different periods showed that each sentence has become more independent with regard to the surrounding text. It introduces a new angle, which means that it becomes less integrated with its neighbouring sentences (Melander, 1993). We thus find a change towards a fact-listing or 'catalogue' style in the modern article.

This tendency towards a catalogue style can be seen as another feature reflecting firmer genre conventions. When texts are organized in a homogeneous and predictable way, there is less need to elaborate on the details. Readers know where in the text they will find different types of content. The tendency towards a more catalogue-like article could also be seen as indicating a strengthening of the scientific community. The knowledge of this community is well established among the specialist readers, and need not be elaborated on.

Other analyses reveal that the number of references per article has increased over time, and that their presentation has become more homogeneous. Another tendency relates to the changed use of personal pronouns. In the articles from the eighteenth century, the pronoun

65

'I' was used quite frequently although it has more or less totally disappeared in the articles from the latter part of the twentieth century. The pronoun 'we', on the other hand, which was quite unusual during the first two periods, had a similar low rank in the medical texts until the last period (1975–1985). The author's explicit marking of article relevance has also changed over time. We here find a shift from a societal orientation in earlier periods to a more internal orientation in the last period.[8]

To sum up, the changes in formal text organization and the rhetorical patterns show the following diachronic tendencies: more headings; more homogeneous text organization; more homogeneous article introductions; more fact-listing; more references; less use of the personal pronoun 'I'; more relevance marking relating to the group.

The medical article has developed towards greater homogeneity – relating to the use of headings, the superthematic text structure, the rhetorical structure of introductions etc. –, a homogeneity that indicates a strengthening of genre conventions. The medical article has become more established as a genre, and its genre conventions have become firmer and thus more homogeneous. This strengthening of the academic article genre, however, is also a sign of a growing and stronger medical discourse community. For the medical discourse community, as for most scientific discourse communities, writing plays an essential role as a group marker, and the establishment of firmer conventions for written text genres is part of the growth and strengthening of this community. The trend towards a more fact-listing and catalogue type of article can also be seen as a sign of a stronger discourse community, in the sense of a more homogeneous and closed community. It is a well-known fact within sociolinguistics that communication within a dense group or network needs to be less explicit and elaborated than communication within an open and less dense one (cf. discussion in Chapter 9).

The modern habit of giving references to the works of colleagues is another sign of a strong discourse community, a discourse community with a clear group feeling. When the group is essential to its members, it becomes important to indicate one's sense of belonging and one's relationship to other group members. Problems relating to the group also become more important than those relating to the world outside the group. The modern tendency to list references, to use 'we' instead of 'I', and to mark relevance in relation to one's own group can be viewed from this social perspective. I would suggest that these text features are part of the construction of an increasingly close-knit (dense) medical discourse community.

There is also a connection between these features and the role of medical scientists in society, i.e. the strengthening of the professional group is paralleled by a process of gradual specialization of the professions. These features are thus also part of the construction of a role for the medical community within society. We can thus see how the social and societal layers interact. Strengthening of the internal group structure is interrelated with the underlining of a role for the group in society.

4.4.3 Linguistic expressions of evaluations

Thirdly, I will relate the linguistic expressions of evaluation and its variation over time to the positioning of the scientist/author on the developmental axes for the three contextual dimensions.

The study referred to was based on an analysis of 30 Swedish scientific medical articles from six periods. All articles dealt with pulmonary diseases. The study, which comprised an analysis of evaluations linked to descriptions of the subjects studied, the diseases and treatments, the introduction of the author's own initiatives, and descriptions of the research and findings of others, focused on three main aspects: (1) what is being evaluated, (2) through whom the evaluation is taking place and (3) how the evaluation is being made.[9]

In articles from all periods, the object of the study and the initiatives of other researchers are evaluated. The author also refers to his own initiatives in most articles.

From a diachronic perspective, however, it is more interesting to consider the second aspect, through whom the evaluation is taking place (author's own voice, author through others, author through facts). A comparison of the medical texts from the eighteenth, nineteenth and twentieth centuries shows that in the earliest texts the evaluation is made by the author himself, using his own voice, whereas in later articles it is allowed to emerge indirectly via facts from others, e.g. in references to articles by others.

A change over time is also found in relation to the third aspect, how the evaluation is being made. When articles from the eighteenth century are compared to articles from the twentieth century, we find increasing temperance with the evaluations in articles from 1730 being expressed more severely. A more obvious change, however, relates to the degree of certainty. Here we find a discernible increase in the use of hedges and other expressions of caution over time.[10]

We thus find a progressive moderation of the author's own voice in the medical articles and increasingly the focus is placed on facts. There is another clear change in the author's relationship to facts, which is revealed in an increase in the frequency of markers of epistemic modality.

These tendencies were also found in analysis of word frequencies. As mentioned earlier, there is a change in the use of the personal pronouns 'jag' [I] and 'vi' [we] in the articles over time. The occurrences of the pronoun 'I' decline by half between period I (eighteenth century) and period IV (1895–1905) and disappear completely during period VI (1975–1985). To some extent the pronoun 'I' is replaced by the pronoun 'we' in the last period. In this case, however, the increased use of 'we' is not mainly explained either by the use of reader-inclusive 'we' or by co-authorship. It could rather be linked to the progressive phasing out of authorial identity in scientific prose.

A comparison of the frequencies of a number of markers of modality in the Swedish medical corpus, revealed an increase over time. All nine markers – 'torde' [is probably], 'tyder' [suggests], 'tycks' [seems], 'tänkbar' [conceivable], 'tveksam' [doubtful], 'sannolik' [likely], 'sannolikhet' [likelihood], 'möjlig' [possible], 'möjlighet' [possibility] – revealed a linear increase in the frequency over the six periods.

This increasing tendency to be cautious can of course be seen as a sign of the progressive extension of medical knowledge, i.e. it can be related to the author's placement on the knowledge axis. The greater the body of collective knowledge, the more aware authors are of its relativity. But it could also be linked to circumstances within the social group, in this case the medical community. In order to survive in a competitive society, which is what the world of medical research undeniably is, one must be careful not to lose face and take care not to threaten the face of others. Ideas of this kind are proposed in Myers (1989). Myers claims that in order to survive in the competitive academic world modern scientists adopt pragmatic politeness strategies and that Brown and Levinson's concepts of 'face saving' and 'face threatening' are relevant also in the analysis of scientific texts (Brown and Levinson, 1987). Scientists tread a narrow path between the need to emphasize their own achievements, on the one hand, and to criticize those of their peers, on the other.

It may well be that the difference in the wording results from the increased knowledge scientists now possess about illnesses and their treatment, i.e. that the difference can be linked to the cognitive dimension. Or it may result from greater awareness of the importance of politeness in a large and well-developed scientific community, i.e. the difference can be linked to the social dimension; doctors/researchers admittedly make evaluations, but they avoid expressing them subjectively and straightforwardly and choose greater objectiveness, thus showing more caution.

4.5 The relationship between text and context for scientific medical writing

In this part of the chapter, I will return to the three scientific stages distinguished earlier (in 4.3) and relate my results more systematically to each one of them. I will also place medical articles from the centuries discussed here, i.e. the eighteenth, nineteenth and twentieth centuries, on developmental axes related to each of the three layers: the cognitive, the social and the societal. Figure 4.1 illustrates the relationship between text and context for medical scientific articles during three centuries.

In the articles from the eighteenth century, e.g. Text 1 cited in part 4.2, we encounter a number of different individuals – the author himself, his colleagues and his patients – and their experiences and judgements are described. The typical article is full of explicit, severe and assured evaluations which concern the object of the study – the illness and method – and also the advocates of the method, its naïve practitioners. In the way the author writes, he places himself fairly obviously towards the left of all three contextual axes in Figure 4.1: he treats individual findings as if they exist *per se*, he describes himself and his colleagues as isolated researchers and he seems to act within society rather than the scientific community.

Cognitive dimension		
18th century	19th century	20th century
Individual findings	Accumulation of findings	Theoretical integration

Social dimension		
18th century	19th century	20th century
Isolated researchers	Academic groupings	Developed scientific community

Macrosocial dimension		
18th century	19th century	20th century
Scientists act within society	Scientists act within society and academic groupings	Scientists act within the scientific community

Figure 4.1 Text and context during three centuries (Gunnarsson, 2001a: 136)

In the articles from the nineteenth century, e.g. Text 2, the typical author adopts a considerably more analytic attitude to the research of others. The author himself figures as an evaluator. He also explicitly adduces the opinions of other researchers. The evaluations are of medium severity and the author marks his doubts in different ways. The author is fair and square in the middle of the contextual axes.

In the articles from the twentieth century (around 1980), e.g. Text 3, the typical author does not express himself in his own voice or explicitly through others. Evaluations take the form of the presentation of facts, supported by references to other works. Summaries of the research of others form an integral part of the description of the illness/method. What characterizes this and other articles in the sub-corpus from this period is above all the attitude adopted to facts. The evaluations are not few in number, but they are weak to medium severe rather than severe and they are presented throughout as less certain – in other words these authors should be placed to the right on the contextual axes.

4.6 Conclusions

Language constructs science in relation to the cognitive layer (the scientific content), the societal layer (the scientists' role in society) and the social layer (relations within the group). This construction process has been in progress since the first doctors tried to establish themselves as medical scientists and it is still continuing. In Sweden this process began in the seventeenth century. However, it was not until the middle of the eighteenth century that Sweden became a national writing community. Before 1740, the language of the learned was Latin, but in the Era of Liberty, from the middle of the eighteenth century, Swedish was gradually accepted as a scientific language, and the construction of medical science and the medical scientific community was related over a long period to the development of the Swedish medical article as a genre. This article has focused on this phase in the Swedish medical history, an account which ended in 1985 (cf. Chapter 6).

What has taken place since then is an accelerating Anglicization of the academic writing community in Sweden. English is now used in medicine as the medium for Ph.D. theses, for conference abstracts and papers, and for articles presenting original research (Gunnarsson, 2001b). *Läkartidningen*, the Swedish medical journal, still exists, but is no longer the prime forum for presentations of new findings. The Swedish medical scientists of today choose to present their research in English in international medical journals. When they write in *Läkartidningen*, the Swedish journal, they have other aims than to present original research findings. The Swedish medical scientific community has thus become diglossic, i.e. English is used for certain purposes and Swedish for others. In the Swedish medical journal, articles offer surveys and present research relating to basic diseases but it is no longer a journal for the original presentation of new research (Gunnarsson et al., 1995).

A development of the kind described here is not country specific. The shift from Latin to the national language took place around the same time in most western countries, and the modern extension of English as a scientific language is universal (Ammon, 2001; Carli and Ammon, 2007). The Anglicization of the medical scientific community and the accelerating use of the Internet as a communicative tool has led to intensified globalization and also homogenization of science and scientific language. From a socio-historical perspective this development is most interesting and will certainly in the future lead to important investigations. In Chapter 6, I discuss a study of the Anglicization of the economic scientific community.

Notes

1. A constructionist perspective on the emergence of scientific discourse and text genres are found within the sociology of science tradition (e.g. Knorr-Cetina, 1981, Latour and Woolgar, 1986). Bazerman (1988) studied the rise of modern forms of scientific communication, focusing on the historical emergence of the experimental article. A social constructivist approach in relation to written texts is also found in Bazerman and Paradis (1991) and in Gunnarsson, Linell and Nordberg (1997).
2. Bergius, P. J. (1782), 'Anmärkningar öfver Fähus-Curen för lungsiktiga', in *Svenska Vetenskapsakademiens Handlingar*. Stockholm, pp. 307–318.
3. Collin, J. G. (1842), 'Underrättelser om Asthma thymicum', *Hygiea*, 6, 256–271.
4. Lindström, F. and Schildt, B. (1980), 'Förenklad behandling av pneumotorax med Heimlich-ventil', *Läkartidningen*, 999–1001.
5. The Uppsala LSP corpus, which consists of 360 articles from three disciplines (medicine, technology and economics), is presented in Gunnarsson et al. (1987) and Gunnarsson and Skolander (1991).
6. This chapter draws on an article in *Encyclopedia in Language and Linguistics* (Gunnarsson, 2005b).
7. In Gunnarsson (1993), this study is presented in more detail.
8. In Gunnarsson (1998), this study is presented in more detail.
9. See Gunnarsson (2001a), for a detailed presentation of the study.
10. Compare Salager-Meyer (1994) and Valle (1999).

5 Non-verbal representation in articles within technology, medicine and economics

The studies on the socio-historical construction of medical scientific discourse in the previous chapter were based on analyses of the verbal elements of texts – on words, phrases and verbal text patterns. All non-verbal elements were excluded from the material used for these analyses. In this chapter, however, it is the non-verbal elements of scientific articles that my analysis will deal with. I will analyse and compare the role of non-verbal elements in scientific articles within technology, medicine and economics from different periods. My material will thus also comprise technical and economic discourse.

A similarity with the previous chapter is, however, that this chapter will also concern the construction of scientific discourse. Here my aim is to explore the role of graphic and other types of abstract non-verbal representation in order to deepen our understanding of the relationship between scientific representation and scientific thinking. As a theoretical background for my study, I will begin with a brief discussion of some ideas developed within the tradition of the sociology of science. In the second part of the chapter, I will present the study and discuss its results concerning graphic representations (5.2.1), formulas (5.2.2), tables (5.2.3) and mainly verbal articles (5.2.4). In part 5.3 I discuss what these results tell us about the scientific discourse practices within the three disciplines. In the concluding part (5.4), I return to the question of the relationship between non-verbal representation and scientific thinking.

5.1 Theoretical background

As the construction of scientific knowledge has largely taken place in written discourse, the verbal presentation of scientific ideas and thoughts have come to play the most essential role for the creation and dissemination of scientific knowledge. In varying degrees due to discipline and time, however, the non-verbal elements have also come to play an important role in the construction of scientific knowledge (Myers, 1988). Though earlier more difficult to transform into text, non-verbal representations have probably always been basic not only to thinking about scientific problems but also to the written discourse about them.

In his article 'Drawing things together', Bruno Latour warns us against mixing scientific thinking with scientific representational conventions, where certainly the invention of print and the modern development of printing techniques have come to make a difference. He states: 'The idea that a more rational mind or a more constraining scientific method emerged from darkness and chaos is too complicated a hypothesis.' (Latour, 1988: 19). The role of the paperwork, i.e. fixing ideas on paper, relates less to the thinking of the scientist than to his or her control of the readers and their interpretation. By means of graphic representations on paper, the scientist can highlight and determine certain perspectives and thus control readers' interpretations. The non-verbal element of scientific texts is important for the construction of scientific knowledge and its gradual accumulation within the scientific communities, and historical changes in the representational conventions tell us something about the state of the scientific discourse at the time.

According to Latour, 'there is no detectable difference between natural and social science, as far as the obsession for graphism is concerned' (p. 39). He means that graphism is basic to scientific thinking. I quote: 'Scientists start seeing something once they stop looking at nature and look exclusively and obsessively at prints and flat inscriptions' (p. 39). Latour stresses the importance for scientific thinking of a perceptual selection and a choice of a perspective from which nature can be viewed. Scientific thinking requires abstraction. According to Latour, scientists 'have to invent objects which have the properties of being mobile – movable from one case to another; from one situation to another – but also immutable – not susceptible to change – and also presentable, readable and combinable with one another' (p. 26).

The question of how non-verbal representation is related to the construction of knowledge has, of course, become increasingly relevant as a result of technical developments, where for instance the increased use of computers has not only made it possible but also relatively simple to work with images, diagrams and tables in the texts produced. During the last decade there have been numerous studies and discussions of the multimodal features of texts. One important issue in this context is, however, what significance the growing use of non-verbal elements in texts may be considered to have for the creation and dissemination of different forms of knowledge. Will increasing multimodality lead to new ways of thinking? Will our multimodality make it easier to share our thoughts? One reasonable assumption is

73

that developments in different disciplines will depend on the interaction of thinking and communication, i.e. that the construction of
knowledge requires researchers to postulate theories and produce
results that can be presented in ways that enable other researchers
to understand and accept them. The interaction of the verbal and the
non-verbal may therefore be assumed to influence the way one thinks
and perceives as well as how this is communicated to others. Images,
diagrams, formulas and tables enable reality to be filtered – offer a
perspective – that is important for both the researcher or writer and
for their audiences.

In this chapter, as stated above, I shall present a survey of scientific
articles from 1730 to 1985. My main question is whether the non-verbal
elements have changed over time, and if this change has differed in
the different disciplines I have studied – economics, medicine and
technology. In the conclusion, part 5.4, I return to the question posed
about the interaction/interplay between thought and representation.

5.2 Non-verbal representation in scientific articles

The study discussed in this chapter compares articles from the three
disciplines of economics, technology and medicine in order to find
out *if* and *how* the role of the non-verbal elements varies in the texts.
The material for this study is taken from the Uppsala LSP corpus,
which consists of 360 articles, 180 scientific and 180 popular articles, from three disciplines and six periods: 1730–1799, 1800–1849,
1850–1880, 1895–1905, 1935–1945, 1975–1985 (cf. Chapters 3 and 4).
Within each discipline, the corpus consists of articles dealing with
two subjects, for instance within medicine we have collected articles
dealing with lung diseases and articles dealing with skin diseases.
In this study of the non-verbal elements I will concentrate my analysis to 90 scientific articles dealing with one subject within each
discipline: within medicine those dealing with lung diseases; within
technology those dealing with electricity; within economics those
dealing with banking and the credit system. My analysis comprises
5 articles dealing with each subject in each of the six periods from
1730 to 1985.

As mentioned in the introductory paragraph, the Uppsala programme on scientific and popular scientific articles did not include
analyses of the non-verbal elements, such as pictures, graphic representations, formulas and tables. The study presented in this chapter,
however, deals with these previously excluded elements. My analysis
will thus focus on the non-verbal elements: (1) graphic representations
(photos, drawings, schemata, curves), (2) formulas and (3) tables.

With the aim of getting a picture of the historical developments within the three disciplines, I have investigated how frequent a certain type of representation was during the six periods. For each of the 90 articles I noted the existence of the various representation types mentioned above. To measure usage I chose to register the number of articles containing each type of representation during each period. As my material consists of 18 text groups with five articles in each group, this means that the value for each group can vary from 0 to 5.

5.2.1 Graphic representations

Graphic representation is used here as the main classification for the following subcategories: photos, drawings/sketches, schemata, curves (including different types of diagrams and charts). Table 5.1 shows the number of articles with graphic representations from different periods and disciplines. The year below the period figure indicates for the first three periods, I–III, the first year of each period, and for the last three periods, IV–VI, the middle year.

One thing we can note here is the difference between the disciplines. Graphic representations are much more frequent in technology than in medicine and economics. They are already found in two out of five technical articles in the first period, i.e. in the eighteenth century. Around 1900, period IV, four out of five technical articles contain graphic representations, while in the last two periods, around 1940 and 1980, all technical articles contain graphism.

For the medical discipline, we only find graphic representations during the last three periods, i.e. during the twentieth century. However, it is only in the last period, i.e. around 1980, that the use becomes more widespread with three out of five articles.

In economics, we find no graphic representations at all until the last period. Then, however, we find that as many as four out of five articles contain graphic representations. Within the economic article genre, we thus find a drastic change between 1940 and 1980.

As Table 5.1 shows, drawings and schemata are frequent during all periods, while curves – and quite naturally also photos – appear first during the twentieth century.

5.2.2 Formulas

Table 5.2 shows the use of formulas in the articles. Just as with graphic representations, there is a major difference in use of formulas between the technical articles on the one hand and the medical and economical articles on the other. The thirty medical articles included in my

Table 5.1 *Graphism in economics, medicine and technology 1730–1985. Total graphic representation, photographies, drawings, schemata, curves. Number of articles in each text group (Table 2 in Gunnarsson, 2005d: 307)*

	Period						Total
	I: 1730	II: 1800	III: 1850	IV: 1900	V: 1940	VI: 1980	
Total graphic representation							
Economics	0	0	0	0	0	4	4
Medicine	0	0	0	1	1	3	5
Technology	2	3	2	4	5	5	21
All	2	3	2	5	6	12	30
Photographies							
Economics	0	0	0	0	0	0	0
Medicine	0	0	0	0	0	2	2
Technology	0	0	0	2	3	4	9
All	0	0	0	2	3	6	11
Drawings							
Economics	0	0	0	0	0	0	0
Medicine	0	0	0	0	0	1	1
Technology	1	1	0	1	3	1	7
All	1	1	0	1	3	2	8
Schemata							
Economics	0	0	0	0	0	0	0
Medicine	0	0	0	0	0	1	1
Technology	1	1	0	1	3	1	7
All	1	1	0	1	3	2	8
Curves							
Economics	0	0	0	0	0	4	4
Medicine	0	0	0	1	1	1	3
Technology	0	0	1	2	4	3	10
All	0	0	1	3	5	8	17

Table 5.2 *Formulas in economics, medicine and technology 1730–1985. Number of articles in each text group (Table 3 in Gunnarsson, 2005d: 308)*

	Period						Total
	I: 1730	II: 1800	III: 1850	IV: 1900	V: 1940	VI: 1980	
Formulas							
Economics	1	0	0	0	1	0	2
Medicine	0	0	0	0	0	0	0
Technology	1	2	4	3	3	1	14
All	2	2	4	3	4	1	16

corpus do not contain one single formula. If we turn to economics, we find two articles containing formulas, one from the first period, eighteenth century, and one from the fifth, around 1940. Among the thirty technical articles, we find 14 which contain formulas. As we can see from the table, the use of formulas in the technical articles extends over time, with least use in the first and last periods. To conclude, the use of formulas seems to be discipline specific rather than period specific.

5.2.3 Tables

In Table 5.3 the term 'table' is used as a cover term for statistical representations in the form of tables and other systematic presentations of quantitative data.

Even for tables and other systematic presentations of quantitative data, technology stands out in comparison with the two other disciplines. Of the thirty technical articles studied, as many as 13 contain tables, while the corresponding figure for economics is eight and for medicine seven. In economics only one or two articles use tables or the like during the first five periods. None of the economic articles from the last period, however, contain tables or the like. As mentioned earlier, instead we find a widespread use of curves in the economic articles from period VI, four out of five.

In medicine, the use of tables is fairly constant over time, with a slight increase during the last two periods.

In technology, as mentioned above, the use of tables is more common than in the other disciplines. In particular we can note an increased use during periods III, IV and V, when tables are found in the majority of the technical articles. During the last period, however, the use of tables as a form of representation has decreased. If we compare the role

Table 5.3 *Tables and other systematic presentations of quantitative data in economics, medicine and technology 1730–1985. Number of articles in each text group (Table 4 in Gunnarsson 2005d: 308)*

	Period						**Total**
	I: 1730	**II: 1800**	**III: 1850**	**IV: 1900**	**V: 1940**	**VI: 1980**	
Tables							
Economics	1	2	2	1	2	0	8
Medicine	1	0	1	1	2	2	7
Technology	0	1	4	3	4	1	13
All	2	3	7	5	8	3	28

of tables in technology with that found for formulas (Table 5.2), we find the same trend for formulas as for tables. The use of graphic representations, however, follows a different path, i.e. we here find an increase in use over time, with a clear peak during the last period (cf. Table 5.1).

5.2.4 Mainly verbal articles

The purpose of the last table is to sum up the role of the verbal and the non-verbal in the studied articles. Table 5.4 shows the number of articles for each period which are *mainly verbal*, i.e. articles which do *not* contain any graphic representations, formulas, tables or other systematic presentations of quantitative data.

Table 5.4 points to a clear difference between technology, on one hand, with only five mainly verbal articles and economics and medicine, on the other, with 18 and 20 mainly verbal articles respectively.

We can further note that the verbal technical articles are all from the first two periods. During the last four periods, from 1850 and onwards, all technical articles in my corpus contain non-verbal elements, i.e. graphic representations, formulas or tables.

As for economics, we find a quite drastic change taking place between period V and VI. During the first five periods, the majority of economics articles were mainly verbal. The last period, however, means a shift, as the economists then seem to prefer curves for the presentation of their data and results.

The medical discipline is the most verbal discipline of the three; two thirds of the articles are mainly verbal. There is, however, also for this discipline a shift in the discourse practice. During period I to IV, nearly all medical articles (4; 5; 4; 4) were mainly verbal, while the corresponding figures for the last two periods, are two and one.

Table 5.4 *Mainly verbal articles in economics, medicine and technology 1730–1985. Number of articles in each text group (Table 5 in Gunnarsson, 2005d: 309)*

			Period				Total
	I: 1730	II: 1800	III: 1850	IV: 1900	V: 1940	VI: 1980	
Mainly verbal articles							
Economics	4	3	3	4	3	1	18
Medicine	4	5	4	4	2	1	20
Technology	3	2	0	0	0	0	5
All	11	10	7	8	5	2	43

As mentioned earlier, this shift cannot be related – as for the economics articles – to the use of one new type of representation. In the medical texts we find, instead, an increased use of various types of representations: tables and other systematic presentations of quantitative data, photographs, curves and schemata. We can thus point to a more general increase in the use of non-verbal elements during the last periods among the medical scientists.

5.3 Discussion

What can these results tell us about scientific discourse practice? I would first like to stress the clear difference found between the practices of scientists within the three disciplines. With due reservation for the limitation of a study comprising only 90 articles, I wish to claim that this study shows a clear difference in scientific discourse practices in economics, medicine and technology, in particular during certain periods.

The print technique is the same for writers of all three disciplines, and there possibilities already existed to print illustrations in the first period, i.e. in the eighteenth. There must therefore be more content bound and community bound reasons for the difference between the three disciplines. The experimental character of technology is of course relevant. Many of the early technological articles deal with attempts to 'make' electricity, and drawings and schematic illustrations show the design of these attempts. Also medicine is experimental in character, and among the early medical articles there are some that deal with experiments, for instance testing new treatment methods. The way these medical 'experiments' are presented however is very case- and patient-bound. The illnesses and the methods are verbally described (cf. Chapter 4). The modern large scale medical experiment is found first in the articles from the twentieth century, and only then do we also find tables, curves etc. As this study has shown, the modern printing technique is used in the medical articles also to display photos of apparatus and part of the deceased human body.

It is interesting to note how the three disciplines start off in a rather similar way with a mainly verbal representation of scientific knowledge. From the nineteenth century and onwards, however, the three disciplines follow different discourse paths: the non-verbal representation practice gains ground within technology, while economics and medicine stick mainly to verbal representation practice.

Over time, however, the three disciplines become more similar in their use of graphic representations and tables. Graphic representations, which during the early periods were only found in technology, gradually gain ground in medicine as well, as they do in the period around 1980 in economics. Tables and figures, which in the early periods were most characteristic of economics texts, gradually become a feature of medical and technological scientific writing. The scientific discourse ideals seem to have become more homogeneous in this respect. And on the whole they point to an increasingly significant role for non-verbal elements within the three scientific disciplines.

5.4 Conclusions

To conclude, I wish to return to the issue about the role of multimodality for the construction of science. My claim in the introductory part of the chapter was that the interplay between verbal and non-verbal elements influences scientific thinking as well as the representation then transmitted to other scientists.

According to Latour, graphic representation is constitutive for scientific thinking. He also argues that 'there is no detectable difference between natural and social science, as far as the obsession for graphism is concerned' (1988: 39). It would probably be precipitate to claim that the results presented here show that Latour's statement on scientific thinking is wrong, or, in other words, that (contrary to what Latour claims) different disciplines vary in terms of the graphical character of their thinking. What these results, however, show is a clear difference in practices, in how scientists within different disciplines transform theories and results into discourse. The varied use of non-verbal elements in the writing of scientists within different disciplines is striking, as is the change in discourse practices over time. It is also worth noticing that economics, medicine and technology have come to be more similar over time in terms of use of graphic representations. Words and tables are no longer considered adequate for the presentation of scientific knowledge in economics and medicine. It is impossible to say anything about if, and in that case how, these changes in article patterns are related to changes in the scientists' thinking without further and more in-depth investigation.

6 From a national to an international writing community: The case of economics in Sweden

Since the Second World War we have witnessed how scientific communities in Europe are gradually turning into English-speaking and English-writing communities. As a number of studies show, this seems to be a fairly general trend (e.g. Ammon, 2001; Carli and Ammon, 2007). In the case of Sweden, English has replaced Swedish as the prime language of Ph.D. theses, academic articles, conference papers, and also of lectures and seminars for Ph.D. students within many disciplines (Gunnarsson, 2001b). We thus find a diglossic[1] situation, with English used for purely scientific purposes and Swedish for more popular ones. Many Swedish scientists are thus agents both within the international scientific community and within the local Swedish one. Although they live and work in Sweden, the local community is not the primary target audience of their scientific writing. Their scientific texts are instead written in English and intended for a global, English-reading scientific community. For science, this has entailed an enlargement of the community and laid the basis for continued specialization. And for science in general this development is probably both necessary and beneficial. For nation states, national languages and local scientific communities, the consequences are more double-edged and not purely beneficial.

In this chapter, I will discuss this development in relation to three claims. First, I would claim that when science adopts English, the result is a change in the situation of the scientific journals in a country as they have to find another aim and content. Secondly, the adoption by science of English can pose a threat to the national language in terms of domain loss. If scientists use English as their scientific language, their national languages, such as Dutch, Swedish, Finnish or Italian, will gradually lose the scientific domain. Within the natural sciences I believe that this is a threat that has to be taken seriously. Thirdly, when science adopts English the situation changes for the scientists, who not only have to write in a foreign language, but also alter the text patterns they employ. An interesting question is of course whether they adapt to English text patterns or establish new ones. As contrastive studies have shown, natives and non-natives do not organize their English texts in the same way.[2] My assumption is that such cultural differences were even greater some decades ago, during the period when scientists had just started to use English for their scientific writing. My claim is thus that when non-natives began to use English as a lingua franca in their scientific writing, one challenge for them was to find a good model.

The study discussed here concerns the writing of Swedish economists during the period, 1955–1985, which encompassed a change of language, from Swedish to English. The Swedish economics community is an interesting example of the globalization process as regards writing and changing text patterns. Its main scholarly journal has changed its language from Swedish to English. *Ekonomisk Tidskrift* was founded in 1899 and was for 65 years the journal in which Swedish economists published articles aimed at a Swedish readership. In 1965, this journal changed its language to English, becoming *The Swedish Journal of Economics.* Ten years later, in 1976, it became *The Scandinavian Journal of Economics.* I will examine this journal in its three variants. One focus will be on the progressive globalization of the scholarly community, as reflected in the design of the journal, its authors, editors and referees, and the general outline of its articles. Another focus will be on the gradual changes in journal and article patterns.[3]

6.1 The Swedish economics community over three centuries

Before turning to my investigation, I will briefly sketch the history of the Swedish economics community.[4] The first period of interest is the eighteenth century. In Sweden, as in many other countries, there was considerable interest in science and technology during this century. No discipline, however, was as highly esteemed as the economic sciences. The Swedish economy was in ruins after a long period of war, and the economic growth of the country became a major political aim. The mercantilist doctrine was declared to be the great saviour of Sweden.

Academically, the eighteenth century saw all the utilitarian sciences flourish, and there was a remarkable increase in written publications of all kinds. It was also during this century that the first journals appeared in Sweden. In the case of economics we find that the first economic periodicals appeared in the 1730s. During the eighteenth century, 34 journals of economics saw the light of day: 13 on political economy, three dealing with trade and 18 concerned with economy and agriculture. In 1741 the Swedish government also decided that its main university, Uppsala University, should have a chair of economic sciences. The chair was attached to the Faculty of Law, but covered the natural sciences, agriculture and trade, as well as law and the economy. During this period, another three chairs in economic sciences were created in Sweden and Finland, which at that time was part of Sweden.

This interest in economics did not last, however. The mercantilist doctrine was found wanting as a saviour of the Swedish economy. Towards the end of the century, new ideas – liberal and physiocratic – became fashionable. After peaking in 1760, the number of economics journals rapidly declined. At an academic level, too, interest in the economic sciences waned. Of the four chairs created in the eighteenth century, three became chairs of botany and one – the Uppsala chair – was devoted more and more exclusively to law.

The economists of the eighteenth century were the reformers of society. They played a role in society, and one that was greatly valued. Quite a few people considered themselves experts and wrote on economic matters. Only to a very limited extent, however, was their aim to debate theoretical or methodological issues among themselves. They were much more concerned with reforming society. Interest in the economy and economic sciences did not lead to the formation of a scientific community, which may perhaps explain why the academic discipline of political economy and the journals disappeared so suddenly when public interest evaporated.

It was not until the latter part of the nineteenth century, that the economy developed and Sweden became an industrialized country, with a diversified network of industries engaged in large-scale production. It now had an elaborate banking system, and laws regulating joint-stock companies. Towards the end of the nineteenth century we also find that a scientific economics community began to emerge. Uppsala University acquired a chair in economics in 1889, and ten years later, in 1899, Professor David Davidson founded a journal, *Ekonomisk Tidskrift*, the story of which will be told below.

The expansion of the field of economics began during the first decade of the twentieth century, when the other Swedish universities also acquired their chairs of economics. The new professors, Davidson, Wiksell, Cassel, Steffen and Heckscher, established economics in Sweden as an academic discipline of high standing and considerable international renown. Their works, in turn, inspired a second brilliant generation which established itself during the 1920s and 1930s. Later to be known as the Stockholm School, it included Gunnar Myrdal and Bertil Ohlin. Modern departments, however, started to develop much later, in the 1950s. The number of departments increased, as did the number of professors. There was also a remarkable increase in the number of dissertations from 1900 to 1980.

The Swedish economics community was thus much larger in 1985 than it had been before. There were many more undergraduate and Ph.D. students, and many more professors. The community's international links had also been expanded and stabilized, a process promoted not least by the Nobel Prize in Economics. In 1968 Sveriges Riksbank (the central bank of Sweden) instituted this prize, and since 1969 it has been awarded to a series of well-known economists. Certainly the prize has been very important for the Swedish economics community. It has strengthened its international networks and placed Sweden firmly on the world map when it comes to economics.

6.2 The change from a journal in Swedish to a journal in English

The story of the Swedish scholarly journal in this field also reflects this process of internationalization. What has happened within Swedish economics is that its main journal has shifted language – from Swedish to English – and thus enlarged its circle of writers and its readership. A national scientific journal has turned into a prestigious international one.[5] From the perspective of a linguist, it is interesting to follow the verbal and textual signs of this development and also to consider its wider social dimensions, i.e. its effects on the national scientific community.

6.2.1 Ekonomisk Tidskrift

I will begin with *Ekonomisk Tidskrift*. It appeared four times a year from 1899 to 1964. Focusing on the twenty last years of this journal, on the numbers published from 1945 to 1964, I found that eight of the twenty volumes did not include any English articles, eight volumes included one article in English and two volumes carried two such articles. There were thus very few articles in English in the volumes from 1945 to 1963. In the very last volume from 1964, however, all sixteen articles were published in English. The Anglicization of the journal thus began the year before it became *The Swedish Journal of Economics*. We can also note that one of the English articles in the penultimate volume (1963) was written by a Swede, further reflecting its gradual shift into an English-language journal. From the point of view of language choice, it should also be noted that six of the articles in the 1948 volume and one in the 1952 volume were published in other Scandinavian languages than Swedish, and that one article in the 1959 volume was written in German.

In *Ekonomisk Tidskrift* the authors are not presented in any way. Their names are given with no mention of their affiliation or title. We can assume that all the authors were well-known to the Swedish readers of the day. The great majority of them were in fact Swedes: in the 1955 volume, 11 out of 13, in the 1960 volume 17 out of 18, and in the 1964 volume 19 out of 20. It thus seems that this was a truly Swedish journal in every respect.

The change to an English journal in 1965, however, was not as sudden as it might at first appear. The first proposal to launch a Scandinavian journal of economics in English came as early as 1926, in other words almost forty years before the language shift actually occurred. Though most of the articles were written in Swedish, the journal could, as mentioned above, include one or two articles in English from 1947 onwards. Another harbinger of the language shift in 1965 is the presentation of the contents on the title page. During the period 1955–1959, the list of articles, comments and book reviews is given first in Swedish and then in English. From 1960, and until the last volume in 1964, the English titles are placed in brackets directly after the Swedish title, i.e. they are integrated with the Swedish ones.

6.2.2 The Swedish Journal of Economics

I will now turn to *The Swedish Journal of Economics*, the story of which covers only 11 volumes, from 1965 to 1975. In the early volumes, the authors were mainly Swedish, but gradually the number of authors from Denmark, Norway, Finland and Iceland, from the rest of Europe, from the United States and Canada, and from other countries around the world increased. Table 6.1 shows the origin of the authors of articles and comments in *The Swedish Journal of Economics*. Abbreviations: Swe (Sweden), Den (Denmark), Nor (Norway), Fin (Finland), Ice (Iceland), Eur (Europe), US (USA), Can (Canada), Other (other countries).

Table 6.1 Authors of articles and comments in The Swedish Journal of Economics (Table 2 in Gunnarsson, 2006a: 30, that is in a book)

Year	Swe	Den	Nor	Fin	Ice	Eur	US	Can	Other
1965	14						1		
1970	11	2	3	3			2	2	1
1975	15[a]	4	11	1		2	6		1

[a] Two articles where written by one Swedish and one American scholar

Note: Swe – Sweden, Den – Denmark, Nor – Norway, Fin – Finland, Ice – Iceland, Eur – Europe, US – United States of America, Can – Canada, Other – Other countries

In contrast to the practice in *Ekonomisk Tidskrift*, in *The Swedish Journal of Economics* all the authors are presented. The way in which this is done, however, is not consistent but varies over time. In the first two volumes the name of the author is preceded by the preposition 'By' and the author is presented in a footnote at the bottom of the page. In the third volume, from 1967, a new practice is established. Here we find the name of the author on one line with a presentation on the line below. In some cases the author's title, e.g. 'Professor', is mentioned, in other cases only the university, town and country. The fact that such presentations of authors were a novel feature in this English-language journal is a plausible explanation for the varied practice. It took some years for the editors to decide on a consistent practice.

Another reflection of the gradual establishment of a new journal is the way its title is presented on the front cover. On the cover of the first two volumes, from 1965 and 1966, we find the name of the journal, followed by that of its Swedish predecessor and the journal's founder. The text on cover was thus: 'The Swedish Journal of Economics, Ekonomisk Tidskrift, Founded by David Davidson in 1899'. This information was omitted from the 1967 volume onwards.

The gradual emergence of a prestigious journal is undoubtedly linked to the Nobel Prize in Economics, which was established in 1969. The journal also highlights this on the front cover of the December 1969 issue, which includes the text 'The First Nobel Prize in Economics'. The following year (1970), the Nobel prizewinner is given even greater prominence on the front cover, with the words: 'The Nobel Memorial Prize in Economics 1970. Assar Lindbeck on Paul A. Samuelsson.' The Nobel Prize is announced in the December issue of each volume. In the same December issues, we also find a list of 'Dissertations in Economics' in Sweden. I mention this as it can be interpreted as another sign that a growing scientific community wished to make an impact on the international economics community.

The change from a Swedish to a Scandinavian journal is further reflected in a gradually more complex description of the editors. In the first two volumes, those of 1965 and 1966, we find four categories on the inside front cover: (1) 'Editorial Board', (2) 'Editors', (3) 'Book reviews' and (4) 'Ansvarig utgivare' [= person legally responsible for the journal]. From 1967 to 1975, there are three additional categories: (5) 'Corresponding Editorial Committee' with the subcategories: 'Denmark', 'Finland' and 'Norway', (6) 'Administrative Office' and (7) 'Distribution'. The participation of professors from the other Scandinavian countries is thus highlighted, e.g. as members of the 'Editorial Committee'. As Table 6.1 above showed, many of the authors in the final volumes of the *Swedish Journal of Economics* came from the other Scandinavian countries: in the 1970 volume we find two authors from Denmark, three from Finland and three from Norway, and in the 1975 volume, there are four Danish authors, eleven Finnish and one Norwegian. The shift towards a Scandinavian journal is thus a gradual one.

6.2.3 The Scandinavian Journal of Economics

In this part I will focus on *The Scandinavian Journal of Economics*. In 1976, the journal changed its title and editorship to cover the whole of Scandinavia. From the presentation of the editors and the editorial board on the inside front cover, we can see that the 'Board of Editors' included members from all the Nordic countries, including Iceland. However, distribution is taken care of by a Swedish publisher, and the person legally responsible for the journal is a Swedish professor. In the 1980 and 1981 volumes there are no national subcategories for the category of 'Board of Editors', although the professors listed under this heading do represent the various Nordic countries. In these volumes a new category also appears, namely 'Associate Editors'. Here we find the names of 11 professors and their universities, which belong to the various Scandinavian countries. Gradually, the administration of the journal seems to have changed. The various Scandinavian countries are not explicitly mentioned, although each country is represented on the 'Board of Editors' and also among the 'Associate Editors'.

A major change can be seen as regards the range of authors writing in the journal. Table 6.2 shows the countries stated in the presentations of authors of articles and comments.

As Table 6.2 shows, the authors are no longer mainly Swedes or Scandinavians. The United States of America, Canada and also Europe are well represented among the authors. The journal has also placed itself among those at the top of the international citation rankings, as mentioned in endnote 5.

Table 6.2 *Authors of articles and comments in* The Scandinavian Journal of Economics *(Table 3 in Gunnarsson 2006a: 33)*

Year	Swe	Den	Nor	Fin	Ice	Eur	US	Can	Other
1976	11	5	4	3		10	16	3	2
1980	7	3	5	3		2	10	1	
1985	14[a]	1	2	5[b]	2	16	10	1	1

[a] One article was written by a Swedish and an American scholar
[b] One article was written by a Finnish and an American scholar

Note: Swe – Sweden, Den – Denmark, Nor – Norway, Fin – Finland, Ice – Iceland, Eur – Europe, US – United States of America, Can – Canada, Other – Other countries

6.3 Homogenization of article patterns

The change from *Ekonomisk Tidskrift* to *The Swedish Journal of Economics* and eventually to *The Scandinavian Journal of Economics* brought with it a more international circle of authors and also a larger readership.

As early as 1969, *The Swedish Journal of Economics* started to print instructions to authors on the inside back cover, at that time headed 'Advice to Contributors'. This tradition was maintained when the journal became *The Scandinavian Journal of Economics*. The inside back cover of the 1976 volume carried a section headed 'Instructions to Contributors'. The following year, in the 1977 volume, these instructions were extended, stressing that the journal editors' wished to promote a common pattern in the articles published.

As these data reveal, the editors tried to homogenize the article structure fairly early on. However, it took some time for this to be achieved in practice in the journal. Below, I will present data on the structure of the articles, as revealed by their explicit organization by means of subheadings. I will also describe the changes that occurred as regards the listing of references.

This study of article structure is based on an analysis of the subheadings in the articles written by Swedes in three volumes of each of the three variants of the journal. In *Ekonomisk Tidskrift*, I studied the articles by Swedish authors in the 1955, 1960 and 1964 volumes, 28 articles in all. In *The Swedish Journal of Economics*, I studied the articles by Swedes in the 1965, 1970 and 1975 volumes, a total of 27 articles. And in *The Scandinavian Journal of Economics*, I studied the Swedish-authored articles in the 1976, 1980 and 1985 volumes, 24 articles in all. I thus covered nine volumes, seven of them chosen at five-year intervals, from 1955, 1960, 1965, 1970, 1975, 1980 and 1985, while two volumes, published in 1964 and 1976, were chosen in order to include issues from around the two changes of title, i.e., 1964–1965 and 1975–1976.

Table 6.3 shows the results of my analysis of article structure, in terms of *subheadings, marked article introduction, marked abstract section,* and *marked article conclusion.* For each article, I have noted whether or not there are subheadings, a clearly marked introduction, an abstract and a clearly marked conclusion. In the table, the figures in the 'No.' column are the numbers of articles containing the features in question.

As Table 6.3 shows, the results of my analysis point to a gradual rather than a sudden shift towards a more homogeneous structure. In *Ekonomisk Tidskrift*, only 75 per cent of the articles had subheadings, compared to 100 per cent and 96 per cent in the later journals.

Table 6.3 Subheadings and marked introductions, abstracts and conclusions in articles written by Swedish economists (Table 4 in Gunnarsson, 2006a: 35)

	Subheadings		Introduction		Abstract		Conclusion	
	No	**%**	**No**	**%**	**No**	**%**	**No**	**%**
Ekonomisk Tidskrift	21	75	3	11	0	0	9	32
Swedish Journal of Economics	27	100	17	63	18	67	16	59
Scandinavian Journal of Economics	23	96	16	67	18	75	17	71

The marking of introductory sections also differs between *Ekonomisk Tidskrift* and its successors. In the oldest journal we find no abstracts, and clearly marked introductions occur in only 11 per cent of the articles. In both *The Swedish Journal of Economics* and *The Scandinavian Journal of Economics*, clearly marked abstract and introduction sections seem to be the norm, although we can note that these features do not occur in all the articles. As regards clearly marked conclusion sections, we find a more gradual development: they are present in 32 per cent of the articles in *Ekonomisk Tidskrift*, 59 per cent in *The Swedish Journal of Economics* and 71 per cent in *The Scandinavian Journal of Economics*.

The patterns of *Ekonomisk Tidskrift* thus vary with regard to both the existence of subheadings and the types of subheadings used. It would probably be incorrect to say that the authors published in the journal before 1965 did not structure the content of their articles; however, they did so in a more heterogeneous way. The majority of the articles have subheadings related to the specific content of the article in question, and only rarely do we find subheadings which describe the structure in terms of the theoretical content of the article, as in this one published in the 1955 volume:

> I Problem [= problem]
>
> II Teorifunktion [= theory function]
>
> III Teoristruktur [= theory structure]
>
> IV Teori och fakta [= theory and facts]
>
> V Sammanfattning [= summary]

In the later volumes of *Ekonomisk Tidskrift* we more frequently find headings such as 'Inledning' [= Introduction] as well as 'Slutsatser' [= Conclusions] than earlier, though this cannot be described as a general pattern.

The advent of *The Swedish Journal of Economics* involves a step towards more homogeneous patterns. In 18 of the 27 articles we find an abstract, in this journal referred to as a summary, and in 17 a section headed 'Introduction'. Most articles also mark a concluding section.

In *The Scandinavian Journal of Economics*, as well, we find a variation in article patterns. Here we find an abstract in 18 of 24 articles, an 'Introduction' section in 16, and a clearly marked concluding section in 17. In the 1985 volume, six of the ten articles analysed contain the three headings: 'Abstract', 'Introduction' and 'Conclusion'. Another sign of a shift towards a more homogeneous structure is that three of the articles also have a section headed 'The Model', two of them a section with the heading 'The Framework' and one a section labelled 'Theoretical considerations'.

Another pattern change relates to the presentation of references and other literature in the articles. Table 6.4 shows the results of my analysis of practices relating to this feature.

As Table 6.4 indicates, the unmarked practice in *Ekonomisk Tidskrift* was to give the references in footnotes at the bottom of each page. Of the 28 articles analysed, only 4 have a list at the end. Three of these lists, all in articles from the 1964 volume, which, as noted earlier, used English, are in alphabetical order. In *The Swedish Journal of Economics*, we find a varied practice: ten give the references in footnotes, eight in a numbered list at the end of the article, with the numbers following the structure of the article, and nine in a list at the end in alphabetical order. As we can see, this latter practice, a list of references or other literature in alphabetical order at the end of the article, has become the common practice in *The Scandinavian Journal of Economics*. Of the 24 analysed articles written by Swedes in that journal, 21 have such a list.

Table 6.4 Lists of references and bibliographies in articles written by Swedish economists (Table 5 in Gunnarsson, 2006a: 36)

	No list	**Reference list/bibliography**		
		Numbers at the end of article	**Alphabetical order**	**Chronological order**
Ekonomisk Tidskrift	24		3[a]	1
Swedish Journal of Economics	10	8	9	
Scandinavian Journal of Economics	2	1	21	

[a] Only in the 1964 volume

To sum up, my analysis of the articles published between 1955 and 1985 reveals an ongoing process of homogenization. The scientific structure of the articles is made more explicit by means of categorization based on their rhetorical structure. This has probably also entailed a more thoroughgoing homogenization of their content, but that is another story.

6.4 Discussion

I have discussed here the evolution of a Swedish journal, originally written in Swedish by Swedish economists for a Swedish-reading readership, into a prestigious international journal with an international circle of authors and, at least in theory, a worldwide readership. The journal was also expanded during the period studied. Its size increased so that there were almost four times as many pages per volume in 1985 as in 1955. The lowest number of pages was found in the 1963 volume of *Ekonomisk Tidskrift*, which comprised only 185 pages, and the highest in the 1985 volume of *The Scandinavian Journal of Economics*, which ran to 682 pages. In parallel with this, the editorial team grew, as did the number of referees. From 1979 onwards we also find a printed list of acknowledgements mentioning all the referees consulted during the year.

The change of language from Swedish to English is not unique to this journal. In 1970 three natural science journals also shifted language: the journal of mathematics, astronomy and physics, *Arkiv för matematik, astronomi och fysik*, which had been established by the Royal Swedish Academy of Sciences in 1903, was replaced with a journal in English with the title of *Physica Scripta*, while the journals of chemistry and zoology were replaced with the English journals *Chemical Scripta* and *Zoological Scripta*.

A feature shared by all these journals, and by *Ekonomisk Tidskrift* and its successors, is that, to begin with at least, the editorship remained Swedish. From a genre perspective it is therefore particularly interesting to study the establishment of journal and article patterns, as this is based on the use of English as a lingua franca both for many of the authors, and for the editors. Swedish economists (and also physicists, chemists and zoologists) not only started to write in English more regularly, but were able to do so in a journal that was produced and edited in Sweden. They could thus shape the patterns of the journal, as they were responsible for the instructions to authors/ contributors and for editing the articles.

From a genre point of view, it should also be noted that a scholarly journal in economics using Swedish as its language was founded eight years after *Ekonomisk Tidskrift* underwent its change of language. *Ekonomisk Debatt* (in translation 'The journal of the Swedish Economic Society') was founded in 1973 with the explicit purpose of bridging the gap between economists at universities and those working in government agencies, business and organizations.[6] It also provided a forum in Swedish for economic scientists, when *Ekonomisk Tidskrift* no longer used that language. The articles in *Ekonomisk Debatt* are of a high academic standard and at the same time try to reach out to economists outside the universities. Swedish economics professors have a history of participating actively in the social sphere as well. Several of the most eminent professors have left academia to take up careers in politics and government admin-istration. The combination of academic research and external issues was thus nothing new for the Swedish economics community. But the existence of two journals in economics, one for a Swedish and one for an international audience must undoubtedly have entailed a divide.

From a contrastive, textlinguistic perspective it would be interest-ing to make an in-depth analysis of the changes in article patterns in *Ekonomisk Tidskrift* and its successors, following these changes dur-ing its gradual evolution from a small, national journal into a large, international one. A question worth looking into would of course be whether the Scandinavian authors write in a different ways from their American and British counterparts. It would also be interest-ing to compare the patterns established in *Ekonomisk Debatt*, founded in 1973, with those pursued in *Ekonomisk Tidskrift* and its English-language successors.

As an example of what such an in-depth analysis of text patterns could reveal, I will refer to some of the results of the Uppsala project presented earlier on writing in science and popular science during three centuries. Within this project, our criteria for the selection of articles were based on field, subject and period. In the case of eco-nomics, our material included ten articles from *Ekonomisk Tidskrift* from the period 1895–1905 and eight from the period 1935–1945. For our final period, 1975–1985, we had to choose another journal, as the Swedish-language *Ekonomisk Tidskrift* no longer existed. Our ten art-icles from this period were selected instead from *Ekonomisk Debatt*.

Looking back at the results of these analyses of economics articles in Swedish,[7] I would claim that the development of writing in Swedish in economics between the periods 1935–1945 and 1975–1985 could also be seen as a shift towards a more popular approach. I will here discuss some of the results of our cognitive analysis. For a description of the methodology, see Chapter 3.

For the purpose of this chapter, I have selected some of the results of our cognitive analysis, comprising an analysis of *cognitive worlds, aspects* and *dimensions*.[8] Table 6.5 contains results based on our analyses of articles in *Ekonomisk Tidskrift* from the period 1935–1945 and in *Ekonomisk Debatt* from the period 1975–1985.

As Table 6.5 shows, the proportion accounted for by the 'scientific world' remained constant between the second and third periods (63 per cent and 62 per cent), while for the 'external world' this figure increased (from 12 per cent to 18 per cent). More interestingly, the proportion of 'theory' within the scientific world declined (from 79 per cent to 68 per cent), while the proportion of 'measures' within the external world rose (from 44 per cent to 69 per cent). I see these changes – i.e. greater emphasis on the external world, less theory and more measures – as signs of a shift towards a more popular and less exclusively scientific perspective.

The change in terms of cognitive *dimensions* could also be interpreted in this perspective: the increase in the proportion of 'cause' (from 7 per cent to 19 per cent) and the decrease in the proportion of 'process' (from 58 per cent to 36 per cent) can be interpreted as a step

Table 6.5 *Cognitive analysis of articles in economics written in Swedish and published in* Ekonomisk Tidskrift *1935–1945 and in* Ekonomisk Debatt *1975–1985 (Table 6 in Gunnarsson, 2006a: 40)*

	Journal and period	
	Ekonomisk tidskrift 1935–1940	**Ekonomisk debatt 1975–1985**
Cognitive worlds		
Scientific world	63	62
Practical world	0	1
Object world	25	19
Private world	1	0
External world	12	18
Cognitive aspects		
Scientific world		
Theory	79	68
Classification	13	19
Experiment	7	13
External world		
Conditions	56	31
Measures	44	69
Dimensions		
Cause	7	19
Phenomenon	11	23
Process	58	36
Change/Result	25	22

towards a more popularizing genre and an attempt to communicate to a lay audience, to whom it is necessary to explain the causes, while the scientific process underlying the results can be omitted.

The conclusion I draw from this is that our analysis of the articles in *Ekonomisk Debatt*, i.e. the articles from 1975–1985, shows the aim of this journal to be both scientific and more popular or societal.

6.5 Conclusions

To conclude I would like to return to the three consequences I mentioned in the introductory part of this chapter. My first claim was that when science adopts English, scientific journals in the national language (if it is not English) have to find another aim and a different content. In economics, as we have seen, there is still a high-quality scholarly journal in Swedish, *Ekonomisk Debatt*. Its aim, however, is to cover both scientific issues and more societal ones. We can thus see a certain shift in aim and content.[9]

My second claim was that the adoption by science of English can pose a threat to the national language in terms of domain loss. If scientists use English as their scientific language, the national language, be it Swedish, Finnish, Italian or whatever, will gradually lose its scientific domain. Within the natural sciences, I believe this is a threat that has to be taken seriously (Gunnarsson, 2001b). In economics, it is probably not yet a threat – and might not become one – as Swedish academic economists also play social roles. Within many disciplines scientists act solely within their scientific communities and leave the task of popularizing their findings to journalists. The tradition within Swedish economics, however, is for professors to play a role in society at large. This is a reassuring fact as far as the survival of the economics domain within the Swedish language is concerned.

My third claim was that the fact that science adopts English also creates a different situation for the scientists, who not only have to write in a foreign language but must also create new text patterns. The study which I have presented here gives examples of the steps taken towards a more international way of writing. The inconsistencies which I have described regarding the presentation of authors, the structure of articles and listing of references are indicative of the difficulties which scientists whose first language is not English face when they try to adopt English. Whether the practices established are in line with British, American or ELF writing is another question that would be worth looking into in future studies.

Notes

1. 'Diglossia' and 'language dominance' and also discussed in Chapter 10.
2. See, for instance, Altenberg (1998), Mauranen (1993), Granger and Tyson (1996), Melander et al. (1997), Petersen and Shaw (2002), and Shaw (2004).
3. The investigation is presented in more detail in Gunnarsson (2006a).
4. In Gunnarsson (1997b: 103–107) I give a historical overview, which will be briefly summarized here.
5. *The Scandinavian Journal of Economics* ranks among the world's most cited journals (Persson et al., 1992: 125).
6. From the entry on 'Ekonomisk Debatt' in *Nationalencyklopedin* (1991: 347).
7. Among our publications in English, I wish to mention in particular these two dealing with economics: Gunnarsson (1997b), and Gunnarsson et al. (1994).
8. The results are presented in full in Melander (1989: 30, 45, 67). Detailed presentations of the textlinguistic analyses carried out within the research project 'LSP texts in the 20th century' are also found in Melander (1991) and Näslund (1991).
9. A more radical change is found in medicine. In Gunnarsson, Bäcklund and Andersson (1995), we present a study on medical articles published in *Läkartidningen*, i.e., the Swedish medical journal. These articles appeared in 1994. What we found was a major change in the contents and patterns of articles, compared with those published in the same journal in earlier periods of the twentieth century. The journal was founded in 1904 and still exists. Because medical scientists have gradually chosen to publish their scientific findings in international journals, *Läkartidningen* has had to change its aim and focus from a purely scientific to a more popularizing one, and thus now includes overviews rather than presentations of original results. See also Chapter 4.

Section 3
Legislative Discourse

This section explores the various communicative processes attached to laws and their varied uses from different perspectives: a function-oriented, or pragmatic, perspective, a psycholinguistic perspective and a sociolinguistic one. In Chapter 7, I present a theory of functional comprehensibility of legislative texts and discuss the results of an experiment designed to test this theory. One question addressed is how knowledge from experiments within psycholinguistics and cognitive psychology can be integrated into a pragmatic theory on the function-oriented, situated use of legislative texts. Another is how an analysis of text comprehensibility can acknowledge the variation in reading purpose and reading strategies between different groups: professionals, semi-professionals and lay people. In the chapter I introduce a model of law-text reading and comprehension which systematically analyses the context base of the law from the point of view of the citizen's use of the text. I also present the alternative law-text which was written based on this model. Comprehensibility was substantially improved by the change of perspective in this alternative text, although the text was still not easy. The experiment, however, points to a way of improving legislative texts and other types of official documents.

Chapter 8 explores the drafting of legislative texts from a combined cognitive-rhetorical and sociolinguistic perspective. Problems of law-text comprehensibility are here related to the legislative writing process. Using an ethnographic methodology, I followed as an observer the drafting process of three segments of consumer law at different stages. My discussion of this study will focus on the stages of the writing process, the professional composition of the committees involved, the societal contextual frameworks and the targeted readers. First, I will claim that the social and societal conditions under which texts are produced result in more or less readable texts. Secondly, I will claim that an analysis of a sustained collective writing process, such as law-drafting, need to consider both cognitive-rhetorical and sociolinguistic parameters. Thirdly, I will claim that a critical sociolinguistic perspective on law-drafting should include an analysis of the targeted readers.

7 The functional comprehensibility of legislative texts

In this chapter, I will present a theory of functional comprehensibility of legislative texts and discuss the results of an experiment designed to test this theory. One question which I will address is how knowledge from experiments within psycholinguistics and cognitive psychology can be integrated into a pragmatic theory on the function-oriented, situated use of legislative texts. Another is how an analysis of text comprehensibility can acknowledge the variation in reading purpose and reading strategies between different groups: professionals, semi-professionals and lay people.

This chapter thus explores the complexity and variety of the reading and comprehension of official documents. Factors of importance for comprehensibility are assumed to be mainly related to the functional perspective of the text, whether a citizen perspective or a court perspective is adopted. In the first part of the chapter, I will introduce a model of law-text reading and comprehension which systematically analyses the content base of the law from the point of view of the citizen's use of the text. Based on this systematic analysis, an alternative text of a Swedish Act of Parliament was produced. The comprehensibility of this alternative text, focusing on the citizen perspective, and that of the original one, mainly focusing on the court perspective, were each tested. The results showed the comprehensibility of the altered version to be greater. The change of perspective led to substantial improvement although the alternative text was still not easy. The experiment points, however, to a way of improving legislative texts as well as other types of official documents. The study, on the whole, deepens our knowledge of how we can analyse text comprehensibility in a way that includes the complexity and variation of the reading process.[1]

7.1 Comprehension and comprehensibility

In the first part of this chapter, I will introduce my theoretical framework. Beginning with a critical view on the psychological laboratory experiment, I will propose a theory of functional comprehensibility.

99

Comprehension and comprehensibility have been studied mainly within cognitive psychology and psycholinguistics. Much of this research has aimed at describing general characteristics of the comprehension process. The purpose has been to describe what is common to all readers and all texts in all situations, and experiments have been carried out in strictly controlled laboratory settings, designed to isolate certain linguistic factors and make other factors – linguistic and extra-linguistic – negligible. In a typical experimental setting, psychology students have been presented with strings of words or sentences, orally on tape or visually on a screen. Generally, their short-term memory of the words or sentences has been tested by recall or recognition tests, but their ability to discover ambiguities or faults has also been investigated.

The applicability of such experiments to comprehension in real-life situations, where a number of factors are involved such as the function of the text, the reading situation, the readers' pre-knowledge and previews, their reading purposes, reading strategies etc., can be questioned. A number of studies within psycholinguistics have thus focused on variations in the comprehension process that are due to characteristics of *the text*, *the reader* and *the situation*. This recognition of variation in the comprehension process does not, however, mean that psycholinguistic experiments have been given a more realistic setting. On the whole only one component – the text, the reader *or* the situation – has been treated as a variable, leading to a marked difference between comprehension studied under laboratory conditions and comprehension in real-life situations.

Furthermore, most research within psycholinguistics and cognitive psychology has only concerned itself with matters like memorization of the text surface or registration of the text content. Such comprehension is, however, only superficial: the reader realizes how the text is constructed syntactically and semantically, but does not see its correspondence with reality. This kind of comprehension has little similarity with the way we comprehend in real-life situations, where the reader's purpose is to apply the text to different situations and different actions. Comprehension in normal reading can be described as the reader's attempt to interpret what the author means by the text by relating it to the author's situation or by trying to apply it to his or her own situation and behaviour. To study such comprehension, we must bear in mind the specific features of the text, the reader and the situation. Our starting point must be an analysis of text function.

My claim in this chapter, however, is that a discussion of the linguistic factors of importance for functional comprehension must take into account the psychological complexity of the reading and comprehension process. Reading is an active, constructive process whereby the reader constructs a holistic description of the text (e.g. Bransford and Franks, 1971; Bransford et al., 1972). This process of construction is governed by the text as well as by the reader's permanent structuring of his or her pre-knowledge, and by his or her occasional structuring induced by the reading purpose and the reading situation.

The theoretical framework, which is the basis for the theory of comprehensibility I develop below, relates to studies within cognitive psychology which have pointed to the variation and flexibility of the reading process, in the sense that the text, the reader and the reading situation determine this process (Gibson and Levin, 1975). This variation has been described as a variation in comprehension depth, with the reading process going through a number of stages. Others have described it as a more flexible kind of variation, in which different levels are focused on and predominate over others. As we know, a text can be analysed into levels, and linguistic factors such as typographical, syntactic, semantic and pragmatic features can be attributed to different text levels. Starting with this perspective of a text, the reading process has been discussed with regard to the text level on which the main focus is placed. Mental activities during reading, e.g. in terms of which level is focused on, have been shown to determine the result of comprehension.

In the theory of functional comprehensibility proposed here, comprehension is described at different depths. Different reading purposes are assumed to cause variations in the direction of the reading process, resulting in different comprehension levels playing a dominant role in the processing of others. The properties of the text are also described at different levels. At superficial text levels we have typography and syntax, at an intermediary level semantics, and at deeper levels pragmatic factors, e.g., concerning perspective and function-orientation. The comprehension level and text level are assumed to correspond in the manner described in Table 7.1. The levels correspond to increasing degrees of depth.

We shall now examine the question of different reading purposes, which are assumed to vary the process. In accordance with pragmatic text theory, texts are mainly considered in relation to actions (cf. Chapter 3). The reading purpose directs the process towards a focus on different text levels. The processing of deeper text levels dominates over the processing of more superficial levels, and different text levels thus become primary to the product of comprehension. The aim of Table 7.2 is to illustrate this correspondence.

The theory suggests that superficial text levels play a different role – and a less important one – when the reading purpose is action-oriented

Table 7.1 *Correspondence between comprehension level and text level (Gunnarsson, 1984)*

Comprehension level	Text level
The reader interprets the letters	Typographical
The reader comprehends the individual words	Word-semantic
The reader comprehends the individual sentence in terms of its structural and conventional meaning	
Comprehension of the syntactic relations	Syntactic
Comprehension of the semantic relations	Sentence-semantic
The reader comprehends the situational Interpretation of the sentence and the text	Pragmatic: Perspective
The reader comprehends what actions the text should lead to	Pragmatic: Function-orientation and perspective

Table 7.2 *Correspondence between reading purpose, reading process and text level (Gunnarsson, 1984)*

	Reading purpose	Reading process	Text level
1	Memorization of the text surface	The exact wording is identified by being related to stored word and phrase structures.	Word semantics and syntax processed primarily. Typography auxiliary level.
2	Registering of the text content as such	The text is related to the message in itself.	Syntax and sentence-semantics processed primarily. Word semantics and typography auxiliary levels.
3	Comprehension of the sender's world description	The text is related to or induces a notion of the sender's situation and his conception of the world.	Perspective processed primarily. Semantics, syntax and typography auxiliary levels.
4	Integration in world conception. (Indirectly action-oriented comprehension)	The text is mainly related to the reader's conception of the world.	Perspective processed primarily. Semantics, syntax and typography auxiliary levels.
5	Directly action-oriented comprehension	The text is related mainly to the reader's own situation, his conception of the world and different alternative courses of action.	Perspective and function-orientation processed primarily. Semantics, syntax and typography auxiliary levels.

comprehension (4–5), than when it is memorization (1) or registering of the text content as such (2). Thus the results from the many studies that have correlated linguistic factors – typographical, syntactic and word-semantic – with the subjects' immediate recall or summary of a text, their rating of its readability or their reading speed, do not capture the levels of prime importance to the comprehensibility of action-oriented texts such as law-texts.

This theory will be related here to the results of the investigations – pilot studies and the main study – that I have carried out involving one Swedish Act of Parliament, namely the Joint Regulation Act.[2] In these studies I tested subjects' ability to 'use' the law-text in reading situations similar to those in real-life, i.e. with reading purpose (5). In each study, the original version of a part of the law was compared with an altered version of the same part. In pilot studies, my altered versions were based on changes at the linguistic surface level. In the main study, however, the alterations also affected the deeper pragmatic text levels.

7.2 Pilot studies

As a background to my discussion of the main investigation, I will give a brief summary of the pilot studies I carried out initially. Starting from a readability approach in the preliminary investigation, I analysed the syntax and vocabulary of the Joint Regulation Act. On the basis of this analysis of the law-text surface, I then worked out an alternative version of some sections of the Act. In two tests, I compared the action-oriented comprehension of these variants with the original versions. In one test, the subjects were students at an upper secondary school and in the other, adult trainees at a vocational training centre for the unemployed. I found in both tests that the linguistic changes I had made did not improve the type of comprehension that was being measured. Qualitative analysis of the subjects' mistakes, led me to the conclusion that more radical changes, based on a pragmatic analysis were needed.

The results of my pilot studies might at first sight seem to contradict the results of other studies on legislative language, e.g. the well-known experiment with jury-instructions by Charrow and Charrow (1979). The two researchers rewrote samples of jury-instructions, making several different linguistic changes at the same time. The changes they made in these texts were of similar types to those I made in the texts for my pilot studies. They changed syntactic structure and vocabulary, and to some extent made the information structure clearer. They then tested the ability of jurors to paraphrase instructions that were presented to them orally, in the original or the altered version. The results of these jury experiments pointed to somewhat better results for the altered versions than for the original.

An interesting question, which I wish to dwell on here, is why the changes made by Charrow and Charrow gave positive results while

103

mine did not. There are, I will claim, important differences between the two series of experiments, which can explain the contrasting outcomes. The main difference between the two experiments is that the methods and the criteria chosen to measure the effects were not at all the same. The Charrows presented oral instructions to the subjects, consisting of two or three sentences. After listening to a short passage, the subjects had to repeat what they had heard. Subjects' immediate recall (memory) was thus being tested. The effect of the linguistic change was measured quantitatively by comparing the number of constituent units in the instructions given mentioned in the subjects' paraphrases. How – and indeed whether – the subjects had understood what they had heard and repeated was not measured. In my pilot experiments, I used longer texts which were presented to the subjects in written form. The subjects were asked to read and solve problems using the text, with no time limit and without needing to memorize the text. The effect of the changes was measured qualitatively as the score on a problem-solving task. I thus measured their deeper understanding of the text. To conclude, this comparison with Charrow and Charrow's study gives further support for a function-oriented approach, i.e. we need to consider the specific features of the text, the reader and the situation.

7.3 Pragmatic analysis of legislative texts

In this part of the chapter, I will explore legislative texts from a pragmatic viewpoint. Beginning with an analysis of the aims (7.3.1) and functions of laws (7.3.2), I will discuss the consequences for reading in 7.3.3. In 7.3.4, I will propose a model of law-text reading and comprehension.

7.3.1 Aims of laws

Lawmaking is a means of determining the development of society. At a macro level the aim can be to change or preserve the existing structures of society, be they political, economic, cultural or social. These structures are, however, products of the actions of individuals or groups of individuals, and at a micro level the aim of legislation is thus to influence people's actions. If the goal is to change structures, legislation is designed to change our norms of behaviour, and is thus an instrument of reform. If the goal is preservation, it is designed to keep our norms of behaviour from changing. Legislation is in the latter case a codification of the existing norms of society.

Most laws probably aim both to change and to preserve, but the primary aim varies. The main aim of criminal law, e.g., can be considered to be to preserve norms of behaviour, while other laws are primarily aimed at changing norms. Throughout the world, we find an increasing number of laws which aim to reform rather than preserve.

7.3.2   Functions of laws

If we now examine the different functions of laws, we can distinguish two main types with different main addresses. As Table 7.3 shows, one is the action-directing function, with ordinary citizens as the main addressees. Ordinary citizens have to abide by the law in various social situations. The other is the control function, with lawyers in court as the main addressees. By their judgments in court, members of the legal profession are expected to exercise control over citizens compliance with the law.

The functions of laws can be further discussed with regard to their aims. For laws that aim primarily to codify existing norms the main function is control-directing, while the function of those whose primary aim is reform is to direct action. In the case of the Joint Regulation Act, the action-directing function is thus primary.

7.3.3   Reader, reading situation and reading purpose

If we first consider the *reader*, his or her pre-knowledge and experience can be described in terms of the various demands made by the text. We can describe the unusual demands that the reading and understanding of the law-text genre place on its reader as compared with those made by normal prose reading. These demands can be classified into requirements of *general law-text knowledge*, of knowledge of different legal and law-text conventions, concerning e.g. the structuring of law-texts, legal terminology, etc., and requirements of *specific knowledge* for the law in question. Knowledge relevant to the Joint Regulation Act includes, e.g., working life, trade unions, etc.

With regard to different readers of law-texts, a relevant distinction with regard to pre-knowledge must be made between lawyers and laymen. In the case of the Joint Regulation Act discussed here a line might also be drawn between readers with work experience

Table 7.3   *Functions of laws (Gunnarsson, 1984)*

FUNCTION	Goal	Main addressees	Use of law
ACTION-DIRECTING	Correct actions	Ordinary citizens	Different social situations
CONTROL-DIRECTING	Correct judgments	Members of courts	Court situations

and those without, and between people with trade union experience and those without. This study therefore involves legal professionals as well as semi-professionals, other professionals and lay people.

As for the *reading situation* and the *reading purpose,* different social situations have to be considered for each particular law. A feature common to all law-text reading, however, is that laws can be read with an indirectly action-oriented purpose as well as a directly action-oriented purpose. We can read them to gain an overall picture of their content or to find out more exactly how to act or judge in particular situations.

As an example, I shall now illustrate some possible reading situations and reading purposes relative to ordinary citizens' reading of the Joint Regulation Act. The citizen groups that are potential readers of this Act are employers, trade union officials and ordinary employees. The reading can be directed towards immediate action to a varying degree, as is shown in the description of possible points of departure and reading purposes in Table 7.4.

Table 7.4 *Points of departure and purposes when reading the Act on the Joint Regulation of Working Life (Gunnarsson, 1984)*

Possible points of departure when reading the Act	Possible purposes when reading the Act	Action which can result from reading the Act
A *Acquiring knowledge*	*Reading the entire Act*	*Indirect influence on action*
Readers read the Act because they wish to acquire a general picture of It.	The purpose is to gain an impression of the overall content of the Act, i.e. what areas it regulates and what the main rights and duties are which it sets out.	Reading the Act forms a basis for subsequent action. Readers have gained an Impression of when they can have recourse to the Act.
B *Solving problems*	*Reading parts of the Act*	*Direct Influence on action*
Readers act on a concrete case they have encountered, e.g. a dispute between employer and union.	The purpose is to find out what the Act lays down In a particular case or question. Readers may want to know, for example, – what duties they/the union/the other party may have – what rights they/the union/the other party may have – what is prohibited – what exemptions from duties apply – how they/the union should act so as to safeguard their rights or fulfil their obligations.	Readers act in accordance with the provisions of the Act or attempt to get round them. They remind their own organization or the opposing party what the Act lays down.

7.3.4 Model of law-text reading and comprehension

I consider the main point of departure to be that of the reader who reads the Act to solve a concrete problem, as in B in Table 7.4. The reader's purpose is directly oriented towards action, to find out what the Act lays down in a particular case he or she has encountered. When reading the law-text, readers can be assumed to actively process the text on the basis of a certain structuring of the concrete case that formed their point of departure, and of the specific question that to which they want to find an answer. Here the functional type of comprehension is relevant – the reader wants to know how to act according to the law. Comprehension can be described as a chain of mental connections from the reader's own situation to relevant parts of the Act and back to the reader's situation.

The *content base* of a law can be described as a collection of rules, each rule consisting of a condition part, which outlines a *framework situation* for the sphere of application of the rule, and a *directive element* stating the obligation it imposes. To comprehend, readers have to link up their own situation with the situation set out in the rule. They must identify the relevant rule by establishing a connection with the correct framework situation. Having found the relevant rule, they must refer from the directive part of the rule back to their own situation and draw the right conclusions for their own action. The model shown in Figure 7.1 attempts to illustrate the functional comprehension of the law. The content of the rule can be analyzed into a framework situation, F, and directive part, D.

The reading process can be described in four steps:

1. The reader looks for the relevant part and section of the law.
2. The reader looks for the relevant rule.

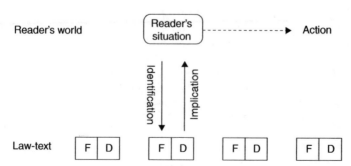

Figure 7.1 *Functional comprehension of law (Figure 1 in Gunnarsson, 1984: 81)*

Note: F – Framework situation, D – Directive part

107

3. The reader realizes what is laid down in the law.
4. The reader realizes the consequences this will have for his or her action.

Steps 1 and 2 describe the *search phase,* steps 3 and 4 the *conclusion phase.*

For law-text comprehension, the reader has to recognize his or her own situation in the text. Comprehension is thus dependent on the correspondence between the reader's perspective – the reader's permanent structuring of the pertinent aspect of reality, and his or her occasional structuring due to the situation – and the perspective of the text.

7.4 Law-texts for different functions

Let us now consider law-texts from a function perspective. The text of a law within the Roman law system, to which Swedish laws belong, can be seen as a summary of the whole content of the law, *the content base.* This content base, which can be found in the original Bill, precedents, practice, etc., can, however, be viewed and summarized from different *function perspectives,* a *citizen perspective* or a *court perspective,* which might result in different law-texts. A law-text adapted to the action-directing function should summarize the content base from the citizen's point of view, and the main content could be described as action rules. A law-text adapted to the control-directing function should summarize the content base from the court's point of view and the main content could be described as judgment rules.

These function perspectives have implications for the content to be expressed in the law-text; certain aspects of the content base are focused on while others are implied. As Table 7.5 shows, the action-directing function leads to an emphasis on actors and action. Furthermore, it leads to the stressing of normal cases, conflict-free cases and initiatives. The control-directing function, on the other hand, places the emphasis on aspects relevant for legal judgment. Exceptions, cases of conflict and obligations are focused on.

Table 7.5 *Law-texts for different purposes (Gunnarsson, 1984)*

FUNCTION	Main content	Cases focused on
ACTION-DIRECTING	Action rules	Normal cases Conflict-free cases Initiatives
CONTROL-DIRECTING	Judgment rules	Exceptions Conflict cases Obligations

The different functions have implications for how the law-text is structured, as it could be structured for use in various social situations or for use in court situations. The different functions also have implications for more superficial text levels such as vocabulary. Legal terminology, e.g., can be used to a greater or lesser extent.

7.4.1   Function perspective in the original wording of a law

On the basis of an analysis of the original text of the Act on the Joint Regulation of Working Life I came to the conclusion that this text is mainly centred on the control-directing function. The court perspective prevails here. Examination of three passages from the original text will serve to illustrate this:

> § 7 By right of association is meant a right for employers and employees to belong to an organization of employers or an organization of employees.

§ 7 focuses on *rule-naming* rather than on *action-stating.* In court, the classification of the case is important. If case A has occurred, rule N has been broken. For breaking rule N, the sentence should be so and so. The fact that the employer and the employee have a right to join an organization is, however, only implied by this legal definition.

> § 14 — If agreement is not reached during negotiations under the first part of this section, the employer shall, on request, also negotiate with a central organization of employees.

§ 14 focuses on obligation rather than initiative. The employer is obliged to negotiate, but only if the employees' trade union takes the initiative to make a request. The law-text focuses, however, on the party under an obligation, and it is indeed this party that can be sentenced in court. Employees are entitled to take the initiative, but cannot be sentenced if they do not.

> § 16 — In a case other than those mentioned in §§ 11–13, a meeting for negotiations shall, if the parties are not otherwise agreed, be held within two weeks of the other party having received a representation concerning negotiations,. . .

§ 16 focuses on cases where conflict arises where 'the parties are not otherwise agreed'. These cases are indeed the ones that result in court hearings. There is no mention of any rules for the cases provided in §§ 11–13, probably because in these cases the parties are to decide jointly (according to precedent), so these cases lead to legal proceedings.

7.5 Schema for function-centred analysis of laws

From the model of law-reading and comprehension described above (7.3.4), I evolved a schema consisting of two parts, rule-component analysis and pragmatic rule-categorization. The purpose of this schema is to provide a model for action-oriented law-text writing.

7.5.1 Rule-component analysis

In the rule-component analysis, the content base of the law-text is described according to its implications in terms of action, and the following components are seen as relevant to the performance of an action:

> Who is to perform the action (AGENT)
> Who is affected by the action (PATIENT)
> What action is to be performed (VERBAL AND OBJECT)
> What framework, i.e. what conditions are to apply (SOURCE)

The terms in parenthesis are the semantic 'deep case roles' (e.g., Fillmore, 1987). It should be noted here that the rule-component analysis is not concerned with the surface level of the original text of the Act, but with aspects of the underlying content base.

Most of the content can be described in terms of *action rules*. In addition, two other classes of rules are introduced, *definition rules* and *stipulation rules*. The stipulation rule differs from the definition rule in that, among other things, it has implications for action. These implications are expressed as resultant action rules.

The three classes of rules are described in a single schema as shown in Table 7.6.

Table 7.6 *Rule-component analysis (Table 6 in Gunnarsson, 1984: 84)*

Rule class	Sphere of application	Directive part			
		Focus	Rule type	Rule content	Party affected
Action rule	Framework situation	Acting party	Right Duty Prohibition Exemption Recommendation	Action + possible conditions	Other party
Definition rule	The entire Act (parts of the Act)	Concept	Definition	Content of definition	First and other party
Stipulation rule	Framework situation	Concept	Stipulation	–	First and/or other party

This schema has been applied to the Joint Regulation Act. For each class of rules the *sphere of application* and the *directive part,* i.e. *focus, rule type, rule content* and *party affected,* are explicitly stated. For most of the rules the sphere of application is a framework situation, outlined in the analysis by the statement of conditions. The focus is the acting party or the concept. The different types of rules are distinguished when the schema is applied to the Act by different verbs. The following modal verbs are used for the five types of action rules: right – *may, is entitled to;* duty – *shall, has a duty to;* prohibition – *may not;* exemption – *need not;* recommendation – *should.* For definition rules *is meant* is used and for stipulation rules *shall apply/ shall not apply.*

In the rule-component analysis, the various possible situations are explicitly stated, i.e. both for cases where conflict has arisen and those where it has not. References to earlier paragraphs and expressions like 'in cases other than . . .' are avoided.[3]

7.5.2   Pragmatic rule-categorization

In the schema, each rule is also classified according to different rule categories. What these categories have in common is that they analyse the rules from a pragmatic viewpoint. The actual choice of categories has been guided by the practical aim of the schema to provide a model for action-oriented law-text writing.

Three categories analyse the rule from a functional viewpoint. They concern the placement of the rule in the text-structure with regard to the importance of the structural levels for action-oriented law-text reading (cf. 7.4). One of these therefore analyses the rule as *main action rule* or *action instruction,* another as *principal case, special case* or *exception* and yet another as *breach of rule* or *not breach of rule.* A finer categorization analyses the rule in terms of the relationship between the acting parties, and also between different rule-actions. Action rules are categorized according to whether they are *symmetrical,* i.e. apply to either party, or *asymmetrical,* i.e. apply to one party only. In some cases symmetrical rules are further classified according to whether they apply to the party of *primary* or *secondary* concern as *mirror-image* roles, i.e. a duty for one party has its counterpart in a right for the other party, and *non-mirror-image* rules. Lastly, action and stipulation rules are classified according to whether they apply automatically when the party in question is in a situation covered by the framework description, *automatic* rules or whether the other party has to act first, *non-automatic* rules, or whether it is a *resultant action* rule as described in 7.5.1.

111

7.6 The alternative law-text

With the aid of this schema, I analysed the Joint Regulation Act and then, following this detailed analysis, wrote an alternative text covering sixteen sections of the Act. Nine legal experts, all of them specializing in labour legislation, verified the legal-pragmatic synonymity of this alternative law-text with the original version. They checked that the alternative text would not have other legal consequences than the original.

The alternative law-text consists of a collection of clearly expressed rules, mainly of action rules for parties, with the framework situation, the acting party, the other party and the action explicitly stated. The rules are structured into a framework situation – in the text marked by the use of italics – and a directive part. This content-structuring is created to facilitate the reading process as described in 7.3.4. For the same purpose, the text also has headings in the margin.

In the alternative text, the cases are clearly stated. Incomplete descriptions of the framework situation, like expressions in the original law-text such as 'otherwise' and 'in a case other than mentioned . . .' (see extract from § 16 below), were avoided. More complete descriptions of the conditions of the framework situation were used instead, such as 'If a request for negotiations has been made to an organization of employers . . .' and 'Where the parties are to negotiate under § 10' (see § 16). Cases where conflict arises as well as conflict-free cases, normal cases as well as exceptions, primary-party cases as well as secondary-party cases, and initiatives as well as obligations are mentioned. Cases more central to the action-directing function have, however, been highlighted.

Conflict-free cases as well as cases involving conflict are clearly stated in the alternative text. Conflict-free cases are, however, given greater emphasis. These cases, beginning with the conjunction 'Where', are thus mentioned first, while the case involving conflict, beginning with the conjunction 'if', follows (see § 16).

Normal cases, i.e. the main cases, are also foregrounded in the text, while exceptions are toned down by the use of smaller print and indentation (see § 11).

In the alternative text, the primary-party cases are stressed. In the case of symmetrical action rules, where one party can be considered the primary-party and the other as the secondary, we thus find that the primary party case is described first, and fully, while the secondary party is only mentioned afterwards and incompletely, e.g.: 'An employer has a corresponding right' (see § 7).

Initiatives are also focused on in different ways. In non-automatic action rules, the initiative is stated in a conditional clause: 'If a request for negotiations . . . the parties shall . . .' (see § 16). In mirror-image action rules, the initiative is further marked by a statement of the right as well as of the initiating action: 'The employees are entitled to central negotiations. If the local or central. . . . requests it . . .' (see § 14). In these types of rules, obligations are left unstressed.

Alternative version[4]

	§ 7
Meaning of the right to organize	An employee has a right to – belong to an organization of employees – take advantage of membership of this organization – lend active support to the organization – attempt to establish an organization. An employer has a corresponding right.
	§ 11
The employer's duty to initiate negotiations before making a decision	*Where an employer is bound by a collective agreement with an organization of employees and where the employer plans* *– an important alteration to his operations, or* *– an important alteration to the working conditions or conditions of employment of an employee who is a member of the organization:* The employer shall himself initiate negotiations on the planned alteration with the organization of employees and conclude these negotiations before making a decision on the alteration. *If exceptional circumstances arise such that the employer cannot postpone making and implementing the decision:* The employer may make and implement the decision before negotiating.
	§ 14 (extract) . . . *If the employer and the local organization of employees do not reach agreement during negotiations:* The employees are entitled to central negotiations. If the local or central organization of employees requests it, the employer also has a duty to negotiate with the central organization.
	§ 16 (extract)
Time and place for negotiations	. . . *Where the parties are to negotiate under § 10:* The parties may together decide on a time for the negotiations. *If the parties have not agreed on a time:* If a request for negotiations has been made to an individual employer or a local organization of employees, the parties shall meet to negotiate within two weeks of that party having received the request. If a request for negotiations has been made to an organiza¯'tion of employers or a central organization of employees, the parties shall meet to negotiate within three weeks of that party having received the request. The parties shall decide on a time and place for the negotiations. *Where the parties are to negotiate prior to a decision of the employer under §§ 11–13:* The parties shall together decide on a time for negotiations and should in doing so take into account how long the employer's decision can be postponed. . . .

113

Original version[5]

§ 7 By right of association is meant a right for employers and employees to belong to an organization of employers or an organization of employees, to take advantage of that membership, and to work for the organization or in order to establish an organization.

§ 11 Before an employer decides on important alteration to his activity, he shall, on his own initiative, negotiate with an organization of employees in relation to which he is bound by collective agreement. The same shall be observed before an employer decides on important alteration of work or employment conditions for employees who belong to the organization. If urgent reasons so necessitate, the employer may make and implement a decision before he has fulfilled his duty to negotiate under the first part of this section.

§ 14 (extract) . . . If agreement is not reached during negotiations under the first part of this section, the employer shall, on request, also negotiate with a central organization of employees.

§ 16 (extract) . . . In a case other than those mentioned in §§ 11–13, a meeting for negotiations shall, if the parties are not otherwise agreed, be held within two weeks of the other party having received a representation concerning negotiations, where the other party is an individual employer or a local organization of employees, and otherwise within three weeks of such representation having been received by the other party. In addition, it shall be for the parties to decide on a time and place for a negotiation meeting.

The alternative text can also be described at more superficial text levels. My intention was to use 'normal' vocabulary and therefore to avoid legal terms wherever possible. Following the schema, I avoided passives and complicated syntax. The sentences follow a subject-verb-object (SVO) structure. The typography marks the content structure. The following extracts from both original and alternative texts are illustrative of my approach.

7.7   Test on functional comprehensibility

7.7.1   Method

The effects on comprehensibility of the systematic change of perspective from court to citizen were measured in a test. In choosing a method to measure comprehensibility, I tried to imitate – as closely as possible – the 'normal' way of reading the Joint Regulation Act and therefore took the analysis of readers, reading situations, reading purposes and reading processes described above (7.3.3 and 7.3.4) as a basis for constructing the test. The test therefore consisted of cases describing possible points of departure for problem-solving reading, and attached questions, stating possible reading purposes. In all, there were six cases covering different situations, and fourteen questions posing a variety of problems. The questions were of the following two types:

(a)   What possibilities does the Joint Regulation Act offer the trade union for getting a better picture of the economic situation? The possibilities are. . . . .

(b) Has L a right to belong to a trade union?

       Yes □   No □

The questions were related to different parts of the law-text, so that of the sixteen law-sections, eleven were covered by questions. The questions also differed with regard to the party focused on. They also varied as to the degree of explicitness and specificity with which the answers were stated in the law-text. Together with the cases and questions, the subjects were given the sixteen paragraphs of the original law-text *or* of the alternative text. (In the order in which they were seated, subjects were alternately given the original law-text or the revised version.) The test lasted for 60 minutes and the subjects had to answer the questions, i.e. give a written answer ((a) above) or mark yes or no ((b) above), underline the relevant passage of the law-text and write a short commentary. The results discussed in 7.7.3 are based on their underlinings, answers and commentaries.

7.7.2   Subjects

The test was taken by 264 adult Swedes, 90 adult trainees at a vocational centre for the unemployed (the EMP group), 126 participants in different courses arranged by the two most important Swedish central trade union organizations (the TU group), and 48 law students (the LAW group). These groups were chosen as representing three relevant types of addressees of this Act, the ordinary employee, the trade union official and the lawyer. Background information assumed to be relevant for law-text reading was compiled on the subjects: sex, age, education, working experience, trade union experience, general law-text knowledge and specific knowledge of the Act. As to these factors (except sex), the three test groups were found to differ significantly.

7.7.3   Results

7.7.3.1   Effects on comprehensibility

The main aim of the test was to measure the effect of the change of perspective. We will first consider the results attained by the three groups tested for the fourteen questions. Correct response frequencies for the questions are shown in Figures 7.2 and 7.3. Figure 7.2 shows the frequencies for those who had the original law-text (-O): EMP-O, TU-O and LAW-O, Figure 7.3 for those who had the alternative text (-A): EMP-A, TU-A and LAW-A. The questions are listed in the order they were presented in the test. The subjects were instructed to answer the questions

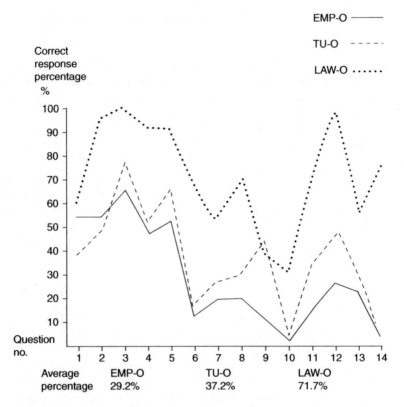

EMP-O ————

TU-O — — — —

LAW-O ......

Correct
response
percentage
%

Question
no.

| Average percentage | EMP-O 29.2% | TU-O 37.2% | LAW-O 71.7% |

* EMP-O = Employed persons given the original version.
   TU-O   = Trade union officials given the original version.
   LAW-O = Law students given the original version.

Figure 7.2 *Correct response frequencies for the 14 test questions achieved by EMP-O, TU-O and LAW-O (Figure 2 in Gunnarsson, 1984: 91)*

in this order, and the lower frequencies for the latter questions therefore partly reflect the lower response frequency for those questions.

As we can see from Figure 7.2, the LAW group had the highest average percentage of correct responses, 71.7 per cent, among those who were given the original law-text. This group had the highest percentage of correct responses for all questions except one (no. 9). If we compare the two non-law groups, we find that TU-O had a higher correct response frequency than EMP-O for most of the questions. The average for TU-O was 37.2 per cent and for EMP-O 29.2 per cent. The average difference between these O-groups was thus 8 per cent.

A comparison of the average results listed below the percentages in Figures 7.2 and 7.3 shows that in all three test groups those who

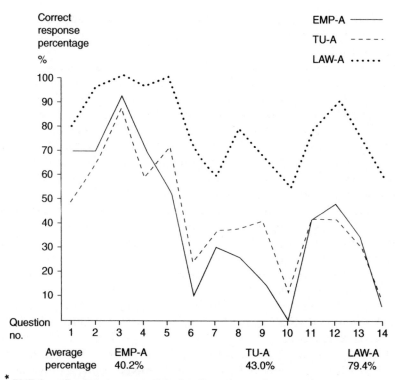

Figure 7.3 *Correct response frequencies for the 14 test questions achieved by EMP-A, TU-A and LAW-A (Figure 3 in Gunnarsson, 1984: 9)*

had the alternative text had higher correct response frequencies than those with the original text. LAW-A had an average of 79.4 per cent, which is 7.7 per cent higher than LAW-O. The TU-A group had an average of 43 per cent, i.e. a gain of 5.8 per cent. EMP-A had an average of 40.2 per cent, an improvement of 11.0 per cent.

As we can see from Figure 7.3, the LAW-A group had the highest percentage on all questions. Even with the alternative text, their comprehension was greater than for the two non-law groups. The correct response frequencies of EMP-A and TU-A can be said to have been on the same level. EMP-A had an average of 40.2 per cent and TU-A 43.0 per cent. The average difference between these two groups was therefore only 2.8 per cent, less than that between EMP-O and TU-O. If we consider the individual questions, we find that TU-A were better on seven questions while EMP-A were better on six.

As for differences between the individual questions, the groups showed similar tendencies. On the whole, all three groups found the same questions easy and difficult, in spite of their different backgrounds. There were, however, a few exceptions. The most noteworthy was question no. 9, where the TU group had a remarkably high frequency (TU-O higher even than LAW-O). For this question, which was 'Has the trade union any way of postponing the shut-down?', the pre-knowledge specific to the trade union officials was thus important. The answer to this question is to be found in § 14 (cf. 6 above) and it can also be noted that the changes made in the alternative text led to a substantial improvement for the law students, LAW-A was 28.9 per cent higher than LAW-O.

Another way to analyse the results is to compare the average number of correct answers, incorrect answers and non-responses, for all subjects and for the groups separately. This comparison points to a higher average number of correct responses among those who were given the alternative text, than among those who had the original law-text, and a corresponding decrease in the average number of incorrect responses. The improvement was greatest in the EMP group, second highest in the LAW group and smallest in the TU group. For all subjects, the differences between the alternative text and the original text were significant at the 1 per cent level, as far as the average numbers of both correct and incorrect answers were concerned. The improvement was, however, not very great. The changes made in the alternative text can best be seen as a step towards a comprehensible law-text. From a further scrutiny of the results, I have come to the conclusion that the alternative text seems to have compensated the EMP group and the LAW group for their lack of trade union experience. It did not, however, compensate the two non-law groups (EMP and TU) for their lack of legal knowledge, or for their lower education. Although the alternative text led to fewer non-responses, the average number of incorrect answers hardly changed. The alternative text was comprehended better, but not more quickly.

These results indicate that the alternative text led to a higher response rate and to more correct answers. The function-centering of the alternative text *as a whole* had a positive effect for the groups tested. I have, however, also analysed the results in relation to the hypotheses made regarding the importance of the different text levels underlying this function-centring.

As we already know, the alternative text was elaborated systematically on the basis of an analysis of pragmatic levels, the content level and the text-structural level. Syntax, vocabulary and typography were used as auxiliary means of realizing the function perspective. The original law-text, however, was not written consistently, as was the alternative text. The differences between the two texts, therefore, vary from rule to rule. I examined this variation between the texts by means of a rule-by-rule analysis of text differences on the following levels: content, text-structural, syntactic, anaphoric, lexical and typographical. This comparison was then used for a detailed analysis of the effect of different text levels on comprehensibility.

I will not elaborate any further on this analysis here, only mention that the results of these detailed analyses support the assumption that function-centering primarily based on changes at deeper text levels leads to improved comprehensibility as far as action-oriented law-text reading is concerned.

7.7.3.2 Difficulties in law-text reading

The degree of explicitness and specificity with which the answers were stated in the text varied from one question to another. According to the hypothesis on law-text comprehension, the result on any particular question should be dependent on the similarity between the posed question and the law-text. To test this hypothesis, therefore, I investigated the relation between the difficulty of the question, on the one hand, and the implicitness of the law-text in relation to the posed question and its specificity, on the other. I listed the questions in order of increasing difficulty, and then drew up one rank order for those who were given the original law-text and another for those who read the alternative text. For each text-variant, the implicitness of the relevant part of the law-text could thus be described. This analysis clearly supports the hypothesis that there is a correlation between the difficulty of the question and the implicitness and specificity of the law-text. The questions which were found easiest were the ones where the case as a whole was explicitly formulated and also specified in the law-text. The most difficult questions were the ones where the case was implicit, i.e. given as negative information in the law-text. The same patterns are found for both the original law-text and the alternative text.

I also analysed the answers given with regard to the two main phases in the reading process described in the model, the search phase and the conclusion phase. I separately described the location in the law-text and the direct answers given to the questions, i.e. marked alternative and commentary. The answers can thus be divided into four categories:

1. Correct in search phase. Correct in conclusion phase.
2. Correct in search phase. Incorrect in conclusion phase.

3. Incorrect in search phase. Correct marking of alt. and commentary.
4. Incorrect in search phase. Incorrect marking of alt. and commentary.

Table 7.7 shows the distribution of the answers among these four categories. The figures indicate the average percentage of given answers (non-responses excluded) for the fourteen questions. Percentages are given for all subjects tested and also divided into those who had the alternative text and those who had the original text.

Considering the total average percentages we find that the majority – i.e. 61 per cent (57 per cent plus 4 per cent) – of the given answers were correct in the search phase. We can also see that of those who had managed to locate the answer correctly in the law-text, only a minority drew an incorrect conclusion. Of the answers 4 per cent came under category and 2. 39 per cent of the given answers were incorrect in terms of locating the relevant section of the law-text (categories 3 and 4). In many cases – 24 per cent of the given answers –, however, the subjects managed, despite failing to locate the answer in the law-text, to mark the correct alternative and give an acceptable commentary. These answers cannot, however, be regarded as correct in the conclusion phase as this must be related to correctly locating the relevant section of the law. If we then compare the figures for those who were given the original law-text and those who had the alternative text, we do indeed find a higher percentage of correct answers among the latter (category 1). As to their distribution among the four categories, however, the figures for O and A show similar patterns. The conclusion that can be drawn from this analysis of the answers with regard to the

Table 7.7 Answers in relation to the phases of the reading process. Average percentages for the fourteen questions. The figures indicate the percentage of all given answers (non-responses excluded). They are given for all subjects, taken together and divided into O-text and A-text readers (Table 10 in Gunnarsson, (1984: 97)

	Type of answer			
	1 Search ph. = C Concl. ph. = C	2 Search ph. = C Concl. ph. ≠ C	3 Search ph. ≠ C Alt + Com = C	4 Search ph. ≠ C Alt + Com ≠ C
TOT (O+A)	57%	4%	24%	15%
O	53%	5%	26%	16%
A	61%	3%	23%	13%

Note: Ph. – Phase, Concl. – Conclusion, Alt – Alternative, Com – Commentary, = C – Correct, ≠ C – Incorrect phases of the reading process is that the main difficulty the subjects experienced was locating the answer in the law-text.

In order to get a better picture of what makes law-text reading difficult, I carried out a qualitative analysis of the incorrect answers. This analysis showed that the main difficulty for the reader is to connect his or her mental representation of the point of departure and the reading purpose with the law-text. Readers tend, e.g., to give a more concrete answer than they should. They tend to locate the answer in an incorrect specific rule instead of in a correct general rule. The analysis also shows that the difficulties experienced when reading a law-text lie not in the understanding of the words as such, but in realizing their relevance to the case in question. In all groups of subjects and for both texts the same types of difficulties were found, though the proportions differed.

7.8 Discussion

The investigation of law-text comprehensibility presented in this chapter is original both in terms of its solid theoretical framework, which combines psycholinguistics, cognitive psychology and text linguistics, and its experimental approach, involving a systematic rewriting of 16 paragraphs of a law-text. The investigation further differs from most experiments in its testing methodology, i.e. that comprehensibility was tested by means of cases, which the subjects were asked to solve (cf. discussion in 7.1).

The experiments with the Joint Regulation Act presented in this chapter point to the importance of the pragmatic text levels – perspective and function-orientation – for law-text comprehensibility. It is my conclusion, also, that these results can be generalized to other laws and also to other action-oriented texts. The changes I made to the Joint Regulation Act for the main experiment substantially increased its comprehensibility. The alternative text was still not easy, however. This text seems, as was suggested earlier, to have compensated the reader more for a lack of trade union experience than for a low level of education or a lack of law-text knowledge. This might be explained by the fact that the alternative text – though closer to a citizen perspective – is still quite similar to the original law-text. The text structure has been changed within the rules, but not between them. The focus on aspects differs in the alternative text, but the choice of rules and facts has not been changed in any radical way. The main conventions for law-texts cannot be said to have been broken, and a more correct description of the perspective achieved in the alternative text would therefore be a *law-conventional citizen perspective.*

In order to further improve law-text comprehensibility, the necessary next step must be to further adapt the text to a *natural citizen perspective*. As we saw, the explicitly stated and the concrete and specified all facilitate mental connections between the reader's point of departure and the law-text. The choice of rules, facts and words must therefore be further analysed from the viewpoint of the citizen's use of the text. The test results also point to the difficulty readers have in finding the relevant sections of a law-text. The next step towards a more comprehensible law-text must therefore entail a more radical restructuring of the text, including a restructuring of the main elements of the law, the sections and the rules. Such a restructuring must be based on closer analysis of the reading situations and reading purposes of different addressee groups.

7.9 Conclusions

To conclude, I wish to stress that the theory proposed in this chapter relates to a wide range of texts. A similar pragmatic analysis of text function and the situated reading and comprehension is relevant for most action-oriented texts. In order to understand why texts are comprehensible for some readers, and incomprehensible for others, we need to acknowledge both the text's function-orientation and the perspective of its various reader groups.

Notes

1. The study is presented in full in a monograph in Swedish (Gunnarsson, 1982). It is also presented in English in an article in *TEXT* (Gunnarsson, 1984).
2. Lag om medbestämmande i arbetslivet (1976: 580), the so-called Medbestämmandelagen, has also been translated into English as 'The Co-Determination in the Workplace Act'.
3. In an appendix to the article in *TEXT* (Gunnarsson, 1984), three examples of the application of the schema to the Joint Regulation of Working Life are given.
4. This is an extract from a translation into English of the alternative version of sixteen paragraphs of the Swedish act Medbestämmandelagen (Gunnarsson, 1984: 87–88).
5. This is an extract from a translation into English of the sixteen paragraphs of Medbestämmandelagen which were included in the comprehensibility experiment (Gunnarsson, 1984: 89).

8 The legislative writing process

In this chapter I will explore the drafting of legislative texts from a combined cognitive-rhetorical and sociolinguistic perspective. Problems of law-text comprehensibility discussed in the previous chapter will here be related to the legislative writing process. In order to investigate this process, I observed the drafting of three pieces of Swedish consumer legislation at different stages. Using an ethnographic methodology, I followed as an observer the discussions at the various committee meetings held over a period of four years. On the basis of this study I will discuss legislative drafting in relation to the stages of the writing process, the professional composition of the committees involved, the various contextual frameworks, and the targeted readers.[1]

Focusing on the relationship between the writing process and text comprehension, I will make the following claims: (1) I will claim that the social and societal conditions under which texts are produced result in less or more readable texts, (2) I will claim that an analysis of a sustained collective writing process, such as law-drafting, needs to consider both cognitive-rhetorical and sociolinguistic parameters, (3) I will claim that a critical sociolinguistic perspective on law-drafting should include an analysis of the targeted readers.

In the first part of the chapter, I develop my three claims. In the second part, I elaborate on the societal constraints on legal writing, distinguishing between general constraints, e.g. legal, political, linguistic, cultural, and specific constraints. Parts 3–5 present and discuss the investigation of the legislative writing process. In part 3, I summarize my results in relation to the societal constraints on Swedish lawmaking. In part 4, I analyse the drafting process and summarize my observations in relation to cognitive and sociolinguistic theories on writing. In part 5, I relate the process to the end-product, i.e. the text. I analyse some paragraphs of the law-texts, the drafting of which I had observed. In the concluding part (6), I discuss the consequences for comprehensibility of a sustained, collective writing process, as law-drafting is.

8.1   Introduction

There is no doubt about the fact that every text reflects the situation in which it is produced. The question is, however, what environmental factors are the most influential and in what ways these are revealed in the final text. In this chapter I propose that conditions related to the writing process as such exert a great influence on texts. In the psycholinguistic laboratory we can quite easily isolate linguistic factors. Academically, we can see the writing process as a pure text-formation and discuss its end result – the text – as a mainly linguistic product. In reality, however, the linguistic factor is very much intermingled with other factors. Writing, or rather text production, is constrained by so many social and societal factors that the linguistic factor seems to be a minor one.

As mentioned above, my first claim in this chapter is that the social and societal conditions under which texts are produced result in less or more readable and comprehensible texts. Problems of text comprehensibility are thus related not only to the writing process as such, but also to the composition of the working group and the various contextual frameworks in which the text is constructed. The social and professional affiliation of those directly involved in the writing process is thus important, as are the social stratification and ideologies within the local linguistic and cultural community. This means that it ought to be worthwhile for scholars interested in comprehensibility issues to look into the writing process and analyse it in its total context. To some extent at least, I believe that the limited results achieved by language reform efforts in many cases are due to the fact that these efforts have focused mainly on end-products. The writing process has less often been connected directly with text comprehensibility.

My second claim is that an analysis of a sustained collective writing process, such as law-drafting, needs to consider both cognitive-rhetorical and sociolinguistic parameters. An assumption guiding this study has been that law writing has similarities to other types of text writing, implying that it is just one particular case of writing. Just as there are a great variety of situational factors surrounding writing – why, when, to whom and in what form people write – the writing process varies. Writing law-texts is indeed a far cry from many briefer types of text writing. It does, however, have similarities with other sustained writing of more formal prose. If different types of text writing were modelled on a continuum from formal and elaborate writing at one end to casual and brief writing at the other, law writing would indeed be placed close to the formal, elaborate end. There are, however, many other types of text writing that would be assigned similar positions.

124

My starting point was therefore that law writing could be described by models similar to those describing 'normal' text writing, i.e. using cognitive-rhetorical models. Though more formal and elaborate, the writing components involved in writing a law-text were assumed to be the same as those involved in writing a poem, an article, a letter, or whatever. The ideas must be generated, organized, and translated into texts. The text must be evaluated and revised.

As this in-depth study of legislative writing has revealed, however, a sustained collective writing process, such as law-drafting, cannot be understood without an analysis of the social and societal contexts. Social variables at group level determine the writing process, e.g. the professional and social background of the members of the drafting committee and the formal and informal social order within the group. The writing process and its end result are also constrained by the various contextual frameworks within which the drafting process takes place.

The study discussed in the previous chapter (Chapter 7) showed the importance for text comprehensibility of perspective and function orientation and of explicitness and concretion. With these results as a background, the hypothesis I put forward in this chapter is that the court perspective, function orientation, implicitness and abstractness of law-texts can to a certain extent be explained by the particular conditions under which these texts are produced.

My third claim is that a critical sociolinguistic perspective on law-drafting includes an analysis of the targeted readers. As was revealed in Chapter 7, the main difficulty for a reader when trying to apply a legal text to a situation experienced is not caused by the text surface – i.e., by the syntax, the morphology, or the functional words – but by deeper text levels. An action-oriented text comprehension is thus primarily correlated to the function orientation and perspective of the text and not to the syntax and vocabulary. If we want to make legal texts radically more comprehensible, we must therefore tackle the problem caused by their abstractness and implicitness. The great problem for the lay reader has always been and still is that so little is actually said in the text and that what is said is presented in a way that suits the needs of the courts, not other groups of readers. The lack of specified content in legal texts makes them incomprehensible, and this I think is not only a legal problem but also a linguistic and socio-cultural one. As I see it, this problem is therefore to a large extent cultural, i.e. related to attitudes among professionals and experts to comprehensibility issues and to their readership. A critical sociolinguistic analysis of law-drafting thus needs to consider who the writers actually view as their targeted readers.

Tackling the problem of the abstractness and implicitness of legal texts is thus very difficult, which is probably one of the reasons so little – actually, nothing – has been done about it. It is no doubt important to analyse and discuss these traits; however, it is impossible to discuss them in isolation. The total situation in which legal texts are produced must be taken into consideration. This leads us to the very heart of the language reform problem, which advocates of clear language all over the world have to face. Language reform is determined by the will to reform and the resources spent on it. There are, however, many other factors as well. The language issue can definitely not be dealt with in a vacuum. On the contrary, it is inextricably bound up with a lot of other issues. Work on language reform is constrained by a multitude of factors. Let us call them societal factors, or societal constraints.

8.2 Societal constraints on lawmaking

In Chapter 2, I developed a theory for the construction and reconstruction of professional discourse and distinguished different societal frameworks – a legal-political, a technical-economical, a linguistic and a socio-cultural. These frameworks are assumed to play essential roles in the forming of all types of professional language and discourse. In this chapter I will focus on the various constraints on lawmaking offered by these various societal frameworks.

To obtain a picture of how the societal frameworks determine lawmaking and the outcome of language reform work, we have to take into consideration general as well as specific constraints. General constraints are those related to the lawmaking process within a society seen in its entirety, while specific constraints are those related to the making of one single law or a few related laws. General constraints are thus related to different systems of a legal, political, economical, socio-cultural and linguistic nature that exist within a society, while specific constraints are related to the particular situation in which the law in question is made.

8.2.1 General constraints

I will first discuss the general constraints, focusing on legal, political, economic, socio-cultural and linguistic factors.

8.2.1.1 Legal Constraints

There are four different factors in the legal constraints determining legal language reform. The first is the drafting system as such. If we look at drafting in different countries we find considerable variation. Within a given country we can also see how the drafting system varies over time, and not uncommonly also from one field to another. We must therefore take into account how this system is constructed. Is it a one-man show or a collective writing process? Do a group of lawyers write the law, or do groups outside the legal world influence the drafting? Does the public have any influence? Is it a one-stage or a stepwise process?

As a second factor of importance I would point to the legal system at work. International, historical and other comparisons reveal great differences, e.g., in how closely interrelated different laws are, how much value is attached to tradition, what roles antecedent laws have, what roles precedents have, what roles practice has and how intertwined the legal system is with that of other countries. There is, of course, a striking intertextuality between the various texts within a legal system, often intended but also due to unconscious compliance with earlier patterns established within the legal community.[2]

The court system is the third legal factor determining lawmaking and law language reform efforts. To get an idea of the societal constraints we must therefore take into consideration what courts there are, how they apply the law, what interpretation rules exist, what role the statute plays in the court's interpretation, what role the underlying government bill has, what role practice plays, what the role of precedents is, and so on.

The fourth legal factor is the system for proclamation of laws. This is a factor that most certainly varies from country to country as well as from period to period. We will thus find variation in terms of how legal texts are published, where we find statute books, government bills, precedents and the like, how information about laws is spread, what roles lawyers play in publicizing laws, what roles schools play, what roles the media play, and so on. We will also find a difference regarding the role of computers; e.g., whether access to legal information is computerized or not.

8.2.1.2 Political constraints

Let me now turn to the political constraints. The first factor to be considered is, of course, the political system. To obtain a picture of the societal conditions determining the lawmaking process we must look at the roles politicians play in the drafting of laws as well as in their interpretation. The bureaucratic system must also be considered, e.g., whether laws are used directly by different local authorities or whether the authorities work with special law translations. We should also look at the role that interpretations by local authorities play in relation to the public.

8.2.1.3   Other societal constraints

Besides these legal and political constraints, there are also a number of other factors that can be seen as societal constraints on the lawmaking process. The technical-economical framework is an important determining factor. To understand the conditions for lawmaking we must therefore look at the influence exerted by industries, trade unions and the like on lawmaking and the interpretation of the law.

The socio-cultural framework must also be considered. We should therefore also take into account whether there are great differences between social classes in terms of power and living standards, and what influence representatives of different social classes and groups exert on lawmaking and law interpretation. Comparisons among countries would probably reveal differences between socialist and capitalist countries, and between highly developed countries and those of the Third World.

The educational system is also an important factor. Lawmaking is definitely related to the average standard of education, and thus indirectly to the proportion of the population able to read a text as complicated as a law-text. Compare, e.g., the proportion of the population who can read a complicated text in countries with a high average standard of education – such as the United States, Germany, and Sweden – with the proportion able to read similar prose in most countries in South America, Asia, and Africa. Lawmaking is also related more directly to the proportion of the population taught to read and apply the law at school, college, work, and so on. That proportion varies from country to country, even in the industrialized world.

8.2.1.4   Linguistic constraints

Finally, to complete my survey of general societal constraints, I will discuss the linguistic factors, pointing first to the role of the language system as such in lawmaking and law reform work. As I will argue later, linguistic questions are of very little concern to lawmakers. This does not mean, however, that laws are written in a linguistic vacuum. When writing the law, lawyers must of course operate within the linguistic system, though they do not consciously deal with linguistic matters. In order to describe the societal conditions for lawmaking and law reform fully, we must therefore take into consideration the differences that exist between various sublanguages within the language system. Is there a great deal of difference between oral and written language? Is there a marked difference between formal and informal varieties in the language? Is there a clear contrast between legal language and ordinary prose?

Other linguistic constraints of importance in law reform work include factors related to the dynamics of the language in question. Is the general language static or undergoing change? What attitudes are there in society towards linguistic changes? How dearly cherished is tradition?

8.2.2 Specific constraints

From these general constraints on lawmaking I will now turn to specific constraints or, in other words, to the role exerted by the particular situation in shaping the law in question. In many ways the making of each law is unique. It is quite obvious that the political situation and the bureaucratic context exert differing influences on the making of different kinds of laws. Some but not all laws are politically controversial so that different parties will adopt different standpoints. Some but not all laws are of great concern to powerful special agencies and authorities. Similar variation is evident if we look at the roles of economic, social and educational factors. Some laws relate to the national economy, the business world, or the labour market, but not all do. Some laws relate to social differences or concern the rights of the ordinary citizen, but again not all do. And so one could go on.

Even legal factors vary to a certain extent from one law to another. If, e.g., we look at the drafting situation, we find that some laws are made and passed in a hurry, while others are the fruit of years of effort. The legal situation as such is also unique in many respects. Much lawmaking can be described – to some or a large extent – as the rewriting of antecedent laws. Other laws, however, are new, but even with these laws there is great variation in how new they are: in the case of many laws, but not all, there exist similar related laws in the country, or there are similar laws on the statute books of other countries. The court situation and the way in which laws are promulgated also vary from law to law. Different types of courts will handle cases relating to different legal domains. A fixed standard practice will exist for some laws, while for others this will be more flexible. The procedures for spreading information also vary for different kinds of laws.

If we then turn to the linguistic situation we can also point to certain traits unique to each law, or at least to each field of law. Different legal domains have somewhat different language traditions, as a comparison of traditions in the classic fields of law, such as contracts and

129

sales, with traditions in a newer field, such as labour law, will show. We find that greater store is set by tradition in certain fields than in others, and that attitudes towards language change vary among lawyers with different areas of expertise.

8.3 The case of Swedish lawmaking

After enumerating all these societal factors I will now analyse the influence they have exerted on the drafting of some consumer laws. As an observer I followed different stages of work on three consumer laws: the work of drafting commissions in the case of two of the laws and scrutiny in the Council on Legislation in the case of the third. I shall discuss a few of the results of this study into the Swedish lawmaking process. I should mention that this study was carried out before Sweden joined the European Union. The lawmaking process described is thus mainly related to the Swedish societal framework.

The lawmaking process in Sweden has the following phases:

(1) government proposal for legislation
(2) consideration by a drafting commission
    (a) long series of full-day discussions within the commission
    (b) hearings
    (c) publication of a report
(3) consideration at the ministry
    (a) circulation of the report for comment
    (b) first draft of the government bill
    (c) Council on Legislation scrutiny of the bill and advice on revisions
    (d) consideration of advice of the Council on Legislation in the ministry
    (e) editing of a second draft of the government bill
(4) consideration in Parliament
    (a) discussion in a parliamentary committee
    (b) report, including possible recommended amendments
    (c) enactment of the law.
(5) promulgation
    (a) the bill, the advice of the Council on Legislation, the committee report in the official journal
    (b) the statute in the yearly statute book
    (c) summaries in pamphlets
    (d) short summaries sent to the mass media

There are variations in the lawmaking process depending on the type of law. For more important laws and laws that concern the ordinary citizen, the process is quite similar to the one I will present below. What we can first note about the Swedish lawmaking process is the fact that it is a long, stepwise process. For the Consumer Services Act the work of the drafting commission took seven years, consideration by the ministry four and a half years, scrutiny in the Council on Legislation five months and consideration in Parliament a few months.

Second, we can note the different participants involved in the process and which roles they play. Using the distinction made in Chapter 1 between 'professionals', 'semi-professionals' and 'non-professionals', we find among the participants both legal professionals, i.e. lawyers, and other groups of professionals and semi-professionals, i.e. politicians and experts from different areas. From the point of view of drafting law, the politicians could of course be said to have a legal expertise as well, as they are part of the body which enacts legislation.

(1) The lawyers: The greatest influence on lawmaking is exerted by highly qualified lawyers. The secretary and in most cases the chair of the drafting commission are lawyers, the officers working on the law in the ministry are lawyers, and the members of the Council on Legislation are lawyers – judges of the Supreme Court. Lawyers might also and very often do act as experts in the drafting commission and as members of the parliamentary committee. At all stages great care is taken in investigating the wordings of earlier and related laws – often also in laws of neighbouring countries, what the interpreting practices of the courts are, and so on.

(2) The politicians: Influence on the drafting process is also exerted by politicians, who are very often members of the drafting commission. For the consumer laws there was one member from the majority party, which at the time was the Social Democratic Party, and one from one of the opposition parties. Politicians are also involved as representatives of different organizations and unions. The main role played by the politicians is then in Parliament.

(3) Experts representing different areas: At different stages representatives of industry, trade unions, government agencies, local government, citizen organizations, and so on play an active part. For more important laws, like the consumer laws I followed, such representatives were attached as experts to the drafting commissions and participated very actively in

the discussions there. Representatives of the public were also called to give their views on the subject matter at hearings. They were also asked to write down their comments on the commission report, which was sent out to a relevant selection of government agencies, schools, organizations and unions.

In a book entitled *Legislative Drafting: A New Approach*, written by the British barrister William Dale (1977), drafting methods in France, Germany, Sweden and the United Kingdom are compared. Dale writes that lawmaking in Sweden is characterized by its intensely democratic nature and by the care taken over drafting. He writes that in Sweden as soon as the government has shaped its proposal for legislation, public referral begins, through a commission, and the views of the public or of bodies outside the government are collected on five occasions: at the successive stages of commission, ministry, Council on Legislation, parliamentary committee and Parliament. He further writes, 'From the outset, therefore, the minds of those who are to formulate the law are fertilised by the ideas of those of the public who are concerned with the subject, the ideas become orderly thoughts, and the thoughts are put into words suitable for the statute book' (Dale, 1977: 104).

I fully agree with Dale about the democratic nature of Swedish lawmaking. I do not, however, agree with his wholly positive picture of the product. From the point of view of comprehensibility I would say, on the contrary, that the Swedish drafting process, due at least in part to its democratic nature, creates texts that are very difficult for readers other than experts to understand. The drafting process is in fact one that creates abstract and implicit texts with content difficult for the lay, non-professional reader to grasp.

The drafting of a law entails a continuous resolution of conflicts, where overt conflicts between different parties and interests have to be democratically toned down. The participants in the drafting process have to come to a certain level of agreement, i.e. the strongest causes of discontent have to be overcome. As for the law being drafted, this often means that its content has to be made less clear and concrete. It is easier to get different parties to accept a vague, abstract rule than a clear, concrete one. Of course this means that the resolution of real conflicts is postponed until the law is applied by courts, government agencies, local authorities, and the like.

8.4 The legal writing process

My analysis of the legal writing process will combine cognitive-rhetorical and sociolinguistic traditions. As a review of earlier literature shows, a major branch of the cognitive theory of the writing process has worked within a rhetorical tradition. The five stages of text production within classical rhetoric (invention, arrangement, style, memory and delivery) have been adapted to modern cognitive theories (Hayes and Flower, 1980; Flower and Hayes, 1984). In these cognitive-rhetorical models writing presents the writer with the problem of evoking a certain state of mind in the reader or otherwise achieving some goal. The writer then directs the text towards a concrete group of people, the intended readers of the particular text.

I will contrast a sociolinguistic view with this cognitive-rhetorical view of text writing. According to sociolinguistic theories, talking and speaking involve a continuous adaptation to the *others*, to the local 'group' and also to the entire 'communicative community'. When we construct a text we thus adapt, consciously or unconsciously, to the norms and attitudes of the communicative community of which we are a part. Collective writing, i.e. when the text is constructed by a group of people, further entails negotiations during the writing process about content, content structuring, wordings, layout etc., which means that the end result – the text – not only reflects the goals, knowledge, norms and attitudes of the group members, but also their interaction during the process.

The sociolinguistic framework is presented in more detail in Chapter 9. I there use the term 'communicative community' (instead of 'speech community' or 'discourse community') to mark that both spoken and written communication, as well as both contact and distant communication, are referred to. In that chapter, I also discuss the sociolinguistic 'group' concept and introduce the term 'professional group'. For the sake of clarity, however, I will here use the term 'legal working group' when referring to a group formed by the committee members. As will be discussed below, the committees involved consist of both professionals and semi-professionals in relation to legislation.

Within sociolinguistics a central concept used for the description of variation is social class. For the purpose of the analysis in this chapter, I have however found it more useful to make a distinction between those members of a community who have an influence on its public discourse and those who have not. I thus make a distinction between the public and private sphere within the communicative community,[3] and between those who belong to the public sphere, e.g. politicians, lawyers, representatives of government, and those who do not, i.e. ordinary citizens. My perspective is here also inspired by critical discourse analysis.[4]

The assumption I will advance in this chapter is therefore that legislative writing entails an adaptation to the 'group' and the legal 'communicative community', and within the community to those who belong to the public sphere.

Let us, however, first return to the cognitive-rhetorical school. As a starting point for a description of the legal writing process I will take the generally based rhetorical writing model presented by Flower and Hayes (1984). Flower and Hayes distinguish three main phases in the writing process: *planning, translating* and *reviewing*. However, I do not find the distinction between the two phases of planning and translating adequate for legal writing. Instead, I suggest the two phases of *construction of a text* and *editing*. By naming the first phase *construction of a text* I am suggesting that everything involved in forming the content of the text should be considered as one phase. This includes both the mental generation of ideas and their formulation in words; rather, formulations cannot be separated from the generation of ideas, as they are part and parcel of them. The legislative drafting process consists of a continuous discussion of the content of a given law, with the different formulations representing different contents.

The second phase of the legal writing process, *editing*, encompasses going from written notes to an adequate text form. This work is mainly done by the secretary and the chairperson of the drafting commission concerned. The third phase, *reviewing*, is the same as that suggested in the rhetorical model for normal writing.

I have thus found that, roughly speaking, the rhetorical writing model captures quite well the main stages of the process of writing laws. However, legal writing is different in certain respects from a more 'normal' type of writing, which I assume is what Flower and Hayes have set out to describe. These differences I would ascribe to the collective, sustained drafting process, which results in a marked, conscious adaptation to the legal working group and the public sphere of the communicative community. Further this adaptation leads to less concern about the reader than the rhetorical writing model assumes.

The writing of a law-text is, as I mentioned above, generally a collective process. This is, e.g., true of the work of the drafting commissions. The actual writing is done by one person, in most cases the secretary, who assumes the role of interpreter and combiner of different ideas. The representation of the text is, however, constructed collectively by all members of the drafting commission. The chairperson and the politicians have decisive roles, but all members of the commission contribute by viewing the issue from their particular perspectives and by thus extending the content of the text.

134

When an individual plans a text, she explores long-term memory concerning the topic, including her concepts and scripts about the subject matter. She thinks about aims, consequences, and so on. This is also what takes place during discussions in the drafting commission. The difference compared with individual planning, however, is that the topic is viewed from many different angles, that many different concepts and scripts are explored, and that many different aims and consequences are considered.

The two drafting commissions whose work I followed concerned consumers' rights – the Consumer Sales Act and the House Sales Act. Both commissions were large, consisting of between ten and fifteen members. The chairpersons were highly placed lawyers, in fact members of the Supreme Court. The secretaries were skilled lawyers with drafting experience. The commissions also included two politicians each. About ten people from different organizations were also attached to each commission as experts. They represented industry and the business world, the trade unions, the ministries, local government, the National Board for Consumer Policies, consumer cooperatives and special courts. Many of the representatives were lawyers or had some legal training. Some experts had participated in the drafting of antecedent or related laws. For years, in the case of the Consumer Sales Act for seven years, the members of the commissions met once a month for a whole day of discussions. Material was circulated in advance of each meeting, mostly different drafts of the statute text and the commentary. These drafts then served as a basis for the commissions' discussions, the aim of which can be described as the construction of a collective representation of the text.

Discussion in the drafting commissions primarily concerns three matters:

(1) exploration of reality: scripts, concepts (What usually happens in different trading situation? What happens in courts?)
(2) exploration of the future: desired aims, possible consequences (What is the purpose of the new law? What might be the consequences of a certain rule?)
(3) exploration of related laws (What is stipulated in laws in adjacent fields? What was stipulated in antecedent laws? What is stipulated in similar laws in neighbouring countries?)

Reality and the future can, however, be seen from different viewpoints; this is exactly what happens in the discussions in the drafting commissions. Figure 8.1 illustrates this aspect of the drafting process. Each matter is viewed from the salesperson's angle, from the consumer

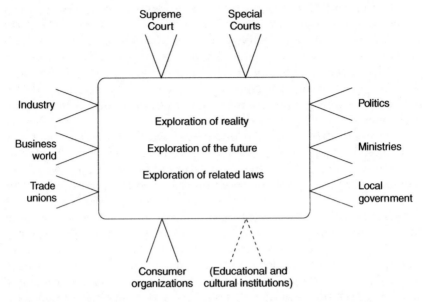

Figure 8.1 *The drafting process (Figure 2 in Gunnarsson, 1989: 100)*

angle, from the court angle, from the ministry angle, from the local government angle, and so on. The long-term memories of the various members of the commissions consist of somewhat varied knowledge, goals, attitudes and norms in the form of scripts and concepts. Their wishes and fears for the future also vary.

Construction of the text thus becomes a multifaceted exploration of reality and imagining what might take place in the future. All of the representatives try to get the others to accept their perspectives. They argue for their own points of view, by presenting different experienced or imagined cases. They build up whole scenarios. It is a time-consuming matter to construct a collective text representation.

As my description of the lawmaking process has shown, the public sphere of the communicative community is not an abstraction for the writers of legislative texts. This sphere – i.e., lawyers, politicians, and representatives of different public organizations – is activated throughout the process. The legal working group is thus formed by individuals who belong to the public sphere of the communicative community. As members of the drafting commission, they can take part in the construction of the text and in the editing and reviewing phases. They can comment on the commission report, they can argue in Parliament.

136

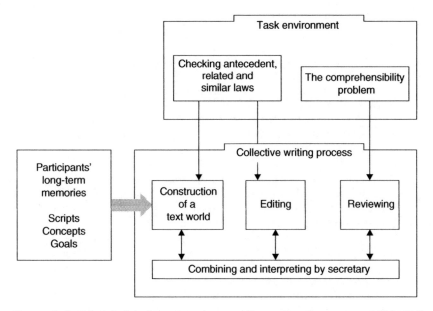

Figure 8.2 *Model of the law-writing process (Figure 3 in Gunnarsson, 1989: 101)*

Adaptation to the prevailing legal traditions within the community is also brought about by thorough and continuous scrutiny of related and similar laws. Throughout the drafting process comparison is also made with antecedent laws and precedents to check that tradition is not violated without an explicit purpose. The goal of the drafting process is therefore to establish intertextuality between texts within the legislative system. The collective law-writing process is described by the model in Figure 8.2.

8.5 The process and its product

If we now look at the product of this collective writing process, we find a very abstract and implicit text. The content of the text constructed after viewing each matter from different sides and arguing for different perspectives becomes very wide. The texts are not made longer: instead, the text content is hollowed out. For each rule the borderlines are described, but the essence is left unspecified.

As an illustration of these statements about the end-product, two sections of the Consumer Services Act are reproduced below: Section 4, which deals with performance and materials, and Section 20, which deals with the remedying of defects.

The Consumer Services Act

Section 4

The entrepreneur shall perform the service in a professional manner. Furthermore, he shall safeguard the consumer's interests with due care and consult the consumer to the extent that this is necessary and feasible.

Unless it may be considered as otherwise agreed, the entrepreneur shall supply requisite materials as part of the service.

Section 20

The consumer is entitled to demand that the entrepreneur remedy the defect *if* this does not entail inconvenience or expense for the entrepreneur that are unreasonably great in proportion to the importance of the defect to the consumer.

Even if the consumer does not demand it, the entrepreneur may remedy the defect if, immediately after a claim has reached him, he offers to do this and the consumer does not have special grounds for rejecting the offer.

The defect shall be remedied within a reasonable time after the consumer has given the entrepreneur opportunity to do so.

The defect shall be remedied without cost to the consumer. This does not, however, apply to expenses that would have arisen even if the service had been performed without defect or, if the defect is due to an accident or other comparable event, expenses for the replacement of material which the consumer, in accordance with the contract concerning the service, has furnished and paid for.

This act, passed in 1985, is supposed to regulate its area of application in detail. If, however, we look closely at its sections we find that it is very difficult to grasp what is actually laid down in the law. The text is filled with abstract nouns and expressions containing indefinite pronouns, adverbs and adjectives. In Section 4 we find the abstract noun 'interests' and the abstract expressions 'be agreed otherwise', 'in a professional manner', 'with due care', 'to the extent that this is necessary and feasible', and 'requisite material'. In Section 20 we also find many abstract nouns and expressions, such as the nouns 'inconvenience' and 'importance', and the expressions 'unreasonably great', 'special grounds', and 'reasonable time'. Though these sections are easy to understand as far as the words used are concerned – i.e., the words are part of the vocabulary of the average adult – it is quite difficult to know how to apply them in concrete situations.

The content is also hollowed out by the way each matter is viewed from different sides. The text of Section 20, e.g., goes back and forth between the consumer side (C) and the entrepreneur side (E). If we look at its first paragraph, we can summarize the content as follows: C is entitled to a, if a does not mean b for E. Even if a means b for E, C is entitled to a if b corresponds to x for C. The background of a text like this is a drafting process involving a constituent step that can be described as a multifaceted exploration of reality and a collective visualization of what might take place in the future (see Figure 8.1).

If we look further at the products of the lawmaking process, we find that the perspective of the text, the functional orientation, the vocabulary and the syntax are shaped to fit in with other laws, with antecedent and related laws. The Consumer Services Act was the first of its kind; Sweden had no act concerning consumer services before 1985 when the act was passed. It is, however, written in the same way as earlier civil laws, such as the Sale of Goods Act of 1905, the Consumer Sales Act of 1973, the Marketing Practices Act of 1975 and the Consumer Credit Act of 1977. Other civil laws will in turn follow the patterns laid down in the Consumer Services Act. The text proposed in the report of the drafting commission responsible for the House Sales Act (submitted in 1986) resembles to a large extent that of the Consumer Services Act. The two sections above, e.g., were used almost word for word. The principle accepted without debate among the members of the House Sales Act commission was that legal tradition should be followed in such matters. This is a general principle followed by Swedish drafting commissions: no interest is shown in structural or language reforms.

In the model in Figure 8.2 we can observe that the comprehensibility box is very small and is placed above the reviewing phase. This is in accordance with my observations of Swedish lawmaking. Language issues, reader issues, text-functional issues and comprehensibility issues are hardly ever discussed by drafting commissions. They are not considered part of the construction of the text. Different interpretations and different formulations are not related to future reader categories and functions. Different reading situations are not considered. No language experts are attached to drafting commissions. No language experts are consulted during the construction and editing phases.

Comprehensibility issues are regarded instead as something to be considered at the very last stage of the process, during the final review in the ministry. Just before the text is printed, language consultants and other lawyers are asked to scrutinize it, i.e. the text surface. At this late stage only minor and superficial changes can be made – one or two sentences can be shortened, one or two functional words can be changed. There is, however, no scope for making the text more concrete and explicit.

From my point of view, the comprehensibility of legal texts is largely a matter of the amount of information in the text and the function orientation of the information presented. These matters cannot be tackled at the last minute: they must instead be considered from the very beginning. The text must be written for different reader groups, not only for the top members of the public sphere. Laws are not only read and used by highly placed lawyers, politicians, and heads of different public organizations, but also by trade union officials and local government officers with varying levels of education and by laypersons.

In order to investigate the actual use of laws by legally untrained people, I initiated a study on the application of laws at local government offices.[5] The aim of this investigation was to explore the use of laws by staff at different offices in five Swedish local authorities of different sizes. Altogether 208 local government officers answered a questionnaire concerning the width of their law application and the depth of their interpretation. Among these officers, of whom most had no legal training, 81 per cent declared that they used law at work. Half of these law users applied between 1 and 3 laws, and half between 4 and 16. 11 per cent applied more than 10 laws at work. We also asked them what types of law material they most frequently used at work: law-texts, bills, precedents, commentaries, journals and other literature. Of the officers 48 per cent reported that they 'always' use the law-text, 27 per cent 'often' and 13 per cent 'sometimes'. I will not dwell any longer on this study, although, I can add, it presented new and very interesting results to the Swedish lawyers. What I wish to stress here, however, is that the law-text is read and used daily by many professional groups who lack legal training. These officials did not have any influence on the lawmaking, although they applied laws in their daily work.

Returning to the drafting process, my view is that if the comprehensibility of legal texts is to improve, comprehensibility issues must be part of the construction of the text. Among the members of the drafting commissions there should be representatives of more distant, non-expert readers as well as the present representatives of the public sphere. (For example, language experts could represent the non-expert reader groups.) Comprehensibility problems could and must be given a larger and more basic role in the lawmaking process. The ideal would be a process more in accordance with the model in Figure 8.3.

In the model of the ideal law-writing process depicted in Figure 8.3, comprehensibility problems relating to reader, function and comprehension play a much more important role than they do now. They come in at every stage of the lawmaking process, in the construction of the text, in editing and in reviewing. They are considered as parts of text content as well as of text surface. The comprehensibility problems play a more prominent role in the writing process, and the reader

140

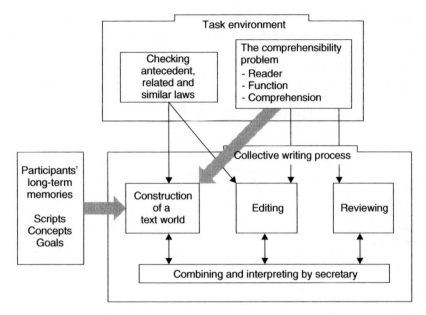

Figure 8.3 *Model of the ideal law-writing process (Figure 4 in Gunnarsson, 1989: 105)*

is brought more sharply into focus. Such an acknowledgment of the fact that comprehensibility issues are a part of text content is the next step that ought to be taken in the work of reforming legal texts.

8.6 Conclusions

The present study has shown how the problems of law-text comprehensibility are related to the legal writing process. The social and societal conditions under which texts are produced result in more or less readable texts. In order to improve comprehensibility radically, it is therefore necessary to change the process.

This study has also pointed to certain similarities and differences between legislative writing and 'normal' text writing. In principle, a model of normal writing can be used to describe law writing. The main phases – text construction (planning), editing (translating), and reviewing – are the same. The differences are due to the collective writing of legal texts and the extremely sustained process involved. In comparison with normal writing, the law-writing process entails a more marked and more conscious adaptation to the legal working group and also, indirectly, to the norms and traditions established within the public sphere of the communicative community. In the law-texts analysed this is shown by the legal perspective and the text's function orientation. The collective, sustained process further means that the text is constructed as a result of negotiations between the members of the working group so that each question is viewed from different angles during the drafting of the text. This is reflected in the abstractness and implicitness of the text.

Notes

1. This chapter is based on an article published in *Written Communication* (Gunnarsson, 1989).
2. Fredrickson (1995) discusses the intertextuality of legal texts.
3. Cf. Habermas (1971).
4. See, for instance, van Dijk (1993), Fairclough and Wodak (1997) and Wodak and Meyer (2001).
5. A detailed presentation of this investigation is found in Gunnarsson and Edling (1985).

Section 4
Workplace Discourse

The following two chapters will explore workplace discourse from a sociolinguistic perspective. Chapter 9 elaborates and evaluates a sociolinguistic framework for the study of communication at work. A sociolinguistic framework is developed, and the two concepts 'communicative community' and 'professional group' are introduced. For the purposes of these concepts, written and spoken discourse are assumed to be intermingled in the communicative process and steered by similar sociocognitive conditions. The chapter further includes a study of communication at a local government office. One aim of this study is to evaluate empirically the sociolinguistic framework proposed. A survey and in-depth interviews are used to study the organization of writing within the office. The communicative processes are also studied, e.g. the interplay between speech and writing and the frequency and type of writing collaboration. The social dimensions of writing are further analysed in relation to different parameters such as structural hierarchy and centrality, the density of the group, group norms, attitudes and identity. This study sheds new light on the social organization of writing within a small, monolingual workplace.

In Chapter 10, my concern is the multilingual workplace. One aim of this chapter is to explore what the term 'multilingual' entails in relation to workplace discourse. Another aim is to discuss the complexity of workplace multilingualism, which means that I will analyse workplace discourse from a variety of perspectives, that of the professional group, the linguistic-cultural community, and the individual employees. In addition to theories related to the forming of a group, my theoretical approach will therefore also include language dominance issues and interactional sociolinguistics. The empirical data focused on emanate from a research project aiming to explore the daily work-related interaction at a public hospital and an international company in Sweden. An ethnographic methodology – comprising interviews, observations at place, recordings and text collection – has been used to study these workplaces. Both environments are multilingual and multicultural in relation to their staff, i.e., a great number of their employees are immigrants in the country and foreign language speakers at work. My discussion of results will concern the organizational structure of text and talk at work, workplace languages and foreign language users' interaction at work.

9 Communication at work: A sociolinguistic perspective on workplace discourse

This chapter elaborates and evaluates a sociolinguistic framework for the study of communication at work. In the first part of the chapter, I discuss different sociolinguistic concepts and theories and introduce the two concepts of 'communicative community' and 'professional group'. For the purposes of these concepts, written and spoken discourse are assumed to be intermingled in the communicative process and steered by similar sociocognitive conditions. In the second part of the chapter, I discuss the application of the theoretical framework to a specific case, the communication at a local government office. This case study comprises analyses of the organizational structure and its effects on writing at work, the communicative process and the role of spoken discourse and collaboration in the construction of documents as well as the social dimension of writing at work. This small, monolingual workplace is found to constitute a professional group of the local-public type, which means that communication at the office is part of a socially based and hierarchically structured set of communicative activities in which spoken and written discourse are closely intertwined.

9.1 A sociolinguistic framework

In this first part of the chapter, I will develop a sociolinguistic framework. The perspective of this proposed sociolinguistic framework is the professional group, e.g. a workplace or a small organization. Writing is viewed as a part of the overall activities of the group and the organization, and the individual is of interest as a member of this group and organization. The individual is given a certain role within the structure, has a certain place within the group hierarchy and exerts certain functions due to this place. Communication, including speech as well as writing, is essential to the group culture and identity and constitutes an essential element in various group activities. Internal structure and external networks influence communication at every level. They are reflected in parameters of openness-closeness and uniformity-diversity. They influence norms, attitudes, identity, and knowledge patterns.

9.1.1 Speech community, network and group

For the early sociolinguists, the concept of 'speech community' was basic. It was from this conceptual unit that a number of analyses of social variation proceeded. As a criterion for such a community, Gumperz (1968) proposed 'difference in language use' between the member of the community and those outside, while Labov (1972) chose 'shared attitudes and norms'.[1]

Another basic sociolinguistic concept is 'network'. A speech community consists, according to Gumperz (1968), of a bunch of basic units, networks, to which the members can belong to differing degrees and in more than one function. The concept of social network represents, one could say, an attempt to conceptualize the variable human being as a social being that is influenced by and can in turn influence others.

A network comprises a variety of relations, and this variation is fundamental to the concept. Boissevain (1987), e.g., mentions the following criteria:

1. The size of the network.
2. The frequency and duration of interaction.
3. The density, i.e. the degree to which members of a network are in touch with each other.
4. Multiplexity, which relates to the type of relations between persons. A uniplex relation is, e.g., that between a teacher and a pupil who have no other relationship, while multiplex relations exist, e.g., between colleagues who are also neighbours and relatives.
5. Clusters refers to the degree to which members are more closely linked to each other than they are to the rest of the network.
6. The directional flow of exchanges between people is related to asymmetry and symmetry.
7. Centrality is another key term. The centrality of a person in a communication network is an indication of the degree to which he or she may be able to influence or manipulate the flow of information. High centrality is thus related to power.
8. The transactional content, i.e. the goods and services, the messages, the information, the confidences, etc. which go back and forth between people who are linked to each other.

Most people are members of many networks. The types of network vary with age. They vary from one environment to another; they are e.g. different in urban areas compared with rural areas. Types of network also vary according to gender, education, profession, position and personality.

A similar set of parameters has been used to describe the sociological 'group'. Groups have thus been characterized in relation to: (1) contact, sympathy or social distance, (2) 'we' feeling and group identity, (3) group cohesion, (4) reference group function, (5) role differentiation, (6) relation patterns and clusters, (7) dominance patterns and power structure, (8) regulation of relation between members by means of rules, routines and rituals. What distinguishes a 'group' from a 'network' is the strength of the internal relations, rather than the character of those relations.

9.1.2 Discourse community

The sociolinguists of the 1960s and 1970s dealt with spoken language, in particular with spoken everyday language. Later, in the 1980s, attempts were made among researchers in the field of the sociology of science and writing rhetoric to enlarge the scope of sociolinguistics to encompass writing as well as speech, and the term 'discourse community' was introduced as a parallel term to 'speech community'.

The term 'discourse community' has been used by many socially oriented American communication researchers, e.g. Faigley (1985) and Swales (1990). For these authors, the difference between the spoken and the written medium is crucial for the type of community involved, and they thus find it necessary to distinguish a separate type of community for written communication. Swales (1990), e.g., contrasts spoken and written discourse: written language is described as the medium for contact at a distance, both geographical and diachronic; written language is standardized and thus less local and provincial. A discourse community is based on functional groupings, while a speech community is based on social groupings. Discourse communities are centrifugal (they tend to separate people into occupational or speciality-interest groups), while speech communities are centripetal (they tend to absorb people into their general fabric). A discourse community recruits its members by persuasion, training or relevant qualification; a speech community inherits its membership by birth, accident or adoption. An archetypal discourse community tends to be a Specific Interest Group, according to Swales. Of course, academic disciplines are special interest groups of this kind, but so too is the stamp collectors' organization he uses as an example.[2]

147

The concept 'discourse community', as used by Swales and the other social perspectivists, is a suitable tool for describing products of communication, but less suitable for describing processes. It focuses on communication between experts, but less on other types of professional discourse. It focuses on communication at a distance and not on communication at close quarters. In this way it offers a tool for describing differences between written genres but not for describing the variation in processes and products due to the different roles, attitudes, norms and identities of acting social individuals. Nor is it a suitable tool for an analysis of communication at places of work, within organizations and the like, where communication is not only professional but also involves socializing and is based not only on distant contacts through written texts but also on close contacts through both spoken discourse and written texts.

9.1.3 Communicative community

In Gunnarsson (1992 and 1997a), I introduce a third concept, namely 'communication community'. This concept covers written as well as oral communication, communication at a distance as well as in close contact, expert as well as everyday communication. It focuses on the communicative process as well as on its products. It thus covers reading and writing as well as the text produced. It covers listening and speaking as well as the discourse produced. The concept 'communication community' is an enlargement of that of speech community. It combines the concepts of discourse and speech community.

Fundamental to the concept of 'discourse community' is, as was mentioned above, the distinction between the oral and the written medium. For an analysis of writing in modern society, however, it is more fruitful to proceed from a concept which covers both media, oral as well as written communication. This does not mean that there do not exist communities, groups and networks which are based solely on oral communication, or solely on written communication. My claim is that most communities are founded on different types of discourse – spoken and written: traditionally transmitted and computer-mediated – and that relations between the members of a local community – and between the members of a distant community – are maintained by both text and talk. The members share habits, norms and attitudes relating to both media, and socialization into a community normally includes the acquisition of knowledge about and attitudes to the patterns, functions etc. of both spoken and written language.

As Figure 9.1 shows, I distinguish four different types of communication communities, based on criteria related to contact distance – from

	Local	Distant
Private	SPEECH writing	SPEECH WRITING
Public	SPEECH WRITING	speech WRITING

Figure 9.1   *Communicative communities (Figure 1 in Gunnarsson, 1997b: 146)*
Note: The main medium is indicated by capital letters

local to distant – and sphere – from private to public.[3] Of course this is a simplification. Private and public are poles on a scale rather than two alternatives, as are local and distant. For the discussion here, however, I will limit myself to these four prototypal communication communities. For each of them, the main medium is indicated by capital letters. For the local-public community and the distant private community, both media are assumed to play equal roles from a communicative point of view.

The four prototypal communicative communities could be described in the following general way.

Local-private. This communication community is established between people who come into direct contact with each other, who interact in a local community of some kind. Speech is of course very important within this type of setting. Writing, i.e. written communication, is however also a part of such local communities. Within the private sphere, e.g. within the nuclear family, communication not uncommonly takes a written form. Notes, lists, short letters and text messages (SMS) are circulated among the members of the family. Of course these habits vary from family to family or rather from environment to environment. Within different families, different peer groups etc. communicative behaviour varies, which means that the role and means of discourse vary too. Speech, however, is the main medium in the private sphere.[4]

Distant-private. The private sphere of course also has its distant community and here I have marked speech and writing as equally important for maintaining contacts. Phone calls, text messages, emails and regular letters are used in communication between relatives and friends living far apart.

Local-public. If we turn to professional and public life, written communication plays an important role in the local community as does oral communication. By using capital letters for both media, I have indicated that they both play essential roles. At workplaces written messages, memoranda, instructions, notices of meetings, minutes, lists, notes and reports are produced and circulated among employees in paper versions or via intranet, and often the workplace develops a special communicative culture affecting patterns, norms and attitudes relating to the use and functions of written language, and relating to spoken language.

Distant-public. The distant-public community has historically been connected by written communication, and has also traditionally been considered the prototype of the written medium. The concept 'discourse community', discussed earlier, is related to this type of community, or more specifically to the distant-public one. For this type of communication community, I have indeed marked writing as the main medium. However, in a modern society mobile phones, internet, email, video etc. make it possible to maintain contact even with persons at a distance. Travelling around makes it possible also to establish speech contact with members of a distant communication community. And if we consider academic disciplines, e.g., communities and networks are established by means of oral as well as written communication, and the special academic use of language relates both to patterns for written texts and to patterns for delivering speeches, conversations etc. Socialization into an academic discipline involves norms governing how, when and why to use written language and also norms for speaking.

9.1.4 Professional group

The four types of communicative community, introduced above, eliminate some of the stereotypes we have about the differences between written and oral communication in general, and about professional discourse in particular. Written texts for professional purposes are produced in the same settings and by the same groups of people as is spoken discourse for professional purposes, and the written and oral communication are interrelated.

The concept 'communication community' serves as a superordinant for different social 'groups' within which individuals, as members of the group, are shaped or socialized with respect to knowledge, norms, attitude and identity.

The 'communicative community' prototypes are meant to encompass different social groups. Within the public spheres, professional groups and networks are found in distant as well as in local settings. One and the same organization, and also one and the same network, can also be spread over several community types, thus covering distant as well as local contacts.

What distinguishes a 'professional group' from a network is the strength of its internal relations. If the formal and official name – enterprise

K, institute X, workplace A – also distinguishes a social grouping with relative strong internal relation patterns, I regard it as a 'professional group'. If there is no such correspondence between formal/official and internal social structure, I consider it a network.

Analysis of the professional group should encompass an analysis of the size and duration of the group. The content should be analysed not only in relation to the goods and services, the messages and information involved but also in relation to speech and writing. The analysis should pose questions such as which medium is used to convey different types of information within the group, and how different individuals communicate with each other to attain different goals.

The internal structure of a group is related to the parameters of hierarchy and cluster, i.e. internal small groupings. Another important variable is multiplicity, and here it is very important to transcend the stereotypes about relations within local and distant communities and within the private and public spheres. The assumption should be that all four prototypes – local-private, distant-private, local-public and distant-public – involve relational patterns of different kinds, social as well as functional, uniplex as well as multiplex.

The density of internal and external relations is also an important parameter for a description of the professional group. The correspondence between these two types of relations describes the openness of the group. A group with a dense internal web of relations and few and less dense external relations is assumed to be less open than a group with less dense internal relations and many and dense external relations. The openness of the group can in turn be assumed to be reflected in its uniformity, which will be manifested in shared knowledge, evaluations, attitudes and norms as to the patterns and use of writing and speech. Uniformity can also assume the form of group identity and the development of a group culture. It can also become visible as a 'we' feeling and group cohesion. Group identity and 'we' feeling are related to attitudes towards one's own group, the in-group, which is viewed positively, and towards others, the out-group, which is viewed more negatively.

9.2 Communication in a local government office

In the second part of this chapter, I will explore the communicative practices within a small workplace, a local government office.[5] I will then examine the following sets of assumptions: the first concerns the social organization of writing at work, which means that I will relate the organization of writing at the office studied to sociolinguistic parameters such as centrality, clusters, hierarchical asymmetries and networks.

The second set of assumptions concerns the communicative processes leading to the construction of documents of various kinds. The focus here will be on the role of spoken discourse and the intertwinement of text and talk. These processes too, which are often collaborative in nature, will be related to social parameters such as hierarchies, clusters and networks. The third set of assumptions concerns social values attaching to writing at work – norms, attitudes, identity and 'we' feeling. These values are assumed to be integrated into a more general value system associated with working life in general and its organization as a whole and related to social dimensions such as internal-external density and openness, group consistency and uniformity.

9.2.1   Presentation of the case study

9.2.1.1   Methodology

The main purpose of this case study thus relates to the writing process and its various sociolinguistic parameters. The prime body of data was collected by means of a survey and in-depth interviews. The survey was based on a questionnaire which was distributed to all the employees at the office – comprising questions on their background, the types of text they wrote and how frequently, their writing procedures, collaboration with colleagues, their role in relation to the texts they wrote – initiative, checking, responsibility –, their influence on writing norms and patterns at the office, and, finally, their attitudes towards writing at work. Altogether, 33 employees answered the questionnaire, which comprised 26 questions. Six members of staff in different positions and with varying bureaucratic experience were interviewed. The purpose of the interviews, which were 1 to 1 1/2 hours long, was to get a more in-depth and diversified picture of the six employees in relation to their role and function in the office network, their writing processes, their norms and attitudes relating to writing and language, and their relationship to the group.

As a complement to these data, on the basis of the individuals' own reports on their writing activities and experiences of writing, more person-independent data were also gathered. In the initial stage of the study, the analysis focused on the total flow of texts, i.e. all the texts emanating from the office during a fixed period. The purpose of these product analyses, covering analyses of text type, purpose, addressee, sender and signature, were to get an overall picture of the actual writing and communication taking place. Official documents presenting the office and its tasks were also studied to provide a basis for an overall description of the organization.

152

A multifaceted methodology was thus used to examine the writing process at the local government office: qualitative as well as quantitative, process as well as product-centered. Though the main core of the results derive from the survey and interviews, the product analyses were of value in that they revealed other aspects of writing activities at the office than those the staff chose to tell us about.[6]

9.2.1.2   The office and its staff

The investigation concerns communication at a local government district office in a Swedish city. This city, which forms one local authority area, is divided into 14 districts, each with a fairly high degree of autonomy. The study centred on the office responsible for one such district. Around 35 employees work at the office itself, serving the district in areas such as social security, education, day care and welfare, libraries, parks, recreation centres and so forth. The investigation covered the writing of all the employees working at the office. In the following I will use a categorization of the staff with regard to their position within the office. I have divided employees on the basis of their salaries into three position groups: high, middle and low position.[7]

9.2.2   The organization of writing at work

I will first focus on the organization of writing at work. The set of questions I will then discuss derives from my first aim, which is to analyse the organizational structure and its effects on writing at work. Sociolinguistic parameters such as centrality, hierarchical asymmetries and clusters will be focused on in relation to the writing activities of the various employee groups. I will discuss results concerning the structure of writing activities (i.e. types of document and addressees) and the structure of influence on writing (i.e. initiative, checking, signing) and on writing norms. The aim of the analysis here is to explore the more concrete meaning of the relationship between the hierarchical structure and writing. The type and form of writing offer one way of capturing not only the formal hierarchy of high, middle and low positions but more importantly the centrality of the writers in the organization.

9.2.2.1   The structure of writing activities

Writing activities occur widely among the staff, and many of the employees in fact consider writing one of their main activities. A wide variety of text types are produced at the office, and not surprisingly the type of document produced varies with the position of the employee. Employees in high positions write more complex documents, such as plans, reports and statements. Those in middle positions are in charge of letters, information papers, memoranda, newsletters, balance sheets and notices of meetings. Staff in low positions are in charge of minutes and lists, in other words the more standardized types of text.

The hierarchical structure is also reflected in the type of writing activities undertaken. Only those in high positions report that they devote any time to the pre-writing stage, to planning and preparation. Although those in middle positions indicated that they often sat thinking for a while before starting to write, they did not report any actual pre-writing activity, such as drafting certain passages or an outline. The answers to the question concerning difficulties also reveal differences for employees in different positions. Overall, staff in high positions reported most problems. It was this group, too, who indicated that they found it difficult to structure texts, to find the correct wording and to get started.

It is of course no coincidence that staff in high positions report most pre-writing activities or that they find writing most difficult, as they are the ones who write the most complex and also the most important texts. Centrality as regards the types of documents one produces also affects the quality of one's writing activities and the communicative process.

The importance of a document – and thus the centrality of the writer – is undoubtedly related to its addressee. What is of interest in a discussion of centrality, however, is not so much how many people are reached by the document, one client or the whole public, as the status of the recipient, ordinary client, i.e. the public, or politicians and authorities.

As the results reveal, none of the documents written by staff in high positions are addressed to the public (private individuals). The majority of their documents are internal, 63 per cent being intended for employees in the office and 24 per cent for those within the district. These figures very clearly reflect the central and leading role played by this group within the internal hierarchy. It is also worth noting that as many as 13 per cent are addressed to authorities, i.e. to the influential district board.

Staff in middle positions write documents aimed at all types of addressees. It should be noted, however, that their documents intended for authorities are of a more routine character, e.g. notices and minutes of board meetings, than those written by staff in high positions. Most documents produced by employees in low positions do not bear an explicit indication of their addressee, e.g. lists, certificates and memoranda. Among the documents with addressees, two-thirds are intended for private individuals within the district, and one-third for other members of the office staff.

When asked about their personal contact with the people who read their documents, employees in low and middle positions answered that they are in frequent contact with the public. Those in high positions, on the other hand, have very little contact with the public but more frequent contact with other government offices and authorities. Also those in middle positions indicated that they had contact with other authorities and offices.

As these findings reveal, actual service functions – writing and speaking to private individuals within the district – are mainly taken care of by staff in low positions and to some extent by those in middle positions, while high-position staff do not deal with these basic service matters at all. They are not in contact with private individuals in the community. This of course says something about the routine nature of these services and also about their low centrality within the organization. Higher centrality is given to contacts with external authorities and with the board, and here the high-position group is involved. The managerial and controlling function of the high-position group in relation to the office and district staff is also clearly shown by these figures, i.e. their writing was mainly aimed at staff within the office and the district. This of course indicates a hierarchical internal structure.

9.2.2.2   Structure of influence on writing

Centrality, clustering and hierarchy can also be assumed to be related to direct influence on writing activities and on the writing norms of the group. Questions about who was perceived as initiating and checking the documents written were intended to provide a picture of how writing within the office was initiated and controlled. Another factor of relevance in this context is who assumes the official responsibility for the document by signing it. From the point of view of the recipient, it is of course the person signing the document who is seen as the actual sender. Internally, too, the signing of documents plays an important role. It is part of the process of establishing an organizational hierarchy.[8]

With regard to initiative, the results reflect the organizational structure of the office. The extent to which the head of the office, here called KC, or other persons initiate an employee's writing reflects his/her position in the hierarchical structure. The middle group are placed more directly under KC, they do his or her writing, while the low-position group are subordinate to other employees inside and outside the office. The high-position group less often stated that KC, or other individuals, were the sole initiator. On the other hand, they reported a greater degree of collaborative initiative than the other position groups. This may be linked to the types of texts they write: statements, reports, plans etc., i.e. texts which are probably more unique and more clearly related to the external image of the office.

Responses about checking and signing different types of documents show that written documents were checked in pretty much the same way in the three position groups. All groups reported that they themselves checked half of the documents. Employees in low and middle positions also signed the documents they wrote themselves in the majority of cases. For those in high positions, however, as many as 43 per cent of documents were signed by KC, the head of the office. In most of these cases the writer also co-signed the document. These results also indicate that the documents written by staff in high positions are of great importance for the office. They have to be signed by the head of the office. Responsibility, however, is shared by him and the writer, who usually co-signs.

The questionnaire also asked staff to indicate if they considered themselves to have any influence on the forms used at the office, existing model texts and internal writing rules. The answers to this question reveal the important role played by the middle group in writing activities. All staff in middle positions indicated that they could influence forms and model texts to a certain or a great extent. Staff in high positions felt that they could influence forms and model texts, too, but to a lesser extent. Their influence seemed to be mainly exerted by reading and commenting on what other people had written. As this study showed, the higher the position, the more often employees read and comment on what others have written.

9.2.2.3 Internal structure

As these results show, to a large extent influence patterns reflect the hierarchical structure. In the interviews, I tried to get a more varied picture of the relationship between internal structure and influence. With regard to influence on writing norms, there are a few key individuals who have a central role. The information officer, here called Ma, who has a middle position in terms of her salary, is a central figure as regards writing activities, and her influence on patterns and norms is greater than that of others. She was also responsible for training. The head of the office, KC, is another key person of great centrality. He checks and signs all important documents. As was revealed in the interviews, his influence relates to the content of the documents, not to their language or style. His influence is thus of a different character than that of Ma (who belongs to middle-position staff). He mainly controls staff in high positions and Ma, in other words the people who write the more important documents, i.e. those reaching the influential political group or a wide readership. Ma, on the other hand, exercises control over all the employees, and in particular over those in low and middle positions, i.e. the people who do the more routine types of writing and the types of writing that are more restricted and dependent on model texts and forms.

The interviews also revealed clusterings within the office. For each of these clusters, or subgroups, one person was the subgroup leader, with high centrality and considerable influence on writing within the cluster. As the figure shows, the clusters are not necessarily centred around a high-position employee: M7 and Lc form one small cluster just as the group with Ha as the leader does. (H, M, L refer to position.)

Figure 9.2 gives a picture of the internal structure with regard to relational patterns (cooperation and influence, centrality and clusters). The vertical axis shows the hierarchy within the office. The

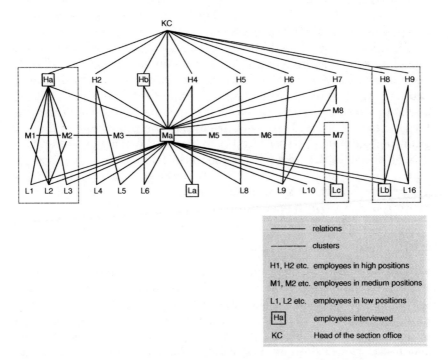

Figure 9.2 *Internal structure. (Figure 2 in Gunnarsson, 1997b: 161)*

head of the office, KC, is placed at the top level, staff in high positions, Ha, Hb, H1 etc., at the second level, middle-position employees, Ma, M1, M2 etc. at the third level, and employees in low positions, La, Lb, Lc, L1 etc. at the fourth level. The horizontal axis reflects centrality within the office seen as a communicative community. The information officer, Ma, who has the central communicative role, is placed in the middle of the diagram. Relations are marked by lines, and internal clusterings by dotted squares. A large number of lines leading to and from a person thus indicates centrality within the internal structure.

As Figure 9.2 reveals, Ha is the leader of an internal clustering with staff in different positions. Hb, on the other hand, works with KC, and one secretary, L6. He is also related to the information officer, Ma, as everyone else is. Clusters also form among staff in middle and low positions, as the cluster around M7 and Lc reveals. These two individuals form a closely knit cluster of their own, as the interview with Lc revealed.

9.2.3 The communicative processes

From this overall picture of the organizational structure of writing activities, I will turn to a more in-depth analysis of the communicative processes in which the employees are involved. The construction of documents of various kinds will be discussed in relation to the role of spoken discourse and the intertwinement of text and talk. As I claimed in the first part of this chapter, we can expect both speech and writing to be socially relevant and important activities in a local-public professional group such as this office must be considered to be. My goal here is to shed some empirical light on this claim, and I will examine a number of issues relating to how and to what extent writing is intertwined with spoken discourse in the communicative processes that occur and to what extent it is collaborative in nature. I will also discuss to what extent speech and writing can be said to be governed by similar sociocognitive conditions.

9.2.3.1 Activity and medium

For an analysis of the role of spoken discourse in communicative processes, the relationship between activity and medium is of relevance. On the one hand there are activities which are fixed to one medium, written or spoken, and those that can use either. In certain contexts a response to a letter from an authority must take written form; a telephone call would not count as a reply. Certain important meetings must have written agendas and written minutes. Larger associations must have written constitutions, and larger organizations must produce written annual reports. There are also events which are restricted to the oral form. Boards of larger organizations must meet regularly to discuss certain issues, and they must hold annual meetings to elect new members, etc. In a few cases the medium is fixed by law. In most cases, however, conventions and practice give one medium priority over the other. We can talk about an oral or a written communicative bias, where this bias not only depends on the content of the activities but also on culture-specific factors. For other activities, however, the medium varies from one case to another. If you want to give a colleague a message, you can either call her, send an email or a text message. To announce a minor meeting you can either tell the persons orally when you meet them, announce it on the intranet, or send around a written circular.

In the chains of communicative events of which cases are normally made up, spoken and written activities are intermingled. If we focus on the interplay between the two media in the communicative process, we find that in certain cases the written text is merely a complement to the spoken main event; an important meeting is preceded by notices of meetings, letters and programmes, and followed by minutes and reports. In other cases, however, it is the written document which constitutes the main event, which in turn is complemented by spoken events; an important report is preceded by telephone conversations, meetings, seminars and followed by public talks and conferences.

Turning now to the results, I have first analysed the role of spoken discourse in the creation of the written documents actually produced at the office. In order to get a picture of how these documents relate to speech, I distinguished three categories:

(1) Documents which complement a spoken main event – a meeting, seminar or conference – in the form of pre- or post-event documents: e.g. minutes, notices of meetings, memoranda, invitations, programmes.
(2) Documents which could have spoken discourse as an alternative, e.g. letters and announcements.
(3) Documents that are more definitely bound to the written form – legally or conventionally –, e.g. reports, lists, certificates, newsletters, balance sheets etc.

Of the 264 documents produced at the office during the period studied, 48 per cent fall into Category 1, i.e. they complement a spoken main event, 30 per cent are possible alternatives to oral communication (Category 2), and 22 per cent are definitely bound to the written form. As this analysis is based on the existing documents, i.e. I tried to characterize these in relation to spoken discourse, it does not say anything about the communicative process in which these documents were embedded: a report (Category 3) may be intricately intertwined with spoken events though its final form is restricted to the written medium.

If we now turn to the communicative processes involved, we find that regardless of which activity is the main event – the meeting, the conference, the report, the statement – the individual activities are normally part of a communicative chain in which spoken and written activities interact. In certain cases we could talk about pre- and post-event activities. In other cases the events give rise to each other in a way that makes it difficult to say which is the main one. A meeting leads to a report which creates a seminar which creates a plan etc.

The normal situation is an interdependence of text and talk; what varies is the length of the chain. An email to the office containing a simple question can be answered by a telephone call or a response by email, which closes the matter. The routine work of the staff in low positions is of this kind. The elaboration of a plan for a part of the city, on the other hand, may take years of work, consisting of a chain of meetings, letters, telephone conversations, outlines, informal discussions and drafts, before the final version of the plan is produced.

9.2.3.2 The communicative processes of two employees

The interdependence of oral and written communication was also studied in the interviews. In one way or another, all six interviews revealed how work at the office comprised both spoken and written discourse and also that these activities often interacted. Nevertheless, it was obvious that this interdependence was stronger, and the communicative chains longer, for those in the highest positions. Writing more complicated documents, as this group did, also meant a great deal of pre- and post-writing activity, in the form of discussions, meetings, telephone calls etc. The role of writing, however, also varied with the type of task for those in high positions.

I will here present some glimpses from two interviews with employees in high positions, Helena (Ha) and Hans (Hb). Compare Figure 9.2, which shows their places in the internal structure.

Helena (Ha)
Helena, who is the leader of one of the sections of the office, gave the following picture of the communication in which she engaged at work:

Her day is taken up more with talking and reading than with writing, she told me. A large part of her working day is devoted to meetings with individuals or groups, and writing is often used as a support for

160

these meetings. She writes an agenda or a list of questions on a piece of paper before the meeting, and writes down decisions and conclusions etc. during the meeting.

Helena stresses that her role at work is to be the leader of the section. She is responsible for what her group produces, and she must be satisfied with the documents written by her subordinates. She is the one who sets the policy, and if she is not satisfied they have to change what they have written.

Her role in the creation of a document is often to sketch its general outline. She discusses her ideas with her group and then asks them to work on the details. Her role in the latter stages varies depending on the outcome. She describes two types of situation. In one, she asks Tom to work on a document. He writes a first draft, Helena comments on it, Tom writes a second version, Helena makes a few corrections and then the document is ready. She may give another document to John to work on. In this case she is less satisfied with John's work, and decides to write the second version herself. When she has done this, she discusses the result with John and makes any corrections they agree on.

For Helena writing is mostly combined with discussion and talking, and in most cases it is a collective undertaking. If she writes something herself, she always discusses the document with the people in her group who might have something to do with the case. She only writes a few types of external and secret documents entirely on her own.

Helena, who has a leading position within the internal office structure, says that though she considers writing to be very important in the life of the district office, she personally prefers talking to people to writing to them. Writing is often a substitute for talking – she cannot get hold of someone on the phone, so instead she writes a letter. It is often a support for talking, as when she writes an agenda for a meeting. And it is often intermingled with talking, as when she initiates, leads and supervises the writing of a document, or when she discusses what she has written with others.

Helena talks about the interdependence of writing and talking, and says that in many cases she chooses which medium to use. She also talks about collaboration, which for her seems to be a frequent basis for writing.

Hans (Hb)

Hans is an internal consultant engaged to carry out special studies. Unlike Helena, he does not have a group of his own but works more directly under the head of the office (KC) with the assistance of a secretary (L6). He is involved in various external networks, however, and a member of several project groups working on various long-term projects.

One of these projects involves rebuilding and extension work at one of the schools in the district, and has been in progress for many years. There have been discussions as to what to do about this badly designed and undersized school for years – just how many, he cannot remember. Hans's role has included producing the basic data needed for the group's description of the 'new' school: what rooms are needed, how many classrooms and group study rooms, and how they should be arranged. The project group is also expected to describe the basic concept of the school. To put together the basic documentation, Hans has been in touch with numerous people, in the district and elsewhere, and sat in on various working groups. The next task is to formulate a draft decision, and although Hans has produced similar drafts before, it will be difficult in this case, since there will no doubt be opposition higher up, i.e. on the district board, to the idea of an expensive rebuilding and extension project at the school.

Hans talks about his other duties – planning and formulating goals. He attends lots of meetings. He is constantly in touch with people outside the office, with members of the district board, with ordinary people and with various professional groups in the municipality. The work of the project group is based to a large extent on the information he gets from his contacts and by listening to what others have to say. Draft texts are often discussed at group meetings and the texts are produced collectively. But sometimes there is no time to do this: individual members of the group then write their own drafts and subsequently phone the other members to check that what they have written is all right. Most of what Hans writes consists of study reports and consultation responses. Here, the written form is important, but the documents are elaborated via spoken discourse.

Hans, then, works primarily in networks involving people outside the office. Within the office, he mainly deals with the head of the office (KC), with whom he discusses major problems and reads through more important documents. These contacts are mainly oral.

Hans's writing takes shape in collaboration with other people and in constant interaction with spoken discourse, in the form of telephone calls, face-to-face encounters and meetings. All aspects of his work seem to involve long chains of interdependent oral and written events.

Figure 9.3 illustrates the interrelationship between written and spoken activities in a fictive communicative chain of the type described by Hans (Hb) in the interview regarding the school building project. The chain is here described as starting with a series of small group meetings (SgrMt) intertwined with informal talk (Talk), letters (Let)

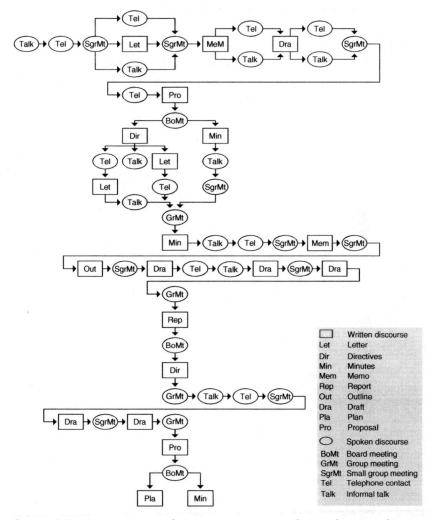

Figure 9.3 *Communicative chain encompassing spoken and written discourse (Figure 3 in Gunnarsson, 1997b: 169)*

and telephone calls (Tel), and leading to a proposal (Pro) to the district board. The board meeting (BoMt) leads to the formulation of directives (Dir), which necessitate the forming of a project group and a series of group meetings (GrMt). The end of this communicative chain is a plan (Pla) for the rebuilding, taken by the district board at a board meeting (BoMt). In the figure, the main events are placed in the middle and marked with circles and squares in bold.

9.2.3.3 The collaborative nature of writing

The interviews presented in the previous section clearly reveal the collaborative nature of the writing activities of the two employees concerned. The role of collaboration at the office, however, was more fully investigated by one of the questions in the questionnaire. The employees were asked to indicate which alternatives were relevant for their writing at work: write together with colleagues; write by oneself, but discuss wording etc. with colleagues; ask colleagues to read and comment on texts; and write by oneself without consulting anyone.

The answers to this question reveal that staff members in high positions seem to collaborate less than the middle- and low-position groups. The form of collaboration, however, differs between the groups. Collaboration in the form of writing the text together with a colleague is thus frequent among staff in middle and low positions, while those in high positions seem to prefer to ask colleagues to read through and comment on texts they have written themselves (89 per cent in high position has indicated this alternative).

From the point of view of the interrelationship of spoken and written discourse, an interesting result is that 'discussions with colleagues' are reported by all groups. Direct collaboration, i.e. writing together, certainly also involves talking as well as writing. Also the alternative 'asking colleague to read and comment' may be assumed to lead to discussions, to spoken discourse.

From a hierarchical viewpoint, the most striking differences is found in relation to this question: 89 per cent of those in high positions said they asked colleagues to read and comment on their texts, but only 25 per cent in middle and 6 per cent in low positions. This is, of course, another indication of the hierarchical difference in the employees' writing activities. Staff in high positions write the most important and difficult documents. They write documents which will have political and legal consequences, such as reports to the board, statements, etc.

9.2.3.4 Conditions for spoken and written discourse

The results presented above point to a close-knit interdependence of spoken and written discourse in the communicative events of the office studied. One activity leads to the other, in a continuous interplay between the two. In the cases discussed above, the actors are mainly the same; the project group of which Hans (Hb) is a member meet, exchange texts and talk over the telephone, with the final aim of presenting a plan for a new school to the board.

The principle that I wish to examine here is to what extent we can assume that the spoken and written activities making up such a communicative chain are steered by similar sociocognitive conditions.

Let us return to the communicative chain illustrated in Figure 9.3. All the activities in this chain are part of a 'case' and can be related back to one problematic situation, the problem with the school building, and to a fixed set of people directly concerned – pupils, parents, teachers, administrative staff, cleaners, etc. The actors involved in the chain, such as the initiators or the members of the small group, and at a later stage the members of the project group, have had to define the problem and provide a solution. They have had to set the goals of the activity chain, to consider the final addressee/audience and to plan the necessary steps/strategies to achieve their goals.

The knowledge, experience, norms and values of the actors, the group members, are of course important in the construction of the problem, goal and strategies. Another important factor is the internal group structure, the role relationships, i.e. who ends up playing what role.

The content of the activity they engage in is constructed by the actors regardless of the medium. The actors' collective construction of the 'case', their gradual definition of the problem, of the people involved and their needs, of the intended goal and the strategies needed to achieve it, determines their communicative activities. Throughout a long chain of activities, we can assume that the 'case' develops. Writing and talking activities are intermingled in the communicative process, which means that no clear borderline exists between the functions of writing and talking or between the norms affecting writing and those affecting talking. The same sociocognitive framework, the same communicative culture, governs both forms of discourse.

9.2.4 Social dimension of writing at work

The third aim of this study relates to the social dimension of writing at work. The first claim I will examine is that the correspondence between the density of the internal and external relations in which the group members are involved, describes the openness of the group. My analysis will focus on the external networks to which the employees belong. The second claim is that the openness of a group is reflected in its uniformity in terms of shared knowledge, evaluations, attitudes and norms, as well as in the form of a group identity. My analysis will focus on results relating to shared norms and attitudes and group identity.

165

9.2.4.1   External relations

To obtain a picture of the social structure of the office, I analysed the external networks in which its employees are involved. One aim of this analysis was to determine whether the office seemed to function as an independent entity (a group), as part of a larger unity (a subgroup) or only as a grouping of different external relations. My assumption was that high communicative openness, a structure with many different and dense external networks, correlates negatively with uniformity and social cohesion within the group. If this is the case, influence over norms and attitudes will be diversified and heterogeneous and the group identity will be weak.

By 'external network', I mean all the external networks (reaching outside the office) in which the members of staff are involved. My analysis relates not only to the existence of a network as such, but also to its degree of externality. I have found it essential to introduce this concept, as the degree of externality of these networks can be assumed to be related to the openness-closeness of the professional group.

External can mean outside and close or outside and distant. Externality has two dimensions. (1) It is related to physical distance; a relationship to someone outside the district is more distant than a contact with someone within the district. (2) It is related to the type of contact. Here I distinguish two types of contact: governmental and non-governmental. A contact with a governmental person in a town outside the studied city, here called Svestad, is considered less external than a contact with a non-governmental professional in the same town.

I can add that my analysis of external networks is based not only on contacts in writing, but on reported contacts of all types: conferences, meetings, courses etc.

The office is a single physical unit, with 35 employees placed in adjacent rooms on the same floor of a building in the local government district of Nylunda (the fictitious name given to the district). The office is called the nucleus. Outside this nucleus, there are different external spheres. The first sphere is the local government district. This in turn is one of fourteen districts of the city Svestad. Outside Svestad, there are other towns and cities within the country, Sweden.

Figure 9.4 shows the district office and its external spheres. Around the office, or the nucleus (Nu), is the district of Nylunda (Ny). The second sphere is the city of Svestad (Sv), and the third the whole country (Co). Within these spheres, different areas are distinguished: (1) a local government area, and within this one section consisting of employees (Emp) and one consisting of local politicians (Pol); (2) a non-governmental professional area, consisting of architects, engineers

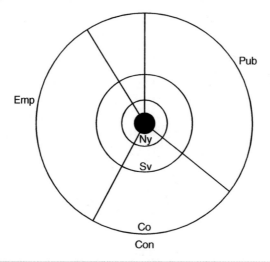

Nu	Nucleus (the section office in Nylunda)
Ny	The district of Nylunda
Sv	The city of Svestad
Co	The country (Sweden)
Emp	Local government employees
Pol	Politicians and others on district boards
Con	Consultants (professionals not employed by local government)
Pub	The public

Figure 9.4 *The local government office and its external spheres (Adapted from Figure 4 in Gunnarsson, 1997b: 174)*

etc. of importance to different undertakings related to the office (Con); (3) the public, i.e. a non-governmental, non-professional area (Pub).

Figure 9.5 summarizes the external relations of the office. It is based on the various findings of this study relating to the external contacts of the group as a whole. The purpose is to give a rough illustration of the network. The lines indicate the distance of the relationships, from the office to the various spheres and areas. Frequency and density is illustrated by the number of lines.

One finding of this study is that the majority of contacts outside the office concern the first external sphere, i.e. the local government district for which it is responsible. The staff have quite frequent contact with other employees within the district, with politicians, with the members of the district board and with the public. They have also some contact with professionals within their own district. These

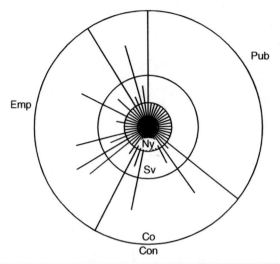

——	The distance of the relation
Nu	Nucleus (the section office in Nylunda)
Ny	The district of Nylunda
Sv	The city of Svestad
Co	The country (Sweden)
Emp	Local government employees
Pol	Politicians and others on district boards
Con	Consultants (professionals not employed by local government)
Pub	The public

Figure 9.5 *The office and its external relations (Adapted from Figure 5 in Gunnarsson, 1997b: 175)*

first-sphere contacts are fairly evenly spread among the individual employees.

The second sphere concerns relations with groups and individuals within the city and its other districts. Contacts with this sphere are considerably less frequent than with the office staff's own district. They are also less evenly spread among the employees.

If we turn finally to the third sphere, which concerns contacts outside the city, the figure shows that they are few in number. The head of the office and staff in high position have contacts outside the city, but the general impression is that these are not very frequent and that they mainly involve other local government officials. They are thus outside but close.

To summarize, we have found that most employees at the office do not participate in dense networks extending beyond their own district. Staff in high positions, and a few in the middle level, are involved in networks reaching outside their own district, but within their own city. Even fewer have contacts outside their own city, and most of these contacts are not dense. The office is thus an entity with a relatively little external openness, which means that the group is likely to function as an independent group with a fairly high degree of group uniformity.

9.2.4.2   Group uniformity

The social structure of a group is reflected in its degree of uniformity with respect to different social parameters. A closed group can thus be assumed to show greater uniformity of norms and attitudes and also a more marked group identity, cohesion and 'we' feeling. The investigation of communication at the local government office therefore also focused on the norms and attitudes of each individual. The employees were asked about their norms concerning a good text and a good writer, and about their attitudes to writing at work. What is of interest in this context, however, is the degree of uniformity of their norms and attitudes. Within a closed workplace – as the office studied was found to be – one can expect uniformity about norms concerning texts and text patterns. One can also expect similar attitudes and values relating to writing and writers. Group uniformity can also be expected to show up as 'we' feeling and group identity.

First of all, as regards the norms of the office staff, a classification of these as group norms would mean that they are both uniform, i.e. related to the group as a whole, and unique, or in other words different from norms at other offices. To begin with, I should point out that there exist standard texts, guidelines, recommendations etc. within the office, which have been developed by the employees around the information officer (Ma). When I asked her about these 'rules', she stressed that the office was completely free to develop its own patterns. It did not need to follow other districts of the city. When asked in the interviews about their criteria of a good text, all the employees gave similar answers. They all stressed the importance of adapting to the reader, choosing an informal, not too bureaucratic style and avoiding difficult words. Many also mentioned that they tried to write in a personal manner. My conclusion is that there seems to be what we could call group norms, or rather that the staff think of their norms as group norms. They consider their style unique in certain respects and typical for their office.

169

The answers to the question on attitudes to writing at work also revealed group uniformity.[9] There was a striking similarity in the attitudes of different groups of staff, regardless of the fact that their writing activities vary largely. My conclusion is that there seem to exist group attitudes towards writing within the office, which prevail independent of the actual tasks the employees have to cope with.

9.2.4.3 Group identity and 'we' feeling

The employees' attitudes towards writing at work are certainly related to their general attitudes towards work and the office as a workplace. Through the interviews I also tried to ascertain their ideas about what the office stood for. I wanted to find out if they considered their own district and their own office different in any way from other districts and other offices, and also if they expressed a 'we' feeling, e.g. by stressing 'we' as opposed to 'others', i.e. people outside the office and the district. The most highly elaborated picture of such a group identity and 'we' feeling was given by Ma, the information officer, who as shown in Figure 9.2, has the highest degree of centrality in the communicative structure. Her description of the in-group, of her own office and district, is very positive, and her description of the out-group, of the others, negative. What is interesting to note is that the other employees also express clear group feelings. In the interviews, both Ha, the leader of one of the office sections, and La, one of the secretaries in a low position, brought up their earlier workplace experiences in order to give a picture of their current workplace, Nylunda, as unique and also better than the others. My conclusion is therefore that a positive group identity, the Nylunda 'we' feeling, permeates the whole office. The office seems to function socially as a professional group.

9.3 Conclusions

One purpose of this chapter has been to evaluate the sociolinguistic framework introduced in the previous chapter. A small workplace, a local government office was investigated. The study comprised analyses of (1) the organizational structure and its effects on writing at work, (2) the communicative process and the role of spoken discourse and collaboration in the construction of documents, and (3) the social dimension of writing at work.

The results of the study lend support to the first basic assumption concerning the social organization of writing at work, with parameters such as centrality, clusters, hierarchical asymmetries and networks as constitutive of the organization of writing activities. In addition, they support the second assumption concerning the collaborative nature of writing at work and concerning the close intertwinement of text and talk in the construction of documents. The nature of these collaborative processes, with text and talk intertwined, was also dependent on hierarchical position; the higher the position, the longer and more complex the communicative chains. The third assumption, relating to the social values attached to writing at work, also found support. Ideas about the organization and work in general were found to be reflected in norms and attitudes vis-à-vis writing at work.

The most important conclusion to be drawn from this study does not lie in the case study as such, but in its role as an evaluation of the sociolinguistic framework. I would suggest that new light could be shed on the writing process by means of a sociolinguistic framework like the one I have discussed here. Internal structure, role patterns, external relations and group uniformity are questions which it is important to study if we are to understand what takes place in writing in real-life settings. Furthermore, I consider the concepts of 'communicative community' and 'professional group' to be a fruitful base for the study of writing in real life, where writing is integrated in communicative activities as a whole and intermingled in its various stages with spoken discourse.

Notes

1. For an overview, see Hudson (1996).
2. Academic disciplines have been assumed to form distinguishable communities, 'discourse communities', which have formed their own social patterns of writing (e.g., Bazerman, 1988; Myers, 1990; Berkenkotter and Huckin, 1995).
3. The latter distinction can be related to the 'sphere' concept as used in Habermas (1971), and the public sphere includes working life.
4. See Barton (1991) for an interesting discussion of the 'literacy events' and 'literacy practices' of everyday life.
5. In a monograph in Swedish, *Skrivande i yrkeslivet. En sociolingvistisk studie* (Gunnarsson, 1992), I give a systematic and full presentation of the investigation. This chapter draws on an article published in *Written Communication* (Gunnarsson 1997b).
6. The product analyses were carried out by Amelie Oestreicher, who also participated in the survey part of the study.
7. 16 members of the staff held low, 8 middle, and 9 high positions at the office during the period studied.
8. In Kaufer and Carley (1993: 113) the term 'handle' is used for the name associated with a document. They write: 'Authorial handles in organizational environments are often used to help the power structure maintain its power. The leader becomes "larger than life" by having a name singularly associated with documents that enjoy the leverage of the group.' The fact that the signing role is often not restricted to one

particular person, can also be analysed in relation to power structure: 'At the same time, authorial handles are fluid enough to allow for the occasional redefinition of power relationships. Some bureaucratic writers remain effaced in organizational handles, but others break through the shield of organizational anonymity and emerge with their own name as handle' (ibid).

9. Using an Osgood scale, we measured the employees' general attitudes towards writing at work. Respondents were asked to indicate on a 7-grade scale, how they felt about their writing at work. We asked them to grade their attitudes with regard to the following variables: enjoyable – boring, active – passive, easy – difficult, varied – monotonous, quick – slow, creative – mechanical, laborious – restful, free – restricted, high-status – low-status, agreeable – disagreeable. By means of this methodology one can capture unreflecting emotional attitudes, rather than precise considered personal standpoints. The employees did not know what exactly we meant by 'free', nor do we know exactly what they meant. This is part of the purpose, which is to capture their imprecise, unreflecting attitudes, attitudes which cannot be captured by means of a clearly defined set of terms.

10 The multilingual workplace: Discourse in a hospital and a large company

All over the world, there are workplaces where some employees – mostly minorities, immigrants or unskilled guest workers – have to use their second, third or fourth language at work. In many organizations, knowledge of the dominant local language is necessary not only for advancement and a career but also for social integration into the working group. Humour, jokes, stories, anecdotes form part of the workplace discourse and contribute to the establishment of friendship and collegiality at work and also to the avoidance of unnecessary conflicts. Social workplace patterns related to friendship, power and dominance often reflect linguistic and communication skills.

The globalized economy also means that large corporations, e.g. multinational companies which operate in countries with different languages, need to choose one language as their lingua franca. Not infrequently, at least in Europe, English is the language chosen. In countries where English is not the mother tongue, this may influence the organizational structure and lead to a divide between those who are fluent in English and those who are not. For employees with a background in countries where English is not a school subject, as is the case in many parts of the world, this adds an additional foreign language to be learnt and mastered for advancement and a career.

In this chapter I discuss some results of a research project which explores the daily work-related interaction in two working environments in Sweden: a public hospital and an international company. Both environments are multilingual and multicultural in relation to their staff, i.e., a great number of their employees are immigrants in the country and use a foreign language at work. There is, however, a difference between the two environments in terms of which languages are used by its staff for professional and socializing purposes at work. The hospital serves the general public and Swedish, the local majority language, is also the main language at work for its employees. The company, which operates in several countries, uses English as its corporate language. This means that some staff use English as a lingua franca for some purposes and Swedish for others.

From a sociolinguistic perspective it is interesting to analyse how linguistic and cultural diversity is handled within these different working environments. How does the organizational structure influence text and talk at work? What does workplace multilingualism entail in the two environments? How do foreign language users cope with the different communicative events they are involved in during a working day?

These questions, the focus of this chapter, relate to theories developed in sociolinguistics and interactional sociolinguistics. First, therefore, I sketch the theoretical framework for my following discussion of results. In the second part of the chapter, I give a brief presentation of the research project: the project team, its methodology and informants. My ensuing discussion of the results will be organized as follows: in part 10.3 I deal with the organizational structure of text and talk at work and then compare the two environments, the hospital and the company, in terms of openness, contact spheres and use of text and talk. Part 10.4 focuses on workplace languages, which means that I will discuss which languages are used during a working day for what purposes and by whom in the environments studied. In part 10.5, my topic is foreign language users at work. I discuss the foreign language users' communicative strategies, participation in humour and joking, and job identities. In part 10.6, I sum up my discussion on workplace interaction with a focus on workplace diversity.

10.1 Theoretical approaches

This chapter will explore workplace interaction from different perspectives, from that of the 'professional group', the 'linguistic-cultural framework', and the 'individual employee and his/her interaction at work'. Here, therefore, I will introduce some relevant sociolinguistic concepts and theories.

In the previous chapter, I introduced a theoretical framework for the analysis of communicative practices within a 'professional group'. Several of the sociolinguistic variables developed there are also relevant for this chapter, e.g. 'openness', 'contact sphere', 'organizational structure' and relation between the 'social and communicative order'.

The discussion of results in this chapter will further include an analysis of the use of different languages at work. I will focus on workplaces which are multilingual in relation to their staff. At these workplaces, employees with different mother tongues work together and interact daily at work. Sometimes different languages are in contact in a particular 'speech event', e.g. in terms of 'code switching' or 'code mixing'. In most cases, however, the use of language at work is more systematically organized, as a consequence of the organizational structure and the linguistic-cultural framework (cf. Chapter 2). My analysis of the relationship between languages at a macro-level will therefore refer to the two sociolinguistic concepts of 'language dominance' and 'diglossia'.[1]

As many sociolinguistic studies have shown, there is often a hierarchy between the languages used in bilingual and multilingual settings which both reflects and strengthens the social structure. In many environments, the main local language, e.g. the national majority language, is the dominant language. This means that immigrants and minorities cannot use their mother tongues in many events, which places them in an inferior interactive position compared to those who can. In supranational contacts, we also find that some languages, e.g. English in large parts of the world, have become the dominant languages and function as a 'lingua franca', i.e. a linguistic denominator between individuals with various mother tongues. In international encounters, therefore, we find that some individuals are able to use their first language while others have to use a second, third or even fourth language. This leads, of course, to an unequal language situation.

Another sociolinguistic concept of importance for my analysis of the relationship between different languages is 'diglossia'. This term refers to a functional divide between languages, with one language being used for some purposes and another language for others. This divide often entails a difference in prestige between the two languages, i.e. one language is considered 'high' and the other 'low'.[2]

The research project dealt with in this chapter focuses on the individual employees and their interactions at work. All the employees studied are immigrants and 'foreign language users' at work, which means that linguistic and cultural issues become salient also from the point of view of the individual. One aim of the project is to explore how these foreign language users succeed in their daily interaction, professionally and socially. In my discussion I will therefore use the concept of 'communicative competence', which was established by Hymes. He asserts that a first language speaker has acquired competence as to when to speak, when not and as to what to talk about with whom, when, where, in what manner (1974). Another relevant concept is 'communicative strategies', which frequently has been used in studies on intercultural communication. According to Tarone (1980), for instance, communicative strategies are used to overcome problems which occur when an individual's language knowledge and language skills are not sufficient to express her thoughts in the communicative event.

Another aim of the project is to analyse if and how the individual is socially integrated into the working group. The analysis of the individual's contributions to spoken and written dialogues are further seen in relation to what the other participants have said or written as well as to how they respond, and the overall aim of the analyses is to find positive and negative communicative patterns within the professional group.

The theoretical base for the micro analysis of the various speech events occurring during a working day has been 'interactional sociolinguistics' with its focus on the joint creation of context and the role of discourse for identity work. 'Context' is a key concept within interactional sociolinguistics. Context, however, is not seen as something outside discourse that impinges on it but rather as created by discourse. Speakers create context by means of linguistic cues. Furthermore, verbal interaction, or discursive practice, proceeds not according to rules but rather by the application of systematic strategies or principles. Listening and speaking are inextricably intertwined, and meaning is the jointly constructed creation of all interactants.[3] For Gumperz (1982a, 1999), one of the key persons within this tradition, all meaning is 'situated interpretation'. Shared contextualization conventions enable a listener not only to interpret what has been said but also to predict what is likely to be said. The ability to make such prediction is necessary for successful participation in a verbal exchange. The listeners must be able to discern, follow and predict the development of the thread of meaning. Their knowledge of what usually co-occurs helps them to predict what will follow, e.g. when speakers raise their voice anger is indicated, which gives a cue to what will come next. Prosody, paralinguistic cues, code or style-switching, choice of particular lexical forms or culturally recognizable formulaic expressions belong to the 'contextualization cues' distinguished in Gumperz (1992).

Work within interactional sociolinguistics typically entails case-study microanalysis of authentic interaction. It is a tenet of interactional sociolinguistics that language can only be studied in its immediate, situated, social context and further that the language of interaction is constitutive of social relationships. Meaning is seen as the joint creation of speakers and listeners in the act of using language to accomplish interactive goals.

According to Gumperz (1999: 453), interactional sociolinguistics has been developed for the analysis of linguistic and cultural inequality:

> Interactional sociolinguistic has its origin in the search for replicable methods of qualitative sociolinguistic analysis that can

provide insights into the linguistic and cultural diversity characteristic of today's communicative environments, and document
its impact on individual's lives.

Many studies within the subfield have also focused on encounters
where there is a clear power difference between the two interactants,
e.g. speech events in which a member of a minority community requires
the approval of a majority-community member to advance professionally or receive a societal benefit.[4] In these gatekeeping encounters, differences in language use have been shown to cause to some extent
or to aggravate social inequality, discrimination, and cross-cultural
stereotyping. In this chapter, however, I will discuss a research project
which had the aim of exploring interaction involving individuals at a
hierarchically more equal level. The dialogical character of the daily
work-related interaction will thus be focused on. Among other things,
I will analyse the individual's participation in small talk, humour and
joking at work.[5] I will also explore how the individual's 'job identity'
is constructed in the interaction with fellow workers.

10.2   Presentation of the research project

The results I will refer to in this chapter emanate from studies within
an ongoing research project at Uppsala University. In this project,
entitled *The communicative situation of immigrants at Swedish workplaces,* spoken and written discourse are analysed with a focus on
employees in different positions and from different parts of the world.
The project team consists of myself as director, Helena Andersson and
Marie Nelson. Andersson's study concerns the hospital, and Nelson's
the company. In the first phase of their studies, they carried out interviews with a fairly large number of immigrants with permanent jobs.
In the second phase, they undertook case studies, five at each workplace. The employees – females and males – were shadowed during a
week, and data related to their workplace communication were collected. The results have been presented in articles and reports.[6] The
full presentation of Andersson's and Nelson's studies will be given in
their forthcoming Ph.D. theses.

10.2.1   Methodology

The procedures chosen for data collection within the project are
related to those developed for empirical studies in the field of interactional sociolinguistics (Gumperz, 1999: 465). Their first step consists
of an initial period of ethnographic research to provide a preliminary understanding and a basis for selecting representative events and

interactions for the next stage, the recordings. In this investigation, a number of introductory interviews were carried out to get to know the workplaces concerned and some of the employees and to gain a picture of their communicative situation at work.

The interviews carried out at the two workplaces were semi-structured in the sense that the goal was to get specific information from all informants, but not necessarily in a particular order or in a particular way. Each interview took place at the informant's workplace during the regular working day. On average, interviews lasted about an hour and were tape recorded. Although the interviews were conducted on the basis of a schedule of questions, the interviewers were always open to topics initiated by the informants, and their answers and comments were followed up with further questions if this was necessary.

The questions were divided into three groups: 'background', 'the communicative situation at work', 'difficulties and experiences' at work.

The main phase of the investigation comprised case studies. Each case study began with a period of observation in which the researchers shadowed the informant for a couple of working days to become familiar with his or her daily life at work and to get a picture of the different communicative activities they were engaged in. When they had gained a general picture of the informants' situation and workplace communication, they started their recordings, using tape recorders and/or video cameras depending on what was appropriate in each situation and what the informant and workplace allow. The overall goal has been to enable analysis of all the different kinds of situations which the informants find themselves in at work. That means that the aim has been to capture not only work-related communication, but also communication in more social situations, such as coffee breaks and lunch hours.

Informants in different positions were chosen for the case studies and as far as possible from different parts of the world. The researchers monitored every aspect and translated their observations into field notes which were supplemented by video and audio recordings, digital photos and collection of texts read and produced by the informants during the period of observation, e-mails included.

During the observed period, on average four working days, all spoken interaction involving the shadowed employee has been recorded (if possible), both interaction for professional purposes – i.e., talk during hospital rounds, at large scheduled meetings, at informal small group events, in collaborative work – and interaction for socializing purposes – talk during breaks and pauses, small talk during work. The spoken interaction has been transcribed and analysed using the technique of conversation analysis.

All texts produced and received by the employees shadowed at the factory that were not considered secret were collected, i.e. emails, notes, sketches and other texts. One focus in the analysis of these texts has been on 'communicative strategies'. At the hospital, where spoken interaction was the dominant medium and all journal texts secret, it was not possible to make an extensive analysis of the written interaction.

10.2.2 Informants

As mentioned above, two different working environments have been studied: a hospital and a major company in Sweden. In the first phase of the study, interviews were carried out with employees with different origins and with different position at work. Eighteen employees were interviewed at each workplace. At the hospital, 3 doctors, 2 midwives, 6 nurses and 7 cleaners were interviewed. Of these 18 informants, only two are men, which reflects the overall situation at the hospital where more than 6,000 of the roughly 7,000 employees are women. At the company, 9 of the informants are office workers and 9 factory workers. Women are represented in both positions, but male workers form the majority, as they do in the company as a whole. The informants came from different parts of the world. Our criteria for choosing informants, however, meant that we did not include informants from the Nordic countries nor from any where English, German or French are spoken.

Five employees from each workplace were selected for the case studies. At the hospital the case studies include two female doctors, one from Hungary and one from Lithuania, two female nurses, one from Iran and one from Lebanon, and one male cleaner from Tanzania. In the company the case studies include two women and three men. Two are factory workers and three office workers, and they come from different continents: a female office worker from Colombia, a female factory worker from Poland, a male office worker from Slovenia, an office worker from India, and a factory worker from the former Yugoslavia.

10.3 The organizational structure of text and talk at work

On the basis of the results of the interviews and the observations of the working environments during the case studies, I will try to explore how organizational structure influences the use of text and talk within the two environments. I will compare the two environments in terms of 'openness', 'contact spheres', and 'use of text and talk'. In order to describe the relationship between the 'social and communicative order' in the studied environments, I will sum up what we have found about differences between employees in different position. For the case of simplicity, I will here make a simple distinction between 'skilled' and 'unskilled' employees. At the hospital, the skilled employees in our study are doctors, midwives and nurses, while the unskilled are cleaners. At the company, the skilled employees are referred to as 'office staff' and the unskilled as 'factory workers'.

10.3.1   Openness

If we first look at the two workplaces in relation to the open – closed variable, we find a striking difference. At the hospital, the doctors, nurses and administrative staff have a continuous contact with new discourse partners, i.e. the patients. In many situations they also communicate with one or more of the patient's relatives. Those working at the hospital encounter a large number of new faces in the corridors, waiting rooms and wards during an ordinary working day. At the company the employees use keycards to enter the different buildings. Most spoken interaction is between individuals who know each other well. Also telephone calls and emails are mainly addressed to or received from someone they have previously been in contact with.

10.3.2   Contact spheres

At the hospital both doctors and nurses interact daily both with lay people and with other professionals. Their contact spheres thus include the local public. For the cleaners, included in our study, all the interaction recorded is internal, i.e. related to other employees.

The employees at the company, on the other hand, have no direct contact with the public. Their professional interaction is with colleagues or other professionals.

10.3.3   Use of text and talk

At the hospital spoken discourse is the main medium both for professional and socializing purposes. Spoken discourse is used in interaction with patients, colleagues and external experts. As our case studies show, doctors and nurses do not write much during a working day. The doctors dictate and a secretary then types up the dictation. Admittedly journals are kept in the wards. What the nurses record, however, consists mainly of names of medicine, the size of the dose and when administered. For both doctors and nurses there are predetermined diagnoses and comments they can use. When they enter a short code in their computer a predetermined phrase appears on the screen, which means that they do not need to formulate the sentences themselves. Many of the texts written at the hospital are confidential. For instance, the journals which are kept are not public and have not therefore been included in our collected data.[7]

The communicative situation for the cleaners at the hospital is quite different from that of nurses and doctors. The cleaners most often work on their own, which means that they do not need to talk to people they meet while cleaning the different wards. Some say that there are days when they do not have contact with anyone in the wards. Their work is organized in a way that means the members of each team do not meet when they are working. Things are different, however, during the breaks. In the coffee room they sit next to colleagues with the same mother tongue, if possible.

At the company, on the whole written discourse plays a much more prominent role than at the hospital. There is, however, a considerable difference between the written production, both in terms of quantity and form, for employees in different position. The office staff, mainly engineers, spend most of their day at their computers reading and writing different types of texts. They write and read emails, letters and reports. For the factory workers, on the other hand, written discourse plays a minor role. They do not use computers and seldom write anything but figures in dockets.

Spoken communication also varies between office staff and factory workers. The office staff participate in many more meetings than the factory workers. Talk seems to have a mainly socializing role for the factory workers and the coffee breaks are considered very important. The breaks not only offer a rest but also small talk and social contact. The conversations at these breaks are very informal and relaxing. The coffee breaks are not a regular – or important – part of the working day for office staff. Each individual chooses his or her own time for a break, and often they take their coffee mug to the computer.

10.4 Workplace languages

In this part of the chapter, I will discuss what workplace multilingualism entails in the two environments, then try to answer the question of which languages are used during a working day, for what purposes and by whom?

The hospital resembles the local government office presented in chapter 9 in many ways. The goal of the hospital is also to provide services for the public in the local community. At the hospital, communication with lay people – patients and relatives – forms an important part of the daily work of the medically trained staff, i.e. of doctors, nurses and midwives. This also means that the majority language of the local community, Swedish, is the dominant language in their work.

The nurses and midwives interviewed say that they mainly use Swedish at work, i.e. the local majority language. One of them reports that she resorts to English when she finds a word difficult to pronounce in Swedish. Some of the nurses also say that they every now and then also use their mother tongue, since many patients come from their countries of origin. They then find themselves in the role of interpreter between patient and doctor. Two of the doctors interviewed report that they use both Swedish and English at work. Swedish is their everyday working language in interaction with patients and colleagues, while English is used in their research and in writing articles for publication. They say that they write a lot in English and sometimes also give lectures in that language. The third doctor, however, says that Swedish is the only language she uses at work.

The communicative situation for the cleaners is, as mentioned above, very different from that of the medically skilled staff. When interviewed the cleaners say that Swedish is used when they speak to their managers, to hospital staff they meet when cleaning their areas and to other cleaners when they do not have a common mother tongue. During coffee and lunch breaks they tend to interact only with those who share the same mother tongue, so there are many subgroups within the larger group of employees. Many of the cleaners have very poor skills in Swedish, and since they mainly interact with others from the same countries, they do not get much practice in Swedish so their proficiency hardly improves, according to the managers who were interviewed. Some of the cleaners actually say that they try to avoid contact with Swedish-speaking people because they are afraid that they will not understand what is being said to them.

In the company, communication is mainly directed to professionals, i.e. to colleagues linked to the same workplace or within the same organization or to other professionals. As the workplace studied belongs to a large, international company for which English is the corporate language, the language practices are of a diglossic nature. English is used as a lingua franca for external purposes, e.g. in written correspondence with colleagues in other countries and in meetings with external professionals, while the local majority language, Swedish, is used for internal purposes and in the daily spoken interaction with colleagues.

From the point of view of language, a clear divide exists between office staff and factory workers. When the office staff were asked about the languages they used at work, three of nine office staff said that they mainly use Swedish, three that they mainly use English, and three that they use English and Swedish to an equal extent. Some of the office staff work on projects involving foreign countries, and this of course affects their choice of language. Both those who mainly use English and who use it half-and-half claim that they write English more often than they speak it. Two-thirds of the office workers say that they have used their mother tongues at work.

Among the nine factory workers interviewed, eight say that Swedish is the language they use at work. One factory floor worker says that much of what she reads is in English but that all spoken discourse is in Swedish. Three of the workers say that they have used their mother tongues at the workplace, while six say that they never have done so. For the office staff, the proportion is the opposite, i.e. six claim to have used their mother tongues at work, while three say they have not done so. The office staff thus seem to use other languages than Swedish (and English) to a greater extent than factory floor workers. The office staff seem to be more involved, e.g., in guiding or taking care of groups and representatives from foreign countries than factory employees. All 18 employees interviewed say that they come into contact with texts in English at work.

10.5 Foreign language users at work

In this part of the chapter, I will view workplace discourse from the perspective of diversity. As I mentioned earlier, both environments are multilingual and multicultural in relation to their staff so that among their permanent staff there are individuals with a range of mother tongues and cultural backgrounds. As workplaces, however, the hospital can be said to be monolingual, using Swedish, the local majority language, for most purposes, while the company is bilingual, using English as corporate language for externally oriented purposes and Swedish in everyday speech and writing. For the immigrants focused on in our investigation, Swedish is a foreign language – often their third or fourth language – which they have learnt as adults.[8] All of them are thus using at least one foreign language, Swedish, during an ordinary working day. Some of them, the office staff at the company, also use a second foreign language, namely English. My summary of results below will concern the immigrants' communicative strategies, their use of humour and joking and their job identities.

I prefer to use the term 'foreign language' instead of 'second language' as I wish to stress that both Swedish and English, which are Germanic languages, are far from the languages which our informants have grown up with. The mother tongues of our informants include languages such as Persian, Turkish, Swahili, Polish, Serbo-Croatian, and Arabic.

10.5.1 Communicative strategies

One of the things which Andersson and Nelson focused on in the interviews was the informants' knowledge of Swedish and whether their language skills were sufficient for all the different kinds of communicative situations that can arise. The majority of informants, both at the company and at the hospital, state that they do not perceive their language skills, or perhaps lack of skills, to be a problem. If they do not understand what is being said to them, they ask the other person to repeat or explain the whole utterance or a word or phrase. They also say that they can always turn to their colleagues for help if they find themselves in some kind of linguistic difficulty.

During the interviews, however, both researchers found that some informants had difficulties understanding the questions or expressing themselves and did not ask for help or repetition. This was true in particular of the interviews with unskilled workers. A few of the factory floor workers also admit that they sometimes do not understand and do not bother to ask. Their reasoning is that if the issue is important, they will hear about it again. They add that they prefer to see the person they are talking to, as they then are able to read faces and body language, which can help them to understand. A few of the cleaners at the hospital also state that every now and then they pretend to understand the message, even though they do not. Sometimes it is because they feel that they have asked for it to be repeated so many times that it is becoming embarrassing, and in the end they simply pretend to understand. Some of the cleaners also use body language and pen and paper to understand. This is of course because many of them have difficulty expressing themselves in Swedish and do not have sufficient skills in English either, so they have to find other ways to understand and be understood.

As the ten case studies have revealed, all the immigrants shadowed have developed communicative strategies which make it possible for them to function properly in their daily spoken interaction, both at professional and socializing speech events. As these individuals were also interviewed, it has been possible to relate what they report in the interviews about their communication to authentic spoken interaction at work. In their comparisons, both Andersson and Nelson have been struck by the linguistic and communicative awareness of their informants. The employees shadowed recognize their difficulties and are consciously using ways to overcome these. The relative success of our informants therefore seems to be associated with an awareness of how to cope with communicative problems of various kinds.

It is particularly interesting to see how the office staff at the company handle language problems when they are writing in Swedish. Writing forms a major part of these employees' daily activities, and they have to write in both English and Swedish. Much of their writing is to recipients outside the company and is fairly official in character, a fact that poses the challenge of being correct and formal. Carolina, one of the office employees, offers a particularly interesting case. She was born in Colombia and Spanish is her mother tongue, and during her working day she writes a great deal in both English and Swedish. Her English is excellent and she has no difficulty in producing texts in English. Her Swedish is also fairly good, but not as good as her English. However, she is working hard to improve her Swedish, and she is very eager to avoid mistakes in her writing. As Nelson has found, Carolina consciously uses different strategies in order to avoid mistakes. She asks colleagues for help, and sometimes she consults her Swedish-born husband. At her computer she uses various tools: grammar and spelling control, lexicon etc. She frequently looks up new words and tries to enlarge her grammar. When preformulated templates are available, e.g. for protocols, she uses these. Another of her writing strategies is to copy other person's formulations. Carolina, herself, considers this to be a way of avoiding potential difficulties but at the same time it involves risk-taking, as the copied words or phrases have to be inserted into her text, i.e. in another textual context.

As this shows, Carolina is very aware of her writing strategies. The other office employees shadowed at the company also show a high degree of awareness in relation to their own text production. They seem also to be successful in their writing. Nelson concludes, on the basis of an analysis of her informants' received mail, that their writing seems to be comprehensible for the intended readers. There were no letters with requests for clarification or any other signs of misunderstanding. The informants thus seem to have found writing strategies which work. However, writing in a foreign language is time consuming. At least, Carolina thinks so. She estimates that writing in Swedish takes 20 per cent longer than writing in her mother tongue or in English.

10.5.2 Humour and joking

Humour, jokes and storytelling are important parts of the daily inter-action at most workplaces. Humour shows solidarity and strengthens the feeling of togetherness within the group. The function of humour, however, is not only to amuse and entertain between equals but also to maintain authority and exert control. Humour can be used to soften face threatening acts such as orders, criticism, of the presentation of unpalatable decisions (Holmes, 2006: 27).

In their analyses of workplace interaction, Andersson and Nelson focus, among other things, on humour and joking. In the interviews, several informants mentioned humour and joking as a particularly dif-ficult aspect of their daily interaction at work. Humour is not only – or mainly – a matter of choosing the right wording; it also entails prag-matic competence concerning what you can joke about, when and with whom. Humour is to a large extent cultural and group specific, which is clearly shown in our investigation. Andersson's analysis, for instance, reveals how humour and joking vary from one hospital ward to the other, and one of Nelson's informants even states that at his workplace, each team has its own way of joking. As the teams prefer to sit together in the staff coffee room, he says that the jargon and styles of joking vary from table to table.

One element of the socialization into a professional group requires employees to learn what is considered funny and how a joke should be presented in this particular context.[9] In order to become a full mem-ber of the professional group, it is also necessary to know who you may joke with. In many cultures joking practices reflect a hierarchical structure, which means that a subordinate, e.g. an ordinary worker, may not joke with a superior, e.g. the manager or boss. In other cul-tures, as for instance at many Swedish workplaces, you may also joke upwards, which means that a worker may joke with her boss.

The analyses of workplace interaction clearly show that the com-municative competence of the employees shadowed includes joking. In the majority of cases they understand their colleagues' jokes and irony. Joking is also a strategy available to them in different situations. Andersson's case studies at the hospital show that both the cleaners and the nurses and doctors frequently joke as a means of establishing solidarity. They tease each other in a friendly way; they joke about themselves, and say funny things to create a good climate. The medic-ally trained staff can also use humour to defend themselves when they are criticized or to deal with difficult situations. Another interesting result is that jokes are also directed upwards, to superiors. In the inter-views, several informants said that a cultural difference which they found difficult to cope with was related to workplace hierarchy, i.e. the Swedish workplace climate was considerably less hierarchical than the one familiar to them from their countries of origin. Andersson's assumption was therefore that the immigrants might refrain from joking with superiors. In the recordings from rounds and meetings, however, she has found several sequences where nurses joke with doctors and other superiors naturally, which can be seen as a sign of their integration into the non-hierarchical Swedish workplace culture. Nelson draws a similar conclusion on the basis of her recordings at the company; it is fully accepted – and quite frequent– for the shadowed workers to joke with their bosses.

10.5.3 Creating a job identity

The frequency and varied ways in which different employees participate in small talk, humour and joking during a working day can also be related to their various 'workplace identities'. Each individual creates – and is assigned – a job identity in the daily social interaction at work. In discourse, this identity is revealed by the way the individual talks about herself and her role at work as well as in the way others talk about her. For Anna, a middle-aged, unskilled factory floor worker, joking and humour seem to be important aspects of her job identity. She is very talkative and jokes with everyone on all occasions. The video recordings and observations further reveal that her jokes succeed in making her colleagues smile and laugh. As she herself states, she even gets a smile from colleagues who are usually quite taciturn. Anna does not hesitate to joke about herself and her appearance, as in this example where she talks to her colleague Nicke:

> *Example*
> Anna: Are you in pain Nicke?
> Nicke: Yes
> Anna: Let me give you a massage later but don't tell me I'm too old ((laughs))

As Nelson concludes (my translation): 'There are grammatical indicators that Swedish is not Anna's native tongue, but pragmatically she operates very skilfully. She knows when and how to speak about what and to whom. Anna's workmates also say that they never have problems in understanding her.' Her communicative competence seems therefore to be very high and it certainly covers humour and making jokes as well. (Nelson and Andersson, 2005: 93–94.)

With her cheerful, talkative personality, Anna helps to create a good social climate at her workplace, which her colleagues also

187

acknowledge. In other ways as well she is important for the social climate. She is engaged in two non-profit working groups, which provide catering services. One of the groups bakes cakes for the coffee breaks and the other runs a non-profit stand where the staff can buy ice creams, chocolate etc. This work is planned during coffee and lunch breaks, where the group members gather at one of the tables. Anna's job identity therefore embodies many social features of the kind stereotypically associated with women in male-dominated workplaces.

From a gender perspective, it is further interesting to note that the other female employee shadowed at the company, Caroline, is involved in non-profit socializing work as well. She chairs the Employees' Club, which organize social activities for its members.

There are many differences between Caroline and Anna. Caroline is a well-educated, young office employee, while Anna is an unskilled, middle-aged factory floor worker. Caroline, who is work-directed, effective and ambitious, avoids unnecessary coffee breaks and does most of her socializing on the computer. The intranet is mainly used for planning the activities of the Employees' Club, so her socializing work mainly entails writing at her ordinary workplace. Anna, on the other hand, uses coffee breaks and lunches to meet the other group members. What the two women have in common, however, is their involvement in non-profit socializing work groups in the company, which none of the three shadowed men are. This difference could of course be due to mere chance, as only five individuals were shadowed at the company. Nelson's findings are, however, in line with earlier workplace studies, which have also revealed that women are involved to a much larger extent than men in practices aiming at 'team building' (Fletcher 1999, Holmes, 2006). Caroline's job identity could thus be said to include features which are stereotypically associated with women at work.

10.6 Workplace interaction from a diversity perspective

In this part of the chapter, I will sum up my discussion by focusing on how diversity issues are dealt with at the hospital and company. Is there a divide between employees due to language knowledge and communication skills? Have the foreign language users become integrated into their working groups? What is the role of the group?

All over the world, we find employees who have not mastered the local workplace language fully. This means that asymmetries between native and non-native users form part of the daily interaction at many workplaces. The asymmetric situation, however, varies from one workplace to another. For instance, we often find differences between organizations which serve the public in the local community and international organizations which operate in many countries.

As this investigation has also showed, the local majority language is used in the majority of events at the public hospital. Nurses and doctors use Swedish in their daily interaction with patients and external experts. They also use Swedish at internal professional events, during rounds and staff meetings, and also to socialize, at lunches, coffee breaks and in corridor small talk. Also the shadowed cleaner, Mustafa, uses the local majority language at work. As no one else speaks his mother tongue, Swahili, at the workplace, he has to stick to Swedish, even though it is fairly poor. His Swedish is mixed with English words, which he seems to use unconsciously. He likes to talk and joke, and he and his colleagues generally manage to understand each other. A variety of communicative strategies, however, have to be used in the interaction involving the cleaners. Nevertheless, Mustafa seems to be fairly well integrated in his working team. However, his limited knowledge of the local majority language restricts his possibilities of getting a better job. Knowing Swedish is of great importance for promotion within the hospital and also for social integration within the workplace.

At the international company studied, proficiency in English creates a divide between the factory floor workers and office staff. Swedish is important for all employees, as most spoken discourse is carried out in the local majority language. For the factory floor workers, Swedish is more or less the only language used at work. The office staff's working day, however, is bilingual in that they use English for certain purposes and Swedish for others. A lack of English is a bar to promotion within the company, a fact that the factory floor workers are aware of.

The communicative situations for the employees interviewed and shadowed are thus different at the hospital and at the company and also within each environment. What all our informants have in common, however, is that they have a permanent job at their respective workplace, and that they seem to be able to perform the tasks they are assigned. Their position at work and the kinds of tasks they are given correspond to their linguistic competence and communication skills. Lack of language skills therefore hinders promotion in both environments: at the hospital good Swedish is necessary for a career and at the company both English and Swedish are required. In the company good writing skills are also important for promotion.

An interesting result of the analysis, however, concerns the way the immigrants – irrespective of position and type of job – have developed communicative strategies, and sometimes also extended their language proficiencies, in a way that enables them to overcome difficulties. Their skills in Swedish – and English – vary, as does their need to read and write at work. In order to cope with the various professional activities during a working day, however, they have developed communicative strategies which help them complete the tasks they are assigned to perform.

Another interesting result concerns our informants' level of pragmatic competence. As our recordings reveal, the immigrants shadowed participate in small talk and socializing events during a working day as full members of their group. Socially they seem to be well integrated into the working groups. For the social integration, pragmatic competence seems to be just as important as correct language use. As our results show, even informants who are not very good at Swedish are able to participate fully in the various socializing events at work. They understand their colleagues' humour and irony, and can also make jokes themselves. When you joke, you run the risk of being misunderstood and misinterpreted. Our informants are obviously not afraid to take this risk, which could be seen as a sign of their membership of the group. At least they seem to feel confident enough among their colleagues to dare to take the risk of making a fool of themselves.

An important purpose of the research project is to explore interaction at work in order to gain an understanding of discursive and communicative factors that have a beneficial effect on the integration of immigrants into the working environment. A sociolinguistic perspective on interaction also means of course that workmates and professional colleagues are considered to be important for the relative success of the individual immigrant. The sociocultural climate at the workplace and within the organizational units can contribute to – or indeed also impede – the immigrant's integration into the group and adoption of a social role. The two women's involvement in non-profit socializing work groups can be seen as a sign of their workplace integration. They are accepted by their fellow workers; they are also seen and allowed to take on socially relevant roles.

The individual's job identity is constructed in the interaction with fellow workers, which means that the relative success of an immigrant also depends on the sociocultural climate at the workplace and within the working group. The fact that the immigrants studied are integrated into their working groups could thus be said to show that these groups are culturally and linguistically tolerant and open to diversity. At least we can say that these groups do not seem to have impeded the integration of the foreign language users.

190

10.7 Conclusions

One aim of this chapter has been to explore what the term 'multi-lingual' entails in relation to workplace discourse. The two working environments studied, the hospital and the company, are both multi-lingual in terms of their workforce in the sense that several of their employees are multilingual and have to use their second, third or fourth language at work. In the company studied, the term 'multilin-gual' also refers to its organizational structure so that it uses English as its corporate language and the national majority language as its local workplace language. As the company operates in several coun-tries, this means that the national majority languages vary from one workplace to the other.

Another aim has been to discuss the complexity of workplace multilingualism. In order to picture this complexity, I chose three perspectives for my analysis: that of the professional group, of the linguistic-cultural community, and of the individual employees. To conclude, I would like to stress here that if we wish to understand how individual employees become – or do not become – profession-ally and socially integrated into a working group, we need to include an analysis of the organizational structure of text and talk, the use of different languages at work and the social climate within the working group. Integration into a group depends not only on the individual but also on their fellow workers and the group climate.

Notes

1. The concepts of 'code switching', 'code mixing' and 'diglossia' are discussed in Hudson (1996). See also Auer (1998) for a discussion of 'code switching in conversation'.
2. Fishman (1970) gives an early definition of the concept of 'diglossia'.
3. For overviews of the field 'interactional sociolinguistics', see Schiffrin (1994) and Tannen (2005).
4. See Erickson and Schultz (1982) and Gumperz (1982b).
5. A number of studies on workplace discourse have been carried out in New Zealand within the Wellington Language in the Workplace Project. Among the large number of publications emanating from this group, here I would like to mention: Holmes et al. (1999), Holmes (2000), Holmes and Stubbe (2003), Marra and Holmes (2004), Holmes (2005).
6. The research project has been financed by the Swedish Research Council. The pub-lications include: Andersson and Nelson (2005), Nelson and Andersson (2005), Andersson (2007), Nelson (2007), and Nelson (2008).
7. In Karlsson (2006), an ethnographic study of literacy at work is presented. The employees shadowed include a truck-driver, a nurse, a shop assistant, a 'pre-school teacher' and a building worker. A similar role of text and writing is found for the nurse in this study as in our study.

8. One of the criteria in our selection of informants was that they should have come to Sweden as adults.
9. This means that the speakers have to know how to 'frame' their utterances. A theory of frames as key to human interaction was elaborated by sociologist Erving Goffman (1974). Parallell to the notion of frame is Gumperz' 'speech activity': the goal-oriented character of an interaction, by reference to which – and only by reference to which – an utterance can be interpreted.

Section 5
Discourse in Large Business Organizations

This section analyses discourse in large organizations. The first chapter explores the complex relationship between enterprise and discourse. The sociolinguistic framework, developed for the analysis of workplace discourse, is here extended to incorporate ideas about business management and national and organizational culture. A model of communication is presented which depicts the multilayered framework of texts within large organizations. With this model as a background, results from a research project on banks and structural engineering companies in Britain, Germany and Sweden are discussed. This project comprised on-site interviews and observations, text collection and corpus construction, and analyses of texts and recorded interviews. The first part of my analysis of results concerns differences between the two sectors (banking and engineering), between organizations within one sector, and differences at national level. The second part presents an analysis of the construction of an 'organizational self' within the three banks. Drawing on data from my in-depth interviews with top-level managers, I view the issue from the perspective of those engaged in the creation of company images. I also present an analysis of the existing bank images. In the last part of the chapter I discuss how the simple sociolinguistic order found at small workplaces, cf. Chapter 4.1, is intertwined in large organizations with various levels of other orders leading to a multifaceted and multi-layered disorder. Societal frameworks at national and supranational levels influence discourse in large enterprises

The second chapter explores companies' websites from a diversity perspective, which means that I analyse the construction of an 'organizational self' from the perspective of the outsiders, i.e. the readers. My sociolinguistic framework is here expanded to include ideas about marginalization within sociology and political science. The reliance of modern companies on the internet for externally addressed information entails a complexity of a new kind while at the same time their policies and practices in relation to language and culture include or exclude reader groups. My analysis in this chapter concerns the customer-related and career-oriented websites maintained by five transnational companies. I explore these websites from a critical, sociolinguistic angle thus focusing on how the companies balance between different concerns and values: local and global, economic and social/societal. In order to grasp how companies balance between local and global concerns I analyse their language use on customer-oriented websites. The balance between economic concerns and social/societal values is studied in relation to the companies' career-oriented websites. First, I focus on the way companies present their culture and core values, i.e. on their statements about values relating to their staff and workplace policy. Secondly, I focus on the policies on workplace language by means of an analysis of the languages required in job advertisements. Thirdly, I focus on the employees featured on company career pages. The aim of this analysis is to grasp the views of companies' on the 'ideal' employee, an issue which indeed is connected to their policies on diversity and multiculturality and the way they handle their corporate social responsibility.

11 The multilayered structure of enterprise discourse: The case of banks and structural engineering firms

From a sociolinguistic viewpoint, the relationship between texts and organization is a two-way relationship. Creating texts is a part, and an important part, of an organization's work. Texts are influenced by their social context, thus reflecting the organization and its social structure, values, knowledge and culture. But texts also play a part in establishing the various social dimensions of the organization. They are not only a product of the social situation, but in their turn shape it. We could therefore distinguish the basic traits of a sociolinguistic order of discourse. Looking at authentic enterprise discourse, however, the most striking feature is its complex and multidimensional nature. The organization functions within various contextual frameworks with different structure, different values, different knowledge and different culture. The various sociolinguistic orders of discourse overlap and intertwine leading to a complex and multilayered structure of discourse.

This chapter explores the various relationships between discourse and organizations. Beginning in part 1 with a discussion of the sociolinguistic order of communication in a small, close-knit working group, when I use the local government office analysed earlier as an example, I introduce in part 2 a model of communication which depicts the multilayered framework of texts within large organizations. This model serves as a background for discussion of the results from a research project on communication within banks and structural engineering companies in Sweden, Germany and Great Britain. The project, which is presented in part 3, comprised interviews and on-site observations, text collection and corpus construction, and analyses of texts and recorded interviews. In parts 4 and 5 I discuss some of the results of this research project. In part 4 I compare discourse in banks and structural engineering companies. In part 5 I analyse the construction of an 'organizational self' within the three banks studied. Finally, in part 6 I sum up my findings on components that have an impact on enterprise discourse.

For the sake of simplicity I will frequently use the term 'text' throughout this chapter. However, one of my central presumptions is that speech and writing are intimately connected and interact not only in the production of written texts but also in moulding the social structure of the organization.

11.1 The sociolinguistic order of communication in a close-knit working group

In Chapter 10 I presented a study of text production at a small workplace with 35 employees. As this study showed, there was an obvious connection between the social and the communicative plane at this local government office. The hierarchical social structure was reflected in the organization of communication at work. Another finding was related to the close connection between 'we-feeling' and communicative patterns. In the interviews I conducted with the employees, I found obvious expressions of a group identity. The staff expressed a 'we-feeling' that distinguished the workplace group from employees in other local government offices. This group identity manifested itself in many ways. But the interesting thing is that the interviewees also made it plain that at this office they not only had the right to cultivate a distinctive style but also made full use of it.

The conclusion, I wish to stress here, is that my interviews with employees at the office showed that language is an element in the growth of the social group identity and culture. At this workplace, therefore, there was a two-way relationship between discourse and the organization, i.e. texts and discourse reflected the social organizational patterns but were also one component in the construction of the 'organizational self', in the shaping of the organization. Group membership therefore became manifest on the planes of both social and communicative content, i.e. with reference to knowledge, norms, attitudes and values in general and to language and texts in particular.

If we look more closely at any specific organization, I am sure we will find that the relationship between texts and organizations is two-way. Producing texts is a part of an organization's activities and an important one. The texts are a reflection of the organization – its social structure, its values, its knowledge, its culture – and at the same time they determine the various social dimensions of the organization. Written and spoken discourse plays a part in the organization's profile. Unconsciously, organizations and their cultures are defined by language. In many cases considerable effort is put into the task of shaping the organization. The employees, the owners, the customers and the general public are the focus of attention. An attempt is made to create a corporate culture that is conducive to creativity and cohesion. The aim is to create an image of the organization that will build up goodwill, confidence, and a good reputation, which in the long run will satisfy the needs of both owners and customers. The knowledge and attitudes that the image-builders attempt to establish are related to history, to the present and to the future. They are the foundation of the organization's culture and image, which are subsequently translated into performance, i.e. actions. The discursive/textual creation of the organization takes place collectively, in interaction between various players, both inside and outside the organization.

11.2 A model of communication in large enterprises

From this brief sketch of the sociolinguistic order of communication in a close-knit working group, I will now turn to large organizations. The main purpose of this chapter is to explore the complex and multidimensional relationship between large organizations and discourse. Looking at authentic enterprise discourse, it becomes obvious that an organization functions within various contextual frameworks with different structure, different values, different knowledge and different culture. The various sociolinguistic orders of discourse overlap and intertwine leading to a multilayered structure of enterprise discourse.

In order to understand real-life communication we must consider the interaction between different environments, the local and distant environment in particular (cf. Chapter 2). Figure 11.1 presents a model which attempts to grasp communication in authentic business organizations.

As Figure 11.1 illustrates, the social context in which business discourse is produced and interpreted can be analysed at different levels: the workplace, the organization, the local sector, the national sector, the national societal context, the sector worldwide. If, e.g., we focus the communication process in a mainly national bank, this can be analysed in terms of: the workplace (the bank office), the organization (Barclays/Deutsche Bank/Handelsbanken), the local sector (banks in Cambridge, Münster/Uppsala), the national sector (banks in Britain/Germany/Sweden), the national societal context (Britain/Germany/Sweden), which of course include other banks but also other companies and branches of international companies in the country in question, i.e. British, German and Swedish structural

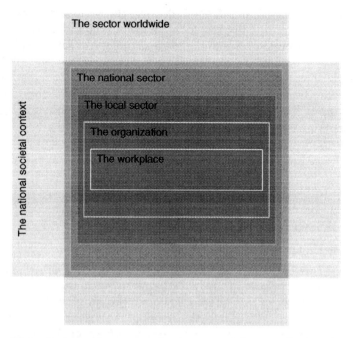

Figure 11.1 Business discourse and its contextual frameworks (Developed from Figure 3 in Gunnarsson, 2005a: 90)

engineering firms, British, German and Swedish branches of international companies etc.), the sector worldwide (banks in Europe/the rest of the world).

With this model of the complexity as a background, I will now discuss some results from two studies on enterprise discourse carried out within a large research project. I will focus on issues related to differences due to the sector, due to the organizational culture and due to the national societal framework. These issues relate, for one thing, to the more general issue of the universality or specificity of genres and text patterns. They also relate to the equally general issue of the relationship between discourse and organizational culture. To what extent are the discourse patterns within an organization unique, i.e. created within the organization in accordance with its organizational culture, and to what extent does discourse reflect more general patterns? These issues also include company images and how top-level managers view the construction of an 'organizational self'. Before I discuss the results of these studies, I will present the research project and its methodology.

198

11.3 Presentation of the research project

In the project entitled *Texts in European writing communities,* we studied communication in mainly national writing communities, such as banks and structural engineering firms, in Sweden, Germany and Britain.[1] One purpose of the project was contrastive, i.e. our aim was to compare Swedish, English and German texts of similar kind. Another purpose was sociolinguistic, i.e. to study the relationship between the (national) societal framework, the organization and discourse.

The choice of settings for the project as a whole was guided by a desire to study national text patterns and organizations which were mainly national in their orientation. Another criterion for our choice of settings was their importance in the local community. Banks and structural engineering firms inarguably play important roles in their respective local communities. For each organization we focused on one local unit. Towns of a similar character were chosen in the three countries: Cambridge, Münster and Uppsala. In banks, however, writing is largely carried out at more central levels than the local branch office, which required us to study offices at a higher level as well, in London and Coventry, in Frankfurt, and in Stockholm.

The study consisted of different phases: (1) an ethnographic study of the setting which comprised interviews and observations at place, (2) text collection and corpus construction and (3) analyses of texts and recorded interviews.

The ethnographic study involved interviews with managers and with the people involved in the various types of writing. The aim of these interviews was to obtain a picture of the insiders' view of their organization. We asked about (1) the history of the organization, (2) the structure of the organization: formal structure, external networks, internal structure, (3) the organization of writing activities, (4) the organizational culture: identity and 'we' feeling, norms, attitudes, socialization/education.

In all, 35 individuals were interviewed in banking and engineering. The interviews, which lasted between an hour and an hour and a half, have been transcribed in full and analysed.[2]

We also collected samples of the types of texts produced in the environment concerned. The texts collected were then used to form the basis of a corpus containing text types that occurred in several environments. The Uppsala contrastive corpus as a whole is large: the bank texts comprise 3,704 macro syntagms and the engineering texts 1590.[3] As will be discussed below, there was a difference as to text types between banks and structural engineering.

In carrying out most of the textual analysis, our point of departure was the multidimensional methodology which I had previously
developed for a study on scientific and popular science texts (see
Chapter 3). In this contrastive project we chose to conduct analysis
at the cognitive, pragmatic and macrothematic levels of the texts.
A separate study concerned images and image creation within the
banks.[4]

In parts 11.4 and 11.5, I discuss some results of this research project. In part 11.4, I compare discourse in banks and structural engineering companies on the basis of interview data and results of the text
analysis at pragmatic level. In part 11.5, I analyse the construction of
an 'organizational self' within the three banks studied. The methodology used for the analysis of images is presented in 11.5.3.

11.4   Discourse in European banks and structural engineering companies

In this part, I deal with discourse in European banks and structural
engineering companies. My discussion relates to our analyses of
three banks: *Barclays Bank, Deutsche Bank* and *Handelsbanken,* and
three structural engineering companies: *Mott McDonalds* in Britain,
Ingenieurbüro Werning + Dr Schmickler in Germany, and *Bjerkings
ingenjörsbyrå* in Sweden. First, I will discuss some results that reveal
differences between the two sectors (banks and engineering firms).
Secondly, I will focus on results that indicate differences between
organizations within one sector, e.g. between the three banks. Thirdly,
I will look at possible differences at national levels.

11.4.1   Differences between the two sectors

Genre repertoire. Interesting differences between the two sectors, i.e.
the three banks studied on the one hand and the three engineering
firms on the other, relate to the genre repertoires in these enterprises.

In order to describe the genre repertoire, I have chosen to distinguish
between two types of texts: *company texts* and *product texts. Company
texts* are texts that present and promote, and can be addressed both
internally and externally. This group of texts includes annual reports,
brochures, advertisements, posters, general presentations, staff magazines, messages to the staff and letters. *Product texts* are texts produced as a part of the production process, i.e. they are supplied to
the customers at different stages of the work they have ordered. This
group of texts includes tenders, project descriptions, reports, investigations, agreements, contracts, minutes and letters.

200

Our analysis of the text production at the three banks and the three structural engineering firms reveals a clear difference between what types of texts they produce within the two sectors. At the three banks the bulk of the texts are company texts while product texts are merely marginal. At the structural engineering firms the situation is the opposite: most texts are product texts, while the company texts form a clear minority.

Writing process and evaluation of writing. Our analysis of the interview data has included a description of the writing process and also of the evaluation of writing in companies within the two sectors. A clear difference was then revealed between the writing process in banks and structural engineering firms. Within the banking sector, we find internal staff who work only with writing. They are professional internal writers. This writing staff has increased since the beginning of the 1990s and is still doing so. The banks also use external writers, i.e. they 'outsource' the production of certain text material. Product texts, however, are written by non-professional internal writers, i.e. staff with financial training who are not professional writers. In the structural engineering sector we find no staff solely involved with writing, i.e. no internally employed professional writing staff. External companies are also seldom used for the production of text material. Most engineers at the structural engineering companies were involved in writing product texts. Of course they were trained engineers but as writers they were non-professionals.

There is also a striking difference with regard to the evaluation of writing within the two sectors. In the banks studied, text writing was as mentioned earlier considered very important and huge resources were devoted to writing. Professionalism was attached to writing, especially writing company texts. When new staff were recruited, writing skills were often taken into account. Internal training in writing was also offered. In the structural engineering firms studied, on the other hand, text writing was not considered important and scant resources were devoted to writing. Though most engineers were engaged in writing product texts, we did not find that professionalism was linked to writing. Writing skills were not taken into account during recruitment and there was no internal training in writing.

As this brief summary of our results has shown, there are clear differences between the two sectors as to genre repertoire, writing process and evaluation of writing and texts. The staff in banks view writing and text production as much more important than the staff in structural engineering firms do. I would like to propose three alternative explanations for this state of affairs.

201

(1) The differences found could be due to differences in company size. The banks studied are larger enterprises than the engineering firms. In support of this claim I could also mention that the largest engineering company, the British one, was more concerned about language than the other two.

(2) The difference could be due to variation between different professional groups: engineers are less aware of the role of language than economists and social scientists. Other studies have pointed to similar results. For structural engineers, discourse is also largely related to drawings, diagrams, photos, etc., a fact that might have contributed to their minor interest in the verbal elements of texts.[5]

(3) The difference could be due to a difference in business activity. Banks are in charge of our money, which makes credibility and trustworthiness important and these are established through language. I would claim, however, that this is not only important for banks but also for many other sectors of the business world.

11.4.2 Differences between organizations within one sector

In my discussion on differences between organizations within one sector, I first summarize what the interviews revealed about differences in culture and ideas within the three banks. Secondly, I present some results relating to differences between texts produced in the three banks. Finally, I discuss differences between the structural engineering companies studied. My focus will be on interview and text data related to advertising.

11.4.2.1 Organizational culture and ideas. The case of banks

From the three banks, 27 people were interviewed: 11 at *Barclays Bank,* 8 at *Deutsche Bank,* and 8 at *Handelsbanken.* In this chapter, I will summarize the interviews focusing on the following dimensions:

(1) internal structure: hierarchical structure – non-hierarchical structure;
(2) communicative structure: centralization – decentralization;
(3) attitudes to proactive communication: belief in advertising – lack of belief in advertising.

Barclays Bank. All the interviews revealed a strongly *hierarchical structure* within each branch and within the organization as a whole. A strictly pyramidal organization was depicted. The organization consists of many levels, with top-down control of all types of communication. Text production is strictly *centralized*. Texts are produced centrally in Coventry or London and sent out to branches for distribution. Instructions accompany these packages, explaining when to use certain posters or brochures, where to put them and how to display them. The uniformity of branches was stressed, as opposed to the uniqueness of the local branch emphasized at Handelsbanken (see below). Customers were viewed as groups – individuals, small businesses, large businesses. No account was taken of possible regional differences; each branch received the same material and the same instructions.

Barclays Bank stressed the importance of standardization – they had standards for all forms of writing and employees were urged to use the standard format and the standard text. The majority of the actual writing was done externally. External professionals were hired for all outgoing writing: to write standard letters, to make posters, to write advertising copy etc. Banking staff gave directives, supervised the process etc., but the actual writing, aimed at customers and the media took place outside the firm. The criterion of a good text was that it was a professional text. The interviews further revealed a *strong belief* in the importance of *advertising*, in the local and national press, on television etc. There was also a very strong belief in the importance of posters and brochures as a means of selling products.

Deutsche Bank. At Deutsche Bank the internal structure is clearly more *hierarchical* than at Handelsbanken. However, the two banks resemble each other in their belief in the idea of *decentralization*. The uniqueness of each branch was stressed, with a unique set of customers depending on the region, part of the town etc. This independence was also stressed in relation to text production and distribution.

From the interviews it also became evident that the idea of decentralization entailed more here than it did at Handelsbanken; i.e. in the Federal Republic of Germany, decentralization encompasses a political dimension as well. As was stressed several times during the interviews with managers and employees at the regional office in Münster, the head office in Frankfurt did not have any direct control over the Münster office; Münster belongs to one state (Land), Frankfurt to another.

As regards advertising, the managers and employees at Deutsche Bank expressed a stronger belief in its value than their counterparts at Handelsbanken, though they were less convinced than people at Barclays. They showed us a video which was part of a television advertising campaign but on the other hand they did not seem to attach very much importance to brochures and posters. I would say that they had a *moderate belief in advertising*.

Handelsbanken. Everyone interviewed at Handelsbanken stressed that the organization was *not hierarchical.* An idea central to this bank is that of a flat internal structure. Any member of staff can pick up the phone and contact head office, if he or she so wishes.

Another central idea underlined in the interviews was the autonomy of every branch office. The uniqueness of each branch was stressed, with a unique set of customers depending on the region, part of the town etc. Text production and distribution were also related to this idea of branch autonomy, i.e. a *decentralized structure* was depicted. Each branch office decided what texts to send out and whether it should produce them itself, buy them from the information department or engage external firms.

The majority of writing was done by banking staff, although external professional firms were engaged for the production of posters and more elaborate brochures. Writing was mainly seen as an 'in-house concern'. In the interviews, staff expressed a strong belief in networking with customers and in personal communication. They very clearly voiced a *lack of belief in advertising* in the media, mass distribution of brochures etc. They expressed a very weak belief in the commercial impact of brochures and posters. On the whole, it can be said that Handelsbanken does not believe written texts to be very important in selling its products.

As these summaries show, I discovered quite a remarkable difference in attitudes within the three banks. Handelsbanken can be described as lacking or at least having very little confidence in the value of advertising, in which it also invests relatively modest resources. Barclays Bank has a very strong belief in the value of advertising and invests a great deal. A large staff is involved in designing advertisements, posters and brochures, and these are carefully tested on groups of consumers to assess their impact. Texts, pictures and colours are selected carefully to suit specific target groups such as small companies, large companies or private individuals. In other words there is a belief in advertising and the possibility of devising advertisements that sell. Deutsche Bank is somewhere in between Handelsbanken and Barclays Bank and could be said to have a moderate belief in advertising.

11.4.2.2 Advertisement discourse in banks

As mentioned earlier, our text analysis was related to different levels. For the case of this discussion, however, I will only bring up some results based on our analyses of the pragmatic structure of the texts. In Gunnarsson (2000), I account for an analysis of the proportion of *sender markings* in bank texts (cf. Chapter 3). We went through the texts marking the existence of sender identification (either the sender's name or a pronoun) in each sentence (in fact in each macrosyntagm). In the example below, I have marked in italics the sender marking, in this case the name 'Barclays'.

(1) That's why you can turn to *Barclays* Complete Mortgage Service and be confident that it will live up to its name. Arranged for you by *Barclays* Mortgage Specialist, the service is designed to make the whole mortgage process simple to understand, convenient and affordable.

In both the quoted sentences in the example, the sender 'Barclays' is mentioned. In our analysis, we have thus counted the sentences, or rather macrosyntagms, where the sender, i.e. Barclays, Handelsbanken or Deutsche Bank, is mentioned by name or referred to explicitly by means of the pronoun 'we', 'vi', 'wir'. We then found a clear difference between the material from the three banks. In the brochures for commercial clients produced at Barclays, for instance, the sender was marked in 61 per cent of the sentences, in the brochures from Deutsche Bank in 13 per cent of the sentences, whereas the corresponding proportion in the Swedish texts is only 2 per cent.

Our text analysis at pragmatic level further focused on illocution (cf. Chapter 3). The type of illocution was identified for each sentence (macrosyntagm) in the text material, with subsequent analysis covering the following illocutionary types: informative, explicative, expressive, argumentative and directive. *Expressive illocutions* were those that contained positive judgements, criticism or expressions of enthusiasm. The example below also comes from a brochure produced by Barclays Bank. What made us classify this sentence as expressive is the formulation 'highly attractive rates' (marked with my italics in the example).

(2) We can offer you a range of mortgages at *highly attractive rates*, like the Barclays Fixed Rate Mortgages featured here.

Also here we find that there is a considerable difference between the texts from the three banks. Of the texts from Barclays Bank 34 per cent were expressive, 9 per cent of those from Deutsche Bank and 13 per cent of those from Handelsbanken.

These results from the text analysis thus point to a great difference between the three banks, especially between the British and Swedish banks. The texts from Barclays Bank contain many more sender markers and expressive illocutions than those from Handelsbanken.

What conclusions can we now draw from these results? To begin with, I would like to suggest that the attitudes to advertising revealed

205

in the interviews are reflected clearly in the texts, for instance, in how frequently the sender is marked or in the proportion of expressive illocutions. I would here like to regard higher frequency as an outcome of more aggressive marketing.

Furthermore, I would like to discuss these differences in texts and in attitudes in relationship to more fundamental differences in marketing philosophy. Barclays Bank is characterized by a traditional approach to marketing, that can be considered in the light of the ideas described for instance in Kotler (1991) and in Kotler et al. (1999). There is a strong belief in mass advertising, in market surveys, in statistics and averages, in the value of texts with mass circulation. The Swedish bank, Handelsbanken, on the other hand, is characterized by a clear service management approach where marketing is concerned, and can be considered on the basis of the ideas described for instance in Grönroos (1990). What is important is the relationship to customers: each customer is seen as unique and each product sold is also regarded as unique. From this point of view personal, oral contact is important. Long-lasting relationships and enduring networks have to be created. In these cases, therefore, the text patterns seem also to reflect more fundamental marketing concepts in the companies, concepts that have found clear expression in the interviews with those responsible for producing texts in these banks.

11.4.2.3 Advertisement discourse in structural engineering firms

It is, of course, interesting to compare the results from our analysis of banks with those from structural engineering firms. In this case it is only relevant to compare the British and Swedish firms, as the German engineering firm is forbidden to use advertisements by German legislation.

The fact that the German structural engineering firm was forbidden to advertise will of course need an explanation. As was revealed in our interviews with the people at Ingenieurbüro Werning + Dr Schmickler, there are some striking differences between the German company, on the one hand, and the British and Swedish, on the other. Legislation in Germany governs the operations of engineering firms in a way that has a direct impact on text production. Engineering firms and architectural practices in Germany are not allowed to compete with each other in the prices they charge. The duties they have to perform and the costs involved are laid down in specific state ordinances. Nor may German engineering firms advertise in the media, which also affects text production in the German companies. As the interviewees told us they would have preferred things to be different. For the purpose of

206

my analysis here, however, I need to exclude the German structural engineering company.

My discussion below, therefore, will only concern the British and Swedish structural engineering companies. On the whole, the role of advertising is less stressed in the interviews with people at the structural engineering companies than in the bank interviews. Not surprisingly the marketing ideas expressed by the interviewees were more in line with service management than with traditional marketing. There is nevertheless a clear difference between Mott McDonald, the British company, and Bjerkings ingenjörsbyrå, the Swedish company, which I would like to refer to briefly. At the British engineering firm there was a fairly strong belief in the role of advertising, at least in comparison with the Swedish engineering company studies, where the stress was solely on the role of personal meetings and contacts. These results thus point in the same direction as those from the banks.

11.4.3 Differences at national level

Though our studies within the project *Texts in European writing communities* have only comprised one bank and one structural engineering company in each country, I would like to connect the differences found in texts and in attitudes in the firms studied with national patterns. In doing so I would like to apply the descriptions of national differences offered by the Dutch sociologist Geert Hofstede. In his extensive analysis of employees in the IBM group in different countries and different continents, Hofstede (1994) came to perceive a number of culturally relevant dimensions, among them avoidance of uncertainty, collectivism versus power distance, self-assertion versus unpretentiousness or, as he also describes it, masculinity versus femininity. Where the masculine-feminine dimension is concerned, according to Hofstede's statistical analyses, Sweden, which is one of the feminine cultures, is different from Germany and the United Kingdom, which are masculine. In his view, a masculine culture, like that of the United Kingdom, rates competition and conflict highly, whereas a feminine culture, like Sweden, values equality, solidarity, avoidance of conflict and negotiation. One possible explanation of the differences in texts discussed here could therefore be that they indicate more fundamental national patterns, linked in this case to the dimension of masculinity – femininity. This dimension also offers potential explanations for several other differences between the texts in our bank corpus. In addition, the differences found between the texts from the British and Swedish engineering company could be explained by means of Hofstede's masculinity – femininity dimension.

11.5 The construction of an 'organizational self': The case of European banks

In this section I will present an analysis of work on image and images in the three banks. The aim of this study is to explore the role of discourse in constructing and maintaining a competitive and trustworthy 'organizational self' in these enterprises. My claim is that discourse is of crucial significance in an enterprise, not only for the success of the various activities it undertakes, but also for its actual survival. Good relations with customers and shareholders are important for a firm's survival. It is also very important that the employees trust the firm and share its ideas and values. Discourse further plays an essential role in the construction of the enterprise as a unique and attractive workplace that can be competitive on both the product and job markets. Texts and spoken discourse are therefore essential for the construction and maintenance of an 'organizational self', both in relation to those affiliated to the company and those outside it. It is by means of discourse that the organization disseminates a picture of its history, its visions for the future, and its current goals, policies and ideas. It is also by means of discourse that companies describe and promote their products and the jobs they can offer. In most organizations substantial effort goes into the promotion of externally and internally disseminated images.

Hofstede includes in the studies discussed earlier (cf. 11.4.3) among his layers of culture an organizational or corporate level, concerned with the way in which employees have assimilated the values and outlooks of their organization or company (1994: 19–20). According to Hofstede cultural differences manifest themselves in several ways (pp. 16–17). What is of interest here is that they also reveal themselves in the imagery connected with the company, in the form of external and internal images.

Images are related to company culture. Within the organization, positive images are part of the construction of an 'organizational self'. They depict the common values of the company. Images show the culture and its value system both to the group itself and to those outside it. In this way, they help to create and maintain the culture. Images are simply there as a natural feature of the self-representation of the corporate entity. But they can also be the subject of a conscious constructive act of will. If the corporate culture is threatened – from without or within – the creation of positive images can be vitally important to the self-esteem of the organization.

Different kinds of images exist within a company: (1) There are *internal images*, relating to the perception of a corporate identity, a corporate self. Such images appear in presentations of the company to prospective and new employees, in staff magazines, in course materials, in letters and notes to staff etc. They can also be part and parcel of the internal discourse. (2) There are *externally addressed images,* relating to the outward presentation of the corporate culture. These images appear in texts and discourse aimed at customers, owners and the general public, i.e. letters, brochures, advertisements, annual reports, press releases, general information leaflets, books about the company etc. They not only depict the company as a corporate unit, but also its relationship to the buyers' market, the stock market, the labour market and society in general. (3) There are images created outside the company. These images reflect the views of the company which are held by 'others' – by those not directly involved. Such *externally constructed images*, which are obviously not always favourable, quite often function as counter-images to the internally constructed ones, and one of the essential aims of conscious image construction within a company is to change such negative, externally created images. Unfavourable images are, of course, also created and circulated within the company – and, clearly, externally created images can also be favourable.

In the following, I shall focus on the images created and transmitted in the three banks included in our project. Though the interviews took place in 1993–1994, i.e. before the internet explosion, they reveal views on business discourse that also relate to modern businesses. What makes my study unique is the combination of in-depth interviews with top-level managers and analysis of a broad range of discourse. The question is not only how the images disseminated within the banks vary, but also why.

11.5.1   The insiders' views on the construction of an 'organizational self'

An interesting question to pose in relation to company images is how the insiders view images and how important they consider work with images to be. I will therefore present some data from my in-depth interviews with top level managers at the three banks. My interviews included the very top level people who were – and felt they were – responsible for the creation and maintenance of a positive 'organizational self' within their respective bank.

Of course, company images are not a new phenomenon. Companies have always been associated with imagery. Nor is there anything new about the management of a company being aware of the importance of images for their company's success and survival, or seeking to create a positive picture of that company.

209

What is fairly new, however, is the emphasis placed on internal images, the effort invested in internal marketing, which involves a purposeful endeavour to create a positive company spirit and a creative company culture. Another new development is the professionalization of image creation, which is of course in turn connected with the greater effort being invested in this area by companies. Within larger enterprises we now find special posts and special units whose functions include developing and nurturing the internal and external images of the companies concerned.

At the time of my investigation of bank discourse, all three banks had a separate body, attached to their central office, in charge of information within the organization and to the outside world. In all cases, however, this body was fairly new as an independent unit, having been established in the early 1990s and having expanded steadily since then.

In all three banks, then, information and image development were considered very important, and the head of the information sector was one of the main posts in the organization. An interesting question is of course why information and image had only recently come to be regarded as important by the banks.

One explanation relates to modern ideas about management, which emphasize the importance of a corporate spirit or culture. The 'excellence' of the organization is contained in the common ways in which its members have learned to think, feel and act (cf. Peters and Waterman, 1982).

Another explanation, stressed by many of those we interviewed, is the increasing significance of relations with the media. Mr Hansson,[6] responsible for press releases at Handelsbanken, talked about a turning point around the beginning of the 1990s, from which date the Swedish bank had begun to play a more active role *vis-à-vis* the media. At the beginning of the 1990s earlier 'very modest' relations with the media were replaced by a proactive approach. Now it was the bank itself which took the initiative and arranged press conferences. All three banks have established a post with responsibility for contact with the press. The individuals holding these posts write or supervise the writing of press releases, arrange press conferences and prepare material for them.

In the three banks, I interviewed, as mentioned earlier, 27 people. For my discussion of image construction in this chapter, however, I shall mainly concentrate on three of these interviews: one with Mr Brown, head of the information department at Barclays Bank; one with Mr Drauber, head of the press department and speech writer for members of the board of Deutsche Bank and one with Mr Hansson, in charge of press relations at Handelsbanken.

What became evident from these and several other interviews was the interest of management in the morale and identity of employees. Internal image construction was stressed very frequently. At Barclays, Mr Brown, head of the information department, showed us a leaflet setting out *The Barclays Values*, which was intended for all employees. According to Mr Brown, the company had problems with its image and its common value system: 'And everybody knew ten years ago what we stood for, and now we are confused.' An economic crisis, resulting among other things in a lot of staff redundancies had led to a loss of the old Barclays spirit. Together with the other managerial staff, therefore, Mr Brown had produced a document describing a set of common values, which were now to be circulated throughout the Group. Everyone was to have a copy of this document – as Brown himself put it: 'Chairman to the lavatory cleaner. Everyone. Or lavatory cleaner to the chairman, if you want.' The idea behind establishing these values was 'partially to raise the morale and the self-belief' of the staff. This type of activity, he said, related to 'corporate identity, the visual identity, especially, of the Group, as distinct from the high street bank'.

Naturally a very important aspect of image construction relates to the external image of the company. Mr Brown sees his role as being 'to manage the reputation of the Group', and he comes back to this expression several times. He distinguishes three audiences: (1) stakeholders in Barclays, in particular smaller private shareholders, (2) customers and (3) lobby groups and the media.

At Deutsche Bank, four people are in charge of external contacts. One of them, Mr Drauber, also writes speeches for the head of Deutsche Bank and for other members of the board. His task, as he explains it, is 'to help the bank speak with one language'. He also writes articles for journals etc. which are published in the name of board members. The addressees are of course shareholders and customers, but also the general public.

The fact that banks also have a more general societal role to play is stressed in several interviews. The state, authorities, politicians and the general public are relevant interest groups for a bank, and much of the effort devoted to external image creation can be related to this societal role. Deutsche Bank sponsors concerts, Handelsbanken sports events. All the banks sponsor research, and publish reports on this research which show their name.

The public interest in banks also has another aspect. The banks themselves have been the subject of research. Researchers have studied Swedish banks, including Handelsbanken, and a volume has been published reporting on these studies. German banks have also been the subject of independent research and in the case of Deutsche Bank these independent studies have been of importance in freeing them of too blameworthy a role during the Nazi era. And interestingly enough, though perhaps not surprisingly, we were given a large volume summarizing these studies on our very first visit to Deutsche Bank. For the reputation of the bank of today, the image of the past is very important.

A bank is of course particularly vulnerable to incidents of fraud and other events that might damage their credibility and trustworthiness. At Deutsche Bank, Mr Drauber talked about a current case involving one of the major property developers in Germany, to whom the bank had lent a very large sum of money. The man had gone bankrupt and fled to Florida, and now Deutsche Bank was being blamed for this affair by the Federal Republic, which was seeking to extradite him. And clearly the press was interested in the affair. What I found most interesting in Drauber's presentation of this case and his own actions in conjunction with it was his sincere concern for the reactions of the bank's employees. As he put it, his efforts to save the reputation of the bank were directed not only towards the press, but also towards the staff. It was very important, he stressed, to ensure that employees were fully informed and that they were given the bank's picture of the affair, and not that of the press. Mr Drauber took the threat to internal self-esteem very seriously. It was important to reassure the bank staff themselves.

What we see here, then, is that banks consider images important. Economic crises, diminishing credibility, scandals etc. lead to intensified and more conscious attention to external and internal images. All these situations pose a threat to the positive image of a bank's value system, to the image which its management wishes to spread within the company and to people outside it. Management consciously seeks to create positive images of the bank and to change existing negative images. Self-evidently, image creation and also image diffusion is a collective and a multifaceted undertaking. The interviewees talk about collaboration on image creation, about how the various publications are a result of chains of spoken and written events involving participants belonging to different groupings. They also talk about the varied media for image dissemination, i.e. publications of different kinds, oral presentations, television, radio, videos etc.

11.5.3   A model of image construction within banks

As a summary of what my interview data revealed, I will present a model of image construction within banks (Figure 11.2). It is important

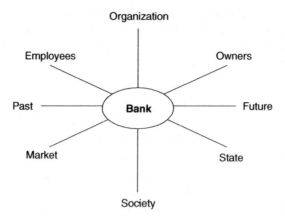

Figure 11.2 *Banks and their relationships (Figure 3 in Gunnarsson, 2000: 3)*

for a bank to take care of its relationship to its past as well as to its present and future. It is important to preserve its internal structure and organization as such, i.e. the bank's relationships to its employees and owners. To survive a bank also needs to take care of its external relationships, both with the market, customers and other banks and with the state and various authorities. Furthermore, banks have to look after their relationship to the undefined public, to society. These relationships could be said to be the target of conscious image construction. They are also the targets of more unconscious efforts to create, through discourse, an organizational culture.

11.5.4 Images of the three banks

In this section of the chapter, I will give a brief summary of my analysis of bank image.[7] This analysis was based on both oral discourse, the taped interviews, and written texts, e.g. general presentations of the company, annual reports and brochures. As shown below, I analysed spoken and written discourse intended for different audiences: researchers (ourselves), employees, customers, owners and the general public.

Discourse analysed	*Intended audience*
Interview data	Researchers
General presentations	New/prospective employees
Annual reports	Owners, employees, public
Brochures	Customers

My analysis concentrated on the images of the banks which they conveyed to us, i.e. on what the individuals interviewed told us about their companies and what was stated in the texts they gave us. The following variables were studied:

Variables analysed

content	what types of values are depicted in *positive* and *negative* images
homogeneity	one image or several images
consistency	the same image over the years or different images
commonality	the diffusion of the image(s) to employees
explicitness	if and how the images are displayed/ made visible

The following is a brief summary of the variation observed between the images of the three banks studied. My purpose is to depict the special character of each bank's image, to capture the differences rather than the common ground. I will not therefore deal with shared, self-evident features of the images presented in the written documents but concentrate instead on the more differentiating features. In the interviews I also explicitly asked about the uniqueness of each bank. 'What is special about Barclays Bank?', 'How would you describe Barclays Bank to a person who knew nothing about the bank?', 'What is special about working at Barclays?' etc.

Let us first look at the images which existed within Handelsbanken at the time of this study. The image of Handelsbanken is a success image, based on the belief that this bank is better than other Swedish banks. This is based on its higher level of profitability, due to an organizational structure based on decentralization and autonomy which makes Handelsbanken unique in comparison with other banks. The bank's success is due to management ideas launched by its chairman in the 1970s. The end result of this restructuring is seen every year, as is stated in the introduction to the chairman's statement in the 1993 annual report, here quoted from the English version of the report (p. 4):

> This result means that for the twenty-second year running we have achieved our goal – better return on equity than the average for the other Swedish listed commercial banks.

This success image was at the time of the study homogeneous, consistent, common and explicit.

214

The images of Deutsche Bank are also success images. In this case the explanation given by the chairman in the annual report stresses the competitive nature of Deutsche Bank, illustrated here by quotations from the English version of the 1994 report (pp. 8 and 9):

> Deutsche Bank, as a universal bank, confronts the competition in Europe and throughout the world wherever there are opportunities to advance its development on a sound basis . . .
>
> Willingness to face competition is a key part of Deutsche Bank's self-perception.

We found the imagery of Deutsche Bank to be fairly homogeneous, consistent, common and explicit.

The image of Barclays, in contrast to those of the other two banks, is far from a success image. The tone of the chairman's statement in the annual report for 1993 is rather low-key, as the following quotations illustrate (pp. 3 and 5):

> Barclays has had a challenging year in 1993.
>
> We know that we have some way to go before we meet our own aspirations.
>
> Meeting changing demand is a carefully-judged process. The process continued in 1993 and it is against this background that our results are to be seen.
>
> This has been accompanied by a reduction in the number of branches in the United Kingdom.

As our analysis of the interviews with the people at this bank showed, there did not at the time exist any homogeneous Barclays image, nor any consistent and common image. On the whole the Barclays images at the time – for there were several conflicting ones – were not very explicit. The conclusion we can draw from this is that non-success images are less clear and explicit than success images. However, as I mentioned earlier, Barclays were aware of their lack of positive images and were consciously working on building up a more favourable image when we interviewed them.

11.5.5 Differences at national level

As this study of image creation and images within banks show, there are clear differences between the three banks in terms of content, homogeneity, consistency, commonality and explicitness of their images. The question of interest here is therefore to what extent the images created by the banks can be said to reflect organization-specific ideas and to what extent they reflect more general patterns.

The difference between Barclays and the other two banks is perhaps mainly a story of economic crisis versus relative economic success, a reflection of its relationship to the national and global economy. Indeed, banks, like all businesses, are dependent on the various societal frameworks, in particular on the technical-economical framework, and economic crisis and success vary from time to time. This does not, however, explain the difference in imagery between Handelsbanken and Deutsche Bank, which both seem to conceive of themselves as having been successful. It is necessary to look for other explanations.

If we first consider the images from the point of view of the management ideas they express, we find that Handelsbanken has built its organizational self on ideas about strong *decentralization* and *autonomy*. The explanation given by the bank for its success is that its organizational ideas are better than those generally held by banks. When I interviewed the head of the information department at Handelsbanken, he began by explaining, in quite theoretical terms, the management ideas of Handelsbanken before the reforms in the 1970s, and those held by the bank since then. What I would stress here is that the image which Handelsbanken repeatedly gives of its organizational self is constructed from the viewpoint of its bank management ideas. And as we have seen, this image is widespread and homogeneous, resting as it does on an explicit theoretical basis.

The image which Deutsche Bank conveys of itself, on the other hand, is that of an old, large, international and competitive bank. What I find interesting here is the stress on competition in the annual report. I quoted two passages, but there are many more references to competition ('Wettbewerb'). In the eyes of its shareholders, customers and employees, Deutsche Bank wishes to be seen as a bank which is rising to the challenge of international competition. This feature makes the German bank's annual report quite different from that of Handelsbanken, which presents the fact that Handelsbanken is opening new offices in the other Nordic countries in far less competitive terms. Turning again to Hofstede (1994) and the distinction he makes between masculine and feminine cultures, I would argue that the difference found between the images of the German and Swedish banks could also be seen as revealing a variation in terms of national culture. The images depicting the German bank as competitive could be seen as a sign of masculine cultural thinking, while the Swedish image, in playing down the acquisition of other Nordic banks, could be seen as a sign of feminine cultural thinking.

My conclusion, therefore, is that in order to understand image construction in banks, we must bear in mind that images are created in a context, e.g. in an existing company governed by ideas and theories

216

about what a company is and how it should be managed. The organization, for its part, exists within a national culture, which in turn exerts
an indirect influence on the creation of bank images.

11.6 Conclusions

This chapter has explored the role of discourse for the creation of an
enterprise as a unique and attractive entity. Enterprises are steered
by ideas, and texts and spoken discourse are part of the dissemination of those ideas, internally and externally. Discourse is a means
for enterprises to reach different markets, at the same time as they
have to adapt to/comply with regulations and conventions that exist at
national and international levels in order to survive.

My main argument in this chapter has been that in order to understand enterprise discourse we must consider its complexity. We must
analyse the sociolinguistic order of the organization both at a local
and distant level and so explore the multilayered structure of enterprise discourse. The simple sociolinguistic order with its correspondence between the *social* and *communicative planes* that we may find
within a close-knit working group is intertwined with various levels
of other orders in large organizations.

In this study, I discussed a study on three banks and three engineering companies. One finding of interest is the homogeneity within each
of the six studied enterprises. The various analyses of texts and interview data from the three banks, and also from the structural engineering firms, gave us a fairly homogeneous picture of each company.

To a certain extent this homogeneity could be related to ideas steer-
ing the companies. My analyses of bank discourse, for instance, have
shown that there is a considerable difference between the three banks
as to marketing ideas. Barclays follows traditional marketing ideas,
as they are described for instance in Kotler (1991). Key words for this
type of marketing are: product, price, distribution, promotion, product
marketing, mass consumption, testing and statistics. Handelsbanken,
on the other hand, follows service management marketing ideas, as
described for instance in Grönroos (1990). Networks and the relationship to the individual customers are considered important. Each customer is viewed as unique as is each product. There is little or no
belief in advertising, and no belief in statistics and testing. What is
considered important within service management is personal contact
and spoken discourse.

To fully understand enterprise discourse we must also consider the
role of the *sector*. Though in many respects each enterprise is unique,
enterprises within one sector also have a great deal in common – due

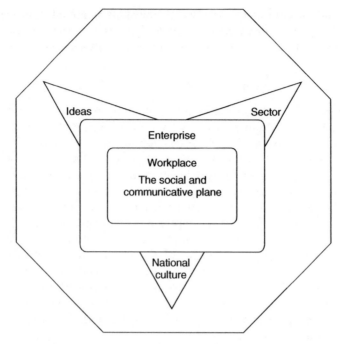

Figure 11.3 *The multilayered structure of enterprise discourse (Figure 5 in Gunnarsson, 2005a: 106)*

to similar professional training, types of activities, relationship to language etc. The enterprise is also part of a wider sectoral network, not infrequently with well-established national and international discourse traditions.

Every enterprise also operates within various societal frameworks: at local, national and international levels. This means that its discourse might be restricted in various ways by legislation and linguistic-cultural patterns. It also means that its discourse is dependent on the technical-economical framework. Internal and external images are created in an existing enterprise governed by ideas and theories about what an enterprise is and how it should be managed. The organization, for its part, exists within larger contextual frameworks, which in turn exert an indirect influence on the creation of images.

Figure 11.3 contains a model with the components that have an impact on enterprise discourse.

Though the degree of importance of the national culture and the international community might vary from one enterprise to the other, the multilayered structure can be assumed to be fairly similar.

218

In national as well as international enterprises, the simple sociolinguistic order of individuals forming a close-knit group is intertwined with various levels of other orders leading to a multifaceted and multilayered disorder.

Notes

1. The research project was carried out at Uppsala University. It involved a team consisting of myself as director, Bo Andersson, Ingegerd Bäcklund, Anna Levin, Ulf Norberg, Lena Norling and Marie Sörlin. The project, which was financed by the Bank of Sweden Tercentenary Foundation, also studied university occupational medicine departments and university departments of history in the three countries. For a detailed presentation of the Uppsala contrastive corpus, see Levin (1997).
2. Sörlin (2000) gives a detailed presentation of the interviews carried out at the banks and structural engineering companies.
3. The unit for text analyses is the macrosyntagm (approximately T-unit), i.e. the main clause and its subordinate clauses.
4. Levin (1997) gives a detailed presentation of the results of the cognitive, pragmatic and macrothematic analysis. An analysis of discourse markers is presented in Bäcklund (1998). Among my own publications from this project I wish to mention Gunnarsson (2000, 2004a, 2004b, 2005a).
5. See also Karlsson (2007).
6. All the interviewee names used here are invented.
7. See Gunnarsson (2005c).

12 Business discourse in the globalized economy: A diversity perspective on company websites

The material for the studies of banks and structural engineering companies discussed in the previous chapter was collected in 1993 and 1994, i.e. in the 'paper era'. As these companies were also mainly national at the time, the texts we analysed – brochures, staff magazines, letters, etc. – were written in the local majority language, English in the enterprises in Britain, German in the ones in Germany and Swedish in the ones in Sweden. What has happened within large enterprises since then is a change from paper as the main medium for internal and external communication to the use of the internet and other computer mediated media. The modern business enterprise uses the internet for a variety of purposes. For large transnational companies, which not only sell their products to customers all over the world but also have branches with employees in different parts of world, the reliance on the internet, has also meant that issues related to language choice and cultural diversity have become crucial and visible.

In this chapter I discuss business discourse in the 'internet era' on the basis of analyses of company websites. In the modern technologized business world, company websites have come to be important tools for rendering the image of a company in relation to different markets. It is by means of its website that a company reaches out to its stakeholders, customers and new employees. Its website plays an important role in the construction of an attractive and trustworthy image of the company. It provides factual information about the company's products and financial results as well as presentations of its goals and values. Most transnational companies endorse values like *diversity, multiculturalism* and *multilingualism,* and to a large extent they rely on their websites to disseminate this adherence to these ethical values. Globally, we find an increased awareness of the ethical dimension of business life, as is shown for instance in the widespread use of a concept like Corporate Social Responsibility, CSR, among business enterprises.[1]

220

My aim in the analyses in this chapter is therefore to explore company websites from a diversity perspective. My investigation will concern texts produced in large, international enterprises. The purpose is to analyse the interface of the organizations with the outside world where the focus is on the way the companies textually create a balance (1) between global and local concerns and (2) between economic concerns and social/societal values. The declared policies and practices of companies in relation to language and culture will be analysed. The material studied consists of texts intended for customers and for prospective employees.

The discourse of large business organizations in the global economy will be explored from a critical, sociolinguistic angle. The societal frameworks, which will be touched upon in the concluding section, are related to issues of language dominance and domain loss (cf. Chapter 6), as well as to issues of social discrimination and marginalization. Within sociology and political science, we find a number of studies on the situation of immigrants in working life which are of relevance for this investigation of language and cultural policy and the practices of large companies (cf. Chapter 10).

The reliance of modern companies on the internet for externally addressed information does indeed entail a complexity of a new kind. Texts on websites necessitate a new type of writing and reading and also a new and challenging way of handling the complex interweave of internet texts.[2]

12.1 The construction of an 'organizational self' on the internet

The need for an enterprise to create positive images of its 'organizational self' and of its culture is nothing new. Company images are not a new phenomenon, nor is there anything new about the management of a company being aware of the importance of images for their company's success and survival. What is fairly new, however, is the use of the internet to disseminate both internal and external images. Products and new jobs are marketed on company websites, emails are replacing letters on paper and internet and intranet texts are replacing printed staff magazines. Computer mediated texts are thus, to a large extent, replacing texts on paper for both external and internal purposes.

One important difference between texts on a company's website and documents on paper is their accessibility. When a company places a text on its website, it has to count on a multiple readership. Global accessibility is a reality for texts on websites. The specified reader of the paper document is replaced by a potential multiple readership: shareholders, journalists, politicians, customers, staff and prospective employees in countries all over the world can open the company website.

Although in theory a company can count on a multiple readership for the texts on its website, it does not mean that the actual number of readers is growing nor that the number of individuals who feel directly addressed by the texts is increasing. The language used on a sub-page includes or excludes reader groups, as does the cultural perspective and focus of the text itself.

One consequence of the increased reliance on the internet is that company policies on linguistic and cultural issues become salient and visible for different reader groups. From a critical, sociolinguistic viewpoint, the company's textual practices on its websites reveal, among other things, its interpretation of the concept of *diversity* – a key term in the modern business world. The languages used on the company's customer-oriented pages reveal which reader groups they wish to sell their products to as well as which reader groups they do not bother to approach. Are the English speaking élite among the intended readers? Do the majority language speakers in a country belong to the intended readers? Are immigrants and other minority language speakers in a country also addressed in a language they fully understand?

The textual practices on a company's career-oriented pages can also be considered from a diversity perspective. How does the company present its culture and core values? Which policy does the company seem to have in relation to workplace language? Which groups of employees are placed in the forefront and pictured as successful? Which groups of employees are marginalized, i.e. not mentioned at all on the career-oriented pages?

The purpose of this chapter is to analyse company texts intended for different reader groups from a diversity perspective. In a globalized business world, organizations have to balance between *local and global concerns* as well as between *economic concerns and social-societal values* in order to be competitive and trustworthy. From a critical, sociolinguistic perspective, it is therefore interesting to see how these balances are textually transmitted on websites intended for customers and prospective employees.

12.2 The balance between local and global concerns

The first part of my investigation of company websites concerns the balance between local and global concerns as this is revealed by the language practices on customer-oriented websites.

In the modern technological business world, the internet has come to play an important role as a means of reaching out to prospective customers with information about a company's products. For large, international companies the goal can be assumed to be to make contact with as many customers as possible throughout the world. In order to explore which readers are viewed as main target groups by large companies I made a study of the language practices of the websites maintained by five transnational companies: ABB, AstraZeneca, Electrolux, Ericsson and Scania.[3] All these companies claim to be world leaders in their fields: ABB is a leader in power and automation technologies that enable utility and industry customers to improve performance while reducing environmental impacts. AstraZeneca is one of the world's leading pharmaceutical companies, Electrolux is the world's largest producer of appliances and equipment for kitchen, cleaning and outdoor use, Ericsson is the biggest supplier of mobile systems in the world and supports all major standards for wireless communication, and Scania is one of the world's leading manufacturers of heavy trucks and buses.

In this study,[4] I focused on the customer-oriented websites, i.e. the companies' '.com' sites. All the companies have a *.com* site in English, functioning as a start page. All five companies also offer the option of selecting a country on the start page. The number of country links varies among the five companies, which of course reflects the global reach of each group: ABB has 112 country links on its webpage, AstraZeneca 105, Electrolux 67, Ericsson 111 and Scania 39 links. My interest here relates to the language practices of the country websites. In which language(s) do the five companies present themselves and their products to customers in different regions of the world. I looked at nine of the country links, namely those for Sweden, Finland, Norway, Germany, Switzerland, France, Spain, Brazil and Japan.

One of the findings of this analysis is that all five companies use the main language of the country to address customers, e.g. Norwegian on the website for Norway, Portuguese on the website for Brazil and German on the site for Germany. Nevertheless, there is a noteworthy difference between companies which address their customers solely in the main local language, and those that use both that language and English. There is also a difference among the companies that offer language options for countries with several official languages, e.g. Finnish and Swedish in Finland, and German, French, Italian and Rhaeto-Romance in Switzerland. However, only one of the companies, Scania, offers an option between Finnish and Swedish for bilingual Finland. Three of the companies, namely Scania, Electrolux and Astra Zeneca, have the option of German or French for Switzerland, while no option is given for the other two languages (Italian and Rhaeto-Romance) used in Switzerland.

On the country websites of Ericsson we find sub-pages in English on all websites. On the ABB websites the main national language is used, but for five countries, namely Sweden, Finland, Switzerland, Spain and Brazil, there is a change language button with English as a second option. On the country websites of Astra Zeneca, Electrolux and Scania, on the other hand, we find only the national language(s). On two of Scania's sites there is a change language button between two national languages, and on one of the Electrolux and AstraZeneca sites there is a similar button.

None of the companies, however, give any information in any immigrant language. As we know, there are large groups in many of these countries, whose mother tongue differs from the main national language. If we take Sweden as an example of the current language situation, statistics show that 11 per cent of the Swedish population and 22 per cent of the workforce (persons aged between 18 and 64) were not born in Sweden.[5] This percentage might be even greater for other countries.

In theory the internet offers global accessibility. In order to reach out to different reader groups, however, companies have to consider regional variation. The language used on a sub-page includes or excludes reader groups as does the cultural perspective chosen for the text. The balance between local and global concerns is therefore related to policy and practice on linguistic and cultural matters. For the five companies studied, however, accessibility seems to be reserved for those prospective customers who either speak the main language of the country or have a mastery of English. Claims by companies to be global and international and to respect the value of diversity do not encompass any interest in the mother tongues of minorities within the different countries.

12.3 The balance between economic concerns and social/societal values

In this part of the chapter, I discuss an investigation of company websites which concerns the textually transmitted balance between economic concerns and social/societal values. This study will analyse the career-oriented websites of the five transnational companies focused on above from a critical, sociolinguistic angle, and sociological studies of marginalization and integration[6] will be drawn upon in the discussion. I will here explore the diversity issue in relation to linguistic and cultural policy and practices. My claim is that from the viewpoint of immigrants' integration into working life the existence – or lack – of multilingualism and multiculturalism in the declared policy and explicit practice of the organization in which they are employed becomes a matter of visibility or marginalization. A relevant question is therefore to what extent a company's website reflects the varied linguistic and cultural backgrounds of its employees. Another question relates to the declared ideology of the company, i.e. to what extent the explicit policy of the company reflects the background of its employees.

The analysis of company websites, which was carried out in June 2006, focused on three types of texts: company presentations (12.3.1), job advertisements (12.3.2) and featured employees (12.3.3).

12.3.1 Company presentations on career-oriented web pages

In order to grasp how the five companies present their workplace and staff policies to future employees, I analysed what the companies claim are their core values on their websites, which for all five companies have statements about values relating to their staff and workplace policies.

ABB has a text entitled 'ABB's Diversity & Inclusion statement', which presents the image they wish to give the reader about the balance they have chosen between economic concerns and societal values. The following quotation is taken from a sub-page on their website:

> *ABB's Diversity & Inclusion statement*
>
> ABB recognizes that a diverse and talented workforce is a key competitive advantage. As a truly global company, our business success reflects the quality and skill of our people. We believe that the wide array of perspectives that results from a diversity and inclusion focus promotes innovation and business success.
>
> At ABB, diversity means difference – differences that make each of us unique. This includes tangible differences such as age, gender, ethnicity, physical disability and appearance as well as underlying differences such as beliefs, ways of thinking and acting.
>
> Inclusion means understanding, valuing and respecting workplace diversity, so that no employee is excluded from the workplace nor the opportunity to develop skills and talents consistent with our values and business objectives.

ABB strongly stresses 'diversity'. It also emphasizes 'inclusion', and points out that diversity 'includes tangible differences such as age, gender, ethnicity, physical disability and appearance as well as underlying differences such as beliefs, ways of thinking and acting'. At the same time they picture economic concerns, such as 'competitive', 'innovation', 'business success' and 'global'.

225

Also AstraZeneca stresses 'diversity' on its website. They express the balance between economic and societal concerns in the following way, thus also combining 'competitiveness and performance' with 'respect for the individual and diversity'.

> Along with our commitment to competitiveness and performance, we continue to be led by our core values to achieve sustainable success
> – Integrity and high ethical standards
> – Respect for the individual and diversity
> – Openness, honesty, trust and support for each other
> – Leadership by example at all levels

On Electrolux's website, the societal values are less explicit. Electrolux has a sub-page entitled 'Mobility', where the company stresses that it 'strongly encourage[s] mobility between countries', which among other things strengthens the 'diversity of our people'. Electrolux thus combines 'diversity' with 'mobility':

> As a highly international company, we strongly encourage mobility between countries, business sectors and functions, as it strengthens the internationalism, professionalism and diversity of our people – and adds to our competitive strength.

Ericsson's site is in English, and here we find a description of 'Our ways of working'. The word 'diversity' is not mentioned on this page. Instead we can read that Ericsson has 'employees in 140 countries'. The term 'core values' appears in the following sentence: 'Our vision, core values and guiding principles inspire behaviours that help us grow as people while we grow our company.'

On Scania's website,[7] we find the following text:

Scania's core values

Our core values shall be instilled in all work within Scania:

- Customer first
- Respect for the individual
- Quality

The core values are given a more elaborated presentation on the sub-page 'About the Scania Group'. 'Respect for the individual' is there described in a way which makes it clear that this respect is related to economic concerns, e.g. 'efficiency' but also 'job satisfaction':

Respect for the individual

Respect for the individual is built by recognising and using all employees' knowledge, experience and attitude of continuously seeking to improve their work. New ideas and inspiration are born out of day-to-day operations, where Scania's employees develop their skills. This helps us ensure higher quality, efficiency and greater job satisfaction.

To sum up, societal values, e.g. 'diversity', is explicitly stressed on the websites of ABB (several times), AstraZeneca and Electrolux, as is the importance of 'competitiveness'. Ericsson focuses on the global character of the company: 'employees in 140 countries', 'behaviours that help us grow as people', and Scania combines 'respect for the individual' with 'efficiency' and 'job satisfaction'.

12.3.2   Job advertisements on company websites

The second part of this study focused on company policies on workplace language. To obtain a picture of what workplace practices the companies wished to promote, i.e. what kind of people they wished to employ, I analysed the career-oriented web pages. I limited my study to advertisements for jobs in Sweden, and therefore turned to www.abb.se, www.astraZeneca.se etc., in other words, to the *.se* pages of the five transnational companies (*.se* stands for Sweden).

For each job advertisement, I noted (1) the language of the advertisement, (2) what languages were explicitly mentioned in it as qualifications for employment: Swedish, English or any other language(s), (3) whether 'communication', 'communication skills', 'clear manner of presentation' etc. were mentioned instead of individual languages and (4) if there was *no* mention of qualifications in terms of language and communication. Table 12.1 summarizes my results. For each company, the first line refers to all advertisements posted (bold), the second to those in Swedish (italics) and the third to advertisements in English.

This analysis of company websites took place in June 2006. I included all the advertisements for jobs in Sweden that were posted on the internet at that time. In all, my study included 100 advertisements: 27 were for jobs at ABB, 23 for jobs at Astra Zeneca, 15 for jobs at Electrolux, 12 for jobs at Ericsson and 23 for jobs at Scania.

As we can see from Table 12.1, 63 of the 100 advertisements forming the corpus for this part of the study are written in Swedish, 32 in English and 5 in both Swedish and English. If these figures are broken down by company, we find that all 12 advertisements for Ericsson are in English, while all 23 for Scania are in Swedish. ABB's adverts, too, are mainly in Swedish, that is to say, 93 per cent (25/27) of them. AstraZeneca has roughly similar proportions of Swedish and English advertisements: 43 per cent in Swedish only and 57 per cent in English only. Electrolux also uses both languages to advertise jobs at Swedish workplaces. In fact, there are five advertisements that mix

227

Table 12.1 *Job advertisements on the internet explicitly mentioning languages or communication skills*

Company	No. of ads	Explicit mention of languages or communication skills				
		Swe	Eng	Other	Comm. skills	None
ABB	**27**	**7**	**21**	**7**	**1**	**5**
In Swedish	*25*	*6*	*19*	*6*	*1*	*5*
In English	2	1	2	1	–	–
AstraZeneca	**23**	**7**	**13**	**0**	**3**	**5**
In Swedish	*10*	*6*	*9*	*–*	*–*	*1*
In English	13	1	4	–	3	4
Electrolux	**15**	**12**	**15**	**0**	**0**	**0**
In Swedish	*5*	*5*	*5*	*–*	*–*	*–*
In English	5	3	5	–	–	–
In Swe + Eng	5	4	5	–	–	–
Ericsson	**12**	**6**	**12**	**2**	**0**	**0**
In Swedish	*–*	*–*	*–*	*–*	*–*	*–*
In English	12	6	12	12	–	–
Scania	**23**	**2**	**9**	**1**	**3**	**10**
In Swedish	*23*	*2*	*9*	*1*	*3*	*10*
In English	–	–	–	–	–	–
Total	**100**	**34**	**70**	**10**	**7**	**20**
In Swedish	*63*	*19*	*42*	*7*	*4*	*16*
In English	32	11	23	3	3	4
In Swe + Eng	5	4	5	–	–	–

Note: All advertisements posted (bold), advertisements in Swedish (italics). Swe – Swedish, Eng – English, Other– Other languages, Comm. skills – communication skills, None – no mention of language or communication

Swedish and English, i.e. some parts of the text are in Swedish and some in English.

If we look at which languages are stated as qualifications for the jobs, seven advertisements mention 'communication skills' or the like but no language, and 20 mention neither a language nor communication skills.

Figure 12.1 places the five companies on three scales on the basis of the languages explicitly mentioned as qualifications for the jobs advertised: English, Swedish or Other languages. Placed at the top of each column are the companies where all the advertisements mention the language in question and at the bottom those where none of the adverts mention it.

As Figure 12.1 shows, English is mentioned in all of Ericsson's and Electrolux's advertisements, while the proportion for ABB is 80 per cent (21/27), for AstraZeneca 60 per cent (13/23) and for Scania 40 per cent (9/23).

		English	Swedish	Other languages
All ads	100%	Ericsson, Electrolux		
	90%			
	80%	ABB	Electrolux	
	70%			
	60%	AstraZeneca		
	50%		Ericsson	
	40%	Scania		
	30%		AstraZeneca, ABB	ABB
	20%			Ericsson
	10%		Scania	
	4%			Scania
No ads	0%			AstraZeneca, Electrolux

Figure 12.1 *Company and language mentioned as a qualification for the job*

Swedish is also stipulated as a qualification for employment in many of the adverts: in 80 per cent (12/15) of those posted by Electrolux, in 50 per cent (6/12) of Ericsson's, in 26 per cent (7/27) of ABB's, in 30 per cent (7/23) of AstraZeneca's, and in 10 per cent (2/23) of those posted by Scania. Of course the language of the advertisement might be relevant to whether Swedish is mentioned as a job qualification. As all of Scania's advertisements are in Swedish, and all of Ericsson's in English, these two companies are not relevant in such a comparison. Looking at the other three companies, however, we find that Swedish is mentioned less in the advertisements in English. Of the five Electrolux adverts written in English only three mention Swedish as a qualification for the job, and of the two ABB ads in English only one mentions Swedish. The biggest difference is found for AstraZeneca, where only 1 of the 13 advertisements in English (8 per cent) mentions Swedish.

From Table 12.1 and Figure 12.1 we can also get a picture of the interest of the companies in other languages. On the whole we can conclude that languages other than English and Swedish are required to a very limited extent. Here ABB is an exception, requiring other languages for 26 per cent of the jobs advertised (7/27),

229

while only 17 per cent (2/12) of the Ericsson jobs and 4 per cent (1/23) of the Scania jobs require any other languages than Swedish and English. It should be noted that these other languages are mentioned together with English and Swedish, i.e. the company seems to wish to hire Swedes with language skills in another foreign language than English. The languages in question are Russian, German and Spanish.

The extent to which language and communication skills are sought varies among the five companies. If we look at the last column of Table 12.1, we find that all the advertisements posted by Electrolux and Ericsson mention languages or language skills as job qualifications. At AstraZeneca, 78 per cent (18/23) of the advertisements posted mention either languages or communication skills, and at ABB the figure is 81 per cent (22/27). Less focus on languages is found in the Scania adverts, where languages or communication skills are mentioned in only 57 per cent (13/23) of the total number or, to phrase this differently, 43 per cent of the jobs advertised by Scania mention neither language nor communication as a qualification.

To sum up, for these five transnational companies multilinguality means bilinguality, i.e. a knowledge of English and Swedish. Of the 100 analysed advertisements for jobs in Sweden only 10 mention any other languages than Swedish and English as a qualification. English, on the other hand, is explicitly mentioned in 70 of the advertisements. Swedish figures less prominently as a qualification, a knowledge of it being explicitly mentioned in only 34 of the adverts. A few advertisements mention communication skills, but as many as 20 mention neither language nor communication skills.

Of course, the variation in terms of the qualifications required depends on the nature of the job. At a general level, however, we can say that multilingualism is mainly related to knowing English and to a lesser extent the main national language, in this case Swedish. The various other languages spoken in Sweden, e.g. Finnish, Persian, Arabic, are not mentioned at all. Of the immigrant languages, only Spanish, Russian and German are mentioned in the advertisements analysed.

12.3.3 Featured employees on company websites

The third part of my study focuses on the employees featured on the company websites. My questions concern which individuals the companies have chosen to feature and what they write about them. We could say that through these presentations the companies are offering readers a picture of their 'ideal' employees, and from a critical, socio-linguistic perspective it becomes interesting to analyse both what is said about them and what is omitted. All five companies included in this study have sub-pages presenting employees, which are linked to their job advertisement pages.

Starting with *ABB*, we find on its Swedish home page a link to 'Att jobba hos oss' ('Working with us'), which is linked to 'Möt medarbetare i ABB' ('Meet ABB employees'). This sub-page featured ten employees in June 2006, giving their full names, photographs and a short presentation. All ten have Swedish-sounding names: Jonas Gärd, Bosse Rosén, Ted Lauritzen, Martin Carlsson, Pernilla Lindström, Lena Johansson and so on. The presentations mention among other things where they work and whether they have worked outside Sweden: Bosse Rosén has worked in Cuba, Iran, Romania and Australia; Ted Lauritzen is working in Brazil; Martin Carlsson is a trainee in India; Pernilla Lindström has worked in Italy and Lena Johansson in Laour, Vietnam.

These presentations give future employees a picture of a global company that offers young Swedes an opportunity to work abroad. This result is somewhat surprising, considering the company's 'Diversity & Inclusion statement', quoted earlier, which stresses the importance of diversity and difference. Another sub-page linked to the Swedish 'Working with us' page, however, lists other values. Here, we can read in Swedish (my translation) about 'creative researchers all over the world', 'opportunities to develop' and 'working abroad', and that 'Jobs abroad are attracting more and more Swedes. ABB is represented in 100 countries throughout the world, offering great potential to gain international experience.' The claims on this sub-page are therefore more closely related to the selection and presentations of the ten featured employees.

AstraZeneca also has a page headed 'Att jobba hos oss' ('Working with us'), with a link to 'Personporträtt' ('Personal portraits'), which presents 11 employees. They all work in Sweden. In the presentation of one of the featured employees, Johnny Rizkallah, it is mentioned that he was born in Lebanon and has moved to Sweden from that country. This information is even included in the heading of his personal portrait: 'Från Libanon till Södertälje' ('From Lebanon to Södertälje', Södertälje being a Swedish town). From the fact that nothing is said about their origins, we can assume that the other ten employees were born in Sweden.

Electrolux does not have a separate sub-page for employees working in Sweden. On www.electrolux.com, however, we can go from 'Joining Electrolux' to 'Career development' and from there to 'Success stories'. On this sub-page we find the stories of five employees. They are

231

presented with their full name, a picture, some data and their history. We are given information about their nationality, what languages they speak and where they are located. Two of the five employees featured are of Swedish origin. At the time they are both working in Stockholm, Sweden. A third person is also working in Stockholm; he is of French origin and knows Swedish. Electrolux also has a page 'For graduates', with a link to 'Why Electrolux'. Here five young employees are presented with their full names, a picture and an appreciative quotation from what they have said about Electrolux. There is no mention of where these individuals were born or where they are located, but on the basis of their names the reader can assume that one or possibly two are of Swedish origin. In the five 'blurbs', presented as quotes from these young employees, we find prestige words such as *global, international, multinational, difference* and *diversity.*

On *Ericsson's* website, we can go from 'Ericsson as an employer' to 'Investing in you', to 'Your commitment' and then to 'New at Ericsson'. On this sub-page, a young Swedish woman, Hanna, was featured in June 2006. We are told that she is Swedish and located in Madrid. On www.ericsson.com there is also a link to 'Our people', where nine employees are presented with their first name, a picture and a short history. For each one we are given information about their country of origin and current location. Besides Hanna, who is also presented on the 'New at Ericsson' page and who works in Spain, another Swede is featured who works in the USA. Neither of the two Swedes therefore works in Sweden. Of the featured employees, however, one born in Scotland is located in Sweden.

Finally, we find a number of young people featured on the Swedish sub-pages of *Scania's* website. On the sub-page 'Student' there is a link to 'Examensarbete' ('Master's thesis work'), which features three students. We are told that one of them, Petra, comes from Germany and is preparing her undergraduate thesis in Sweden. It is also noted that she learnt Swedish in Germany and is fluent in the language. In addition, Scania features employees on its sub-page 'Möt tidigare traineer på Scania' ('Meet earlier trainees at Scania'). Among the four people presented here we find Mehdi, described as coming to Sweden from Iran when he was nine years old. Individuals are also featured on the page 'Sommarjobb' ('Summer jobs'). Here we find interviews with seven engineering students, who – judging from their names – all seem to be of Swedish origin. Of the 14 young people featured on Scania's website, two were not born in Sweden.

To sum up, I would distinguish two groups among the five companies studied on the basis of how they feature their employees. First, the international exchange made possible by their employment strategies is highlighted by three of the companies, namely ABB, Electrolux and Ericsson. ABB features ten Swedes who are or have been working abroad, while Electrolux, through its success stories, constructs a picture of a company that gives its employees, who should know several languages, an opportunity to work in many countries and meet people from other cultures. Ericsson, too, highlights the opportunity for international exchange, i.e. the company gives its employees the possibility of working abroad. In contrast to Electrolux, however, it makes no mention of employees' language skills.

Secondly, two of the companies, AstraZeneca and Scania, highlight the diversity of their Swedish workplaces. Of the 11 employees featured on AstraZeneca's web pages, one is an immigrant to Sweden, born in Lebanon, and of the 14 featured on Scania's site, one is an immigrant to Sweden, born in Iran, and one a visiting student from Germany. Both these companies could be said to give a fairly good picture of the current Swedish job market. As regards Scania, it should be noted that the German master's degree student is said to be fluent in Swedish. The company's monolingual Swedish culture (cf. part 12.3.2) is thus not altered by the presence of this German girl. It is also worth noticing that the country of origin is omitted in the presentations of the majority of the featured employees in both companies. The assumed norm is therefore that employees at Scania and AstraZeneca were born in Sweden and people of foreign origin are presented as exceptions and outsiders.

Relating these results to our findings discussed earlier regarding the language requirements set out in the companies' job advertisements, we find that the three companies in the first group (ABB, Electrolux and Ericsson) also mention languages as a qualification for employment to a greater extent than those in the second group (AstraZeneca and Scania). Ericsson, Electrolux and ABB are placed highest in the 'English' column in Figure 12.1, Electrolux and Ericsson in the 'Swedish' column, and ABB and Ericsson in the 'Other languages' column. The focus of the companies in the first group on international exchange is thus paralleled by a greater emphasis on languages, while a more accepting 'policy' towards immigrants is paralleled by less focus on language skills.

12.4 Discussion

The studies presented in this chapter analyse the interface of large, international enterprises and the outside world with a focus on the way the companies textually create a balance between global and local concerns, on the one hand, and economic concerns and social/societal values, on the other. The construction of an 'organizational self' has been investigated here in relation to explicit value statements by the companies and also to their actual practices in relation to language and cultural diversity. These studies have revealed some features related to the complexity of business discourse in the globalized economy.

Previous to the internet era, large companies, like for instance Barclays Bank, distributed a variety of documents on paper, each intended for one or a few specified reader groups (cf. Chapter 11). Company brochures were intended for specified customer groups, letters for individual customers, staff magazines for specified employee groups, press releases for journalists etc. A great effort was made to design information in a way to suit each reader group. Today, large companies rely on the internet for their externally and internally addressed information. This relates to banks as well as to transnational companies like Electrolux and Ericsson. Products and new jobs are marketed on their website, emails are replacing letters on paper, and internet and intranet texts are replacing printed staff magazines. Computer mediated texts are thus replacing texts on paper for both external and internal purposes, and for both general and individualized purposes. The internet is not only a means to reach out to large readership, but also a means to establish and maintain individualized relationships. Individualized contacts between a company and a customer not infrequently follow from the customer's reading of the company website. General company texts and individualized email messages are therefore often linked for the reader. Also this fact is relevant to discussion of company websites.

When a company places a text on its website, it has to count on a multiple readership, both in relation to who the reader is and in what context the reading takes place. Global accessibility – and also simultaneous access by different reader groups – is a reality for texts on websites. The innate addressee complexity of the Internet means that the specific character of each document is replaced by a possible relationship between texts on various sub-pages of the company website and that 'passive' reading is intermingled with interaction.[8]

One of the things that the analysis of websites in this chapter has shown is how the language used on a sub-page includes or excludes reader groups. The English speaking élite and the majority speakers in a country are found to be the customer groups which the companies address. The many people who speak neither English nor the majority language of the country, however, cannot read about the products of these companies in their own languages on their websites. This implicit policy on linguistic issues is also found on the career-oriented pages. The language requirements are English and the majority language, and the 'ideal' employee is a person who has worked in different countries. The global concern is strongly stressed on the career-oriented pages of the companies studied, where diversity is more related to global mobility than to local diversity.

One shared feature in the work on images in all companies is the focus on financial issues. Large enterprises need to present themselves as highly competitive and attractive on the various markets, which means that strong claims like 'world leading', 'innovative', 'profitable', 'international', 'global', 'large' and 'best' are frequently made in texts which describe their organizations and products.

The challenge for a company, however, is to find a way to combine their claims on profitability with an explicit attachment to social/ societal values. One central social value in today's business world is *diversity*, a value which is not infrequently mentioned explicitly in company texts. Some companies have a separate 'diversity statement', other companies mention diversity as one of their core values, and others still include the word 'diversity' in their general description of their staff policy. From a critical, sociolinguistic angle, it is relevant to look closer at how companies interpret the concept of diversity. Does the interpretation include multilinguality and multiculturality? The analysis presented here compared some companies' explicit value claims with their textual practices, and the research issue was how the company had interpreted the concept of *diversity* in terms of language and culture. The balance between economic concerns and social/societal values was thus related to policy and practice on linguistic and cultural matters.

12.5 Conclusions

The textual construction of their organization is a great challenge for companies in the globalized internet era. The complexity has increased, one reason being the closer relationship between the various societal framework systems. A global organization has to construct its 'organizational self' in relation to local and national frameworks as well as to global ones. It has to compete on a global economic market and also follow laws and practices established at various levels: within the local community, the state and the superstate.

On the internet, a company's presentation of its 'organizational self' in one text is also intermingled with other texts, and other reader-oriented text endeavours. It is no longer possible to direct the image of the company to one specific reader group as it was in the 'paper era'. Instead companies have to count on possible multiple reader-ships for their websites, which poses the challenge of not rendering

235

the image of the company in a way that will lead to the marginalization of certain reader groups. From a discrimination perspective, it is of great importance to relate the image which the company gives of its 'ideal' employees and its culture to the actual workplace situations. An effective way to marginalize certain groups of employees is to omit any mention of their existence in presentations of the company (cf. Boréus, 2006).

The advice which should be given to practitioners within companies with a diverse readership and workforce is thus to consider the complexity of internet discourse. They need to find a way to cope with language issues in relation to readers with different language backgrounds. How can they reach out to a socially stratified readership, i.e. also to readers who do not speak the majority language of a country or have mastery of the English lingua franca? They also need to find a way to present their personnel which does not marginalize groups of employees. How can they include all groups of employees in their 'success stories'?

Notes

1. There are several guidelines for CSR, e.g. Social Accountability International's SA8000 standard.
2. See, e.g., LeVine and Scollon (2004) and Norris and Jones (2005).
3. This study, which first was presented in Gunnarsson (2006b), also included IKEA. For the purpose of the homogeneity of this chapter, however, I have decided to leave out the results related to this company here.
4. The main part of the study was carried out in June 2006. In July 2007, Brazil was included in the study.
5. There are five official minority languages in Sweden: Finnish, Sami, Meänkeäli, Yiddish and Romani. Most speakers of those languages, however, are brought up bilingually and thus have a very good command of Swedish.
6. Cf. Waldinger and Lichter (2003), Behtoui (2006) and Boréus (2006).
7. Scania's website was studied on 1 November 2007.
8. Compare, e.g., Castells (1999), Lemke (2002), Qvortrup (2002) and Wiberg (2005).

Section 6
Conclusions

The last chapter of the book is entitled 'Professional discourse in the twentieth century'. Beginning with a discussion of the possible effects of technological advances and globalization on professional discourse within the different domains dealt with in this book, I turn to some problems facing large organizations in the twentieth century, e.g. in relation to internal management and external marketing. I also deal with multilingual workplaces, both those with English as a lingua franca and those with workforce diversity. I then continue with a discussion of workplace discourse in the 'new work order' and speculate about possible consequences for the individual employee. Lastly, I sketch some topics for future research on professional discourse and sum up the main tenets of the book.

13 Professional discourse in the twenty-first century

One purpose of this book has been to explore the dynamic and complex socio-historical reconstruction of professional discourse. Several chapters have focused on how and why professional discourse varies from domain to domain and why it has changed over time. In this chapter the focus will be on the future, on professional discourse in the twenty-first century. A relevant question for our understanding of modern professional life is related to the effects of technological advances and globalization. The conditions for professional discourse have indeed been influenced by a series of changes which have taken place in recent decades. In this concluding chapter I will discuss the consequences these changes might have for the domains and environments focused on in the various sections of this book.

I will first discuss more generally the ongoing changes in relation to professional discourse within the scientific and academic domains, the legal and bureaucratic domains, and the economic and technical domains. Secondly, I will focus on some problems facing large organizations in the twenty-first century, e.g. in relation to internal management and external marketing. Thirdly, I will deal with multilingual workplaces, both those with English as lingua franca and those with workforce diversity. In the fourth part I will discuss workplace discourse in the 'new work order' and speculate about possible consequences for the individual employee. In the fifth part I will sketch some topics for future research. Finally, I will sum up the main tenets of the book.

13.1 Professional discourse in different domains

If we first turn to the scientific and academic domain, the growth of knowledge and specialization which characterized the earlier development of science (cf. Chapter 4) is now aligned with a globalization and homogenization of scientific knowledge and also of scientific discourse. Students and senior scholars move between universities and colleges as well as from one country to another. Books and articles are written in global languages, e.g. in English, and circulate among large readerships (cf. Chapter 6). The expanded use of the internet has accelerated this development. It is easy to establish global contacts, to circulate papers and articles worldwide, to study from a distance and to cooperate with scholars in other parts of the world. The internet has also lead to new means of circulating publications and in many areas open access journals are replacing earlier printed ones. The roles of editors and publishers change.

The increased international exchange and globalization of publications have consequences for academic discourse. English predominates, which means that smaller, less global languages are threatened by domain loss. Students whose mother tongue is a smaller language face problems understanding course material in academic English. Researchers used to presenting their results in English face problems using their mother tongues for academic purposes, and this could well lead to domain loss for smaller languages (Ammon, 2001; Gunnarsson, 2001b; Duszak and Urszulska, 2004; Carli and Ammon, 2007). Linguistic and cultural diversity are also becoming important issues also for universities and colleges to deal with. Mobility among students and scholars also places gender issues in a new, socio-cultural framework, as women are not treated in the same way all over the world. The changes related to the scientific and academic domains are thus related to the linguistic and socio-cultural frameworks.

The conditions have changed also for discourse related to the legal and bureaucratic domain. The formation of superstates, such as the European Union, has created a new kind of complexity in relation to the drafting and application of laws and other regulations (cf. Chapter 8). Laws and regulations have to be ratified at various levels of the political–legal framework system, and the original version has to be translated into several different languages. Translation and interpretation have become important activities in the European superstate. In this way the issue of comprehensibility is also intertwined with the norms and traditions established in different linguistic communities (cf. Chapter 7).

Technological advances have also made an impact on discourse within the legal and bureaucratic domain (cf. Chapter 9). In the twenty-first century oral contacts between government agencies and citizens are handled by remote service and call centres – sometimes operating 24 hours a day – while emails, chat and questionnaires are used for the written contacts. You ask for information, request a service and also discharge your obligations, e.g. declare your taxes, via the internet. Technological advances intended to reduce costs are indeed a facilitating tool on many occasions. However, they have led to a new divide between people, one between a privileged group of technically adept individuals and a non-privileged group of those without such skills. Not infrequently this divide is related to age, education and income. Participation in democratic procedures and access to social benefits have thus come to be aligned with the ability to use modern technology. Various societal frameworks are related to this social equality issue, the legal-political, the socio-cultural and the linguistic frameworks.

Finally, if we turn to the economic and technical domains, we will find that technological advances have facilitated a globalization of working life, while lifelong learning, flexibility, mobility and diversity have come to be key values in the global economy. In organizations throughout the world, we find a widespread use of technology and increased reliance on the internet for internal and external communication. Another striking feature, made possible of course by the technological advances, is the globalization of the business world and the job market. Throughout the world, we find transnational companies which use English as their corporate language and employ multilingual people who can move between jobs, between branches and between countries. The workforce mobility and workplace diversity which characterize a globalized economy also bring issues of multilingualism and multiculturalism to the surface, both in relation to the organization as a whole and to workplace practices. For employees this new situation has come to entail different and increasing demands for literacy and communication skills.

13.2 Large organizations in the twenty-first century

From the point of view of the top management of large – national and international – organizations one problem area is related to the creation of external and internal images of the organization which can be accepted in various local settings, another is how to create a coherent organization working for the same visions. As was discussed in Chapter 11, texts and spoken discourse are very important in the creation of an 'organizational self' as well as for the presentation of the organization as an attractive unit in the eyes and ears of those outside and inside it.

13.2.1 Internal management and marketing

Modern management theory talks about the need for internal marketing, e.g. as a means of creating and controlling organizational culture, and most top managers are fully aware of this. Discourse is at the heart of this internal construction of the company as a unique and

241

attractive entity, and most organizations attach great importance to disseminating news and storytelling within the organization. Stories of success and failure are told and retold in organizations, thus disseminating knowledge of the behavioural patterns to be followed or avoided in the future (Linde, 1999). In the internet era they are also found on the companies' websites. Stories not only about the company and its history, but also about individual employees and successful customers are found on various sub-pages (cf. Chapter 12). Although their explicit goals vary, these stories all help construct an organizational self intended not only to attract new customers, owners and prospective employees but also to help maintain the existing organizational culture.

In modern organizations, top managers devote a great deal of time to creating mission statements and organizational visions (Swales and Rogers, 1995; Isaksson, 2005). A problem, however, is that a top-down communicative strategy does not always lead to the same message permeating the whole organization, and organizational visions are not infrequently interpreted by employees as unintelligible and insignificant. Johansson (2003) presents a case study which tries to probe this problem. Using a combination of methods, including participant observation, discourse analysis and interviews, she analysed the organizational communication about strategy in a Finnish–Swedish enterprise. Communication about the strategy followed a typical top-down model, starting at group level and ending at department level. She found that visions formulated by top managers met different realities constructed by managers at lower levels in the company. Managers' attitudes, knowledge and interpretations were important individual factors that influenced communication about the strategy. Employees did not have the same detailed knowledge of the strategy as the managers, nor were they given the same opportunities to acquire it. Power structures, conflicts, individual attitudes and perspectives contributed to the successive distortion of the top management's visions. Johansson's study is interesting as an attempt to grasp the whole process.

13.2.2 External communication and marketing

The role of discourse is no less obvious in relation to the construction of an externally addressed image which promotes success and growth. It is obvious that many enterprises have succeeded in spreading a uniform image of themselves which is accepted in a variety of countries and cultures. Logos, advertisements, shop design, stories contribute to this uniformity as well as the products as such. In some cases, the national origin of the company has come to be an essential part of its image and the construction of uniformity. A well-known symbol for American culture is McDonalds with its branches all over the world. Uniformity at every level – from the product to the design of its restaurants – characterizes this franchising company. In many countries, however, the image of McDonalds has come to be seen as representing the negative aspects of American culture at the same time as the company sells its hamburgers. A less ambiguous connection between national culture and corporate image has been created by IKEA. Swedishness has become one element in IKEA's trademark, and it has obviously managed to turn Swedishness into an image that sells. The company's products are given Swedish personal names, like Bosse, Björn etc. One goal in its naming policy is to present an image of 'trygghet' (familiarity and security) to the Swedish audience, and an image of a Nordic product to the international audience. Names with the Swedish letters å, ä and ö are therefore not avoided, but in fact deliberately used to strengthen IKEA's exotic image.[1] The ways in which customers are addressed are also aimed at strengthening the sense of Swedishness. In countries like Austria, e.g., employees address customers in speech and writing using 'du' instead of the normal 'Sie'. As part of its Swedish image, in other words, IKEA wishes to introduce the more egalitarian and familiar language and forms of address that have been used in Sweden since the second person pronoun reform in the 1960s (cf. Gunnarsson, 2001c).

Other companies have been successful in using strategies that permit greater cultural variation. An interesting model for text production is described in Jämtelid (2001, 2002). The concept of 'parallel writing' is used for the analysis of the multilingual production of text in the Electrolux corporate group, where English is the official language (cf. Gunnarsson and Jämtelid, 1999). This study, which is based on interviews and text analysis, reveals an interesting model for the balance between the local and the global. To provide a basis for company texts, e.g. brochures for vacuum cleaners, a textual base in English is devised at the main office in Stockholm, Sweden, and circulated to the sales companies in the other countries. The textual base then provides the raw material for the various consumer brochures produced in different languages and intended for different cultures. As Jämtelid's analyses show, the different sales companies have chosen to incorporate different ideas from the textual base circulated by head office. She also found marked differences in the arguments for the product presented in the brochures, the choice of illustrations and the styles used. There were thus clear differences between Electrolux brochures written in different countries about the same vacuum cleaner and based on the same original. The differences found between the texts of the brochure in the various countries could indicate culturally derived differences (Jämtelid, 2002). This text production strategy, which was established by the Electrolux group in the 1990s for the production of printed brochures, is interesting as it combines the need for top-down control and group unity with the need for local and national variation. In addition, it allowed for both linguistic and cultural variety.

As Chapter 12 showed, computer-mediated texts are, to a large extent, replacing printed texts for external purposes. Products are marketed on the companies' websites and emails are replacing letters on paper. One important difference between texts on a company's website and printed documents is their accessibility. When a company places a text on its website, it has to count on multiple readerships. Global accessibility is a reality for texts on websites. The specified reader of the printed document is replaced by a potentially manifold readership: shareholders, staff, journalists, politicians, former and prospective customers in countries all over the world can view the company website. Although the company can, in theory, count on multiple readerships for the texts on its website, it does not mean that the actual number of readers increases, nor any rise in the number of individuals who feel themselves directly addressed by the company's texts. The language used on a sub-page includes or excludes readership groups as does the cultural perspective and focus of the actual text.

13.3 The multilingual workplace

The ongoing globalization has also consequences for workplace discourse. The correspondence between organizational structure and discourse, discussed in Chapter 11, gets even more complex in large, global organizations where language and culture become socially relevant issues. Although the multilingual workplace is not a new phenomenon, the growing workforce mobility in today's economy entails workplace diversity of a varied and somewhat new kind. Issues of multilingualism and multiculturalism are brought up to the surface, as are issues of dominance and marginalization.

13.3.1 Multilingual workplaces with English as lingua franca

The globalized economy means that transnational organizations, i.e. organizations which operate in countries with different languages, need to choose one language as their corporate language. Not infrequently, at least in Europe, English is chosen for this purpose. In

countries where English is not the mother tongue this creates different communicative problems, in relation to both outgoing and internal
communication.

A number of recent studies have analysed communication with
English as the lingua franca in large, European, organizations and also
focused on the various problems related to this practice. I will here
discuss some studies which view the problem from a Scandinavian
perspective. For all the Scandinavian countries, English has come
to be the natural choice of language at an international level:
Swedish, Danish, Norwegian and Finnish are not understood outside Scandinavian, which indeed necessitates a global language in
external communication. In the last decade, English has also come
to be used as the common language in Nordic mergers, e.g. in the
Finnish–Swedish company *Stora-Enso*. Kankaanranta (2005a: 42)
describes the communicative practices within this company in the
following way:

> In practice, this language choice means that corporate-level docu-
> mentation and all reporting is done in English, and communi-
> cation between different units is mostly in English. This type of
> communication can be characterized as internal communication
> as it is taking place "in-house" in contrast to communication
> between buyers and sellers in which foreign languages have been
> traditionally needed in international business. For an individual
> writer of an email message, the choice is a pragmatic one: any-
> time there are recipients whose mother tongue is not that of the
> writer's, the message is in English. This means that a Swede (or a
> Finn) will receive an English message from another Swede (or a
> Finn) if the list of recipients includes non-Swedish speakers.

As was shown in Chapter 12, the use of English as a corporate language also has impact on the recruitment of the workforce. Many large
business organizations operating in Sweden choose to write their job
advertisements in English only, and include among the job requirements fluency in English rather than Swedish.

I will now turn to some studies which focus on the various problems related to the use of English as corporate language. When Jämtelid
interviewed people involved in writing at different levels of the
Swedish Electrolux group, she found that they themselves referred to
their corporate English as 'bad English' (2002: 44). A widespread belief
was that native speakers of English found their corporate English
poor. The director of corporate communications, however, makes it
clear that 'bad English' is not accepted in texts aimed at a wider readership. 'Although a presentation brochure obviously has to be correct,
it still has to be possible to send a message or a letter or minutes to

one another without them being a hundred per cent correct.' He also elaborates on the necessity for Scandinavians to speak up even if their English is bad:

> Then of course the corporate language is quite clearly "bad English". Otherwise, you easily end up with only Americans, Brits and well-educated Swedes talking at meetings, while Germans and Italians remain silent. What happens, rather, is that we deliberately avoid difficult words, and that people shouldn't feel ashamed at all if they use bad grammar in an internal memo in English. (My translation.)

Another consequence relates to a levelling of cultural differences in favour of a more homogeneous style. In ongoing studies of Nordic mergers, the cultural issue has attracted attention. In her analysis of emails written in English by Swedish and Finnish employees of Stora Enso, Kankaanranta[2] also looked at possible cultural differences. She was able to point to certain differences between the Swedish and Finnish writers:

> In spite of the macro-level similarities, the messages written by Finns and Swedes also exhibited differences on the level of the moves, that is, the realization of the requests. Finns seem to favour direct requests in their writing, while Swedes use more indirect alternatives, thus supporting the notion of the more direct Finnish communication. (Kankaanranta, 2005a: 54.)

Nevertheless, her main conclusion relates to homogenization, in that her study suggests that 'lingua franca interactions are characterized by a high degree of cooperativeness and a consensual style; together the communicators aim at smoothness, and together they construct the situational meanings' (p. 55).

Other studies have been more negative about the levelling of cultural differences in international meetings. Fant (1992) gives the following picture of the situation on the basis of his analyses of cross-cultural negotiations:

> If systematic longitudinal research had been carried out over the past, say, three or four decades in order to investigate the evolution of national patterns of doing business within what is commonly being referred to as the western world, the results would probably have indicated that, in the first place, things have changed a great deal globally, and, secondly, that national differences have diminished, yielding place to some sort of 'Americanized' style, which has served as a model to, and has reshaped, to a greater or lesser extent the local patterns. (Fant, 1992: 125.)

246

The same applies to Börestam (2005), who has analysed meetings within Nordea, another Nordic company with English as its official language. Her study covered meetings held in different countries (Denmark, Finland, Norway and Sweden) and in different languages. Her conclusion is that the levelling of cultural differences which for instance relate to the overall structure of the meeting discourse tends to favour a more Americanized style (p. 71). Fant's and Börestam's conclusions can thus be seen as pointing to a more general problem involving the consequences for small languages and small national discourse communities of the dominance of English and the American culture (cf. Gunnarsson 2001c).

A problem, which should not be neglected, relates to the consequences of the divide between those with mastery of English and those without. In many organizations, the local language dominates the spoken discourse, while the more official documents are written in English. Language knowledge and language deficiencies are likely to create new hierarchies and social orders. New communicative problems become salient: Who can communicate with the top management? Who understands which texts? Who can perform which job within the organization? Who can communicate with whom in the workplace?

Johansson (2003) presents a case study of communication on corporate strategy within a transnational company with its head office in Sweden. She recorded and analysed the information flow relating to a strategy document produced at the top level of the company. The document was written in English and formulated by senior managers. Managers at lower levels were then supposed to present the contents to the employees. Johansson interviewed top and middle managers and also employees and recorded meetings at which the strategy document was presented and discussed. Her conclusion is that the visions formulated by top managers were transformed by the middle managers in accordance with their attitudes and conceptions of reality. The employees who acquired their information via the middle managers did not have the same detailed knowledge of the strategy as the managers, nor were they given the same opportunities to obtain it. Johansson's study shows, among other things, that the use of English for important internal documents might increase the distance between senior management and ordinary employees.

The divide between those with mastery of English and those without in many cases increases the gap between native and non-native speakers. The choice of English as corporate language in the Scandinavian context is quite natural from the perspective of those who grow up there. Everyone attending school in Sweden, for instance, is taught

English as their first foreign language. People growing up in Sweden have also been exposed to English every day, as programmes on television (news, movies, comedies etc.) use Swedish subtitles and the original (mostly English) sound track. English is also used in much of the pop music produced and listened to in Sweden. The increased use of the internet has also meant that many Swedes daily read and write English for various purposes. A new type of 'elite bilingualism' is thus gradually developing in Sweden among young people and educated adults. For individuals who have moved to Sweden as adults, however, English is not always as easy as for those born in Sweden. Many immigrants have received their basic schooling (not uncommonly a very short one) in countries in the Middle East, Africa, Asia, South America and the former Eastern Europe, which means that they might not have been taught English at all, or at least not as their first foreign language. For them, the use of English poses greater problems than for people who have received their basic education in Sweden. The foreign language they have to learn first, when moving to Sweden, is of course also Swedish and not English.

In organizations which use English as their official language these individuals' opportunities to advance are dependent on their acquisition of not only one foreign language, the main national language in the country, but also English. Based on interviews with immigrant factory floor workers and office staff employed in a Swedish transnational company, Nelson gives this picture of the need for language knowledge at different levels:

> to be able to get an office job with this company, you do not necessarily need to know that much Swedish, but you do need to at least understand English. On the factory floor, on the other hand, you would probably not only become lonely but also have problems if you did not speak Swedish. (Andersson and Nelson, 2005: 34; cf. Chapter 10.)

13.3.2 Multilingual workplaces with workforce diversity

All over the world, there are workplaces where some employees, mostly minorities, immigrants or unskilled guest workers, have to use their second, third or fourth language at work. In many organizations, knowledge of the dominant local language is necessary not only for advancement and a career but also for social integration into the working group. Humour, jokes, stories, anecdotes form part of the workplace discourse and contribute to the establishment of friendship and collegiality at work and also to the avoidance of unnecessary conflicts. Social workplace patterns related to friendship, power and dominance often reflect linguistic and communication skills.[3] In Chapter 10 I discussed the results of a research project on the day-to-day communicative situation of immigrants employed in two different working environments: a major Swedish company and a large hospital. Among other things, these studies based on interviews and recordings reveal the collaborative character of workplace discourse. Language problems are overcome and humour and jokes are constructed in collaboration between the second language speakers and colleagues speaking their mother-tongue.

13.4 Workplace discourse in the 'new work order'

The conditions for professional discourse have been influenced by a series of changes taking place in recent decades. Technological advances have coincided with a globalization of working life and lifelong learning, flexibility, mobility and diversity have come to be key values in the global economy.

Below, I will sum up research which has analysed workplace discourse in technological organizations and workplaces. I will also speculate about what consequences the 'new work order' might have for the individual employee.

13.4.1 Technological advances and workplace discourse

In organizations throughout the world, we find a widespread use of technology and an increased reliance on the internet for internal and external communication. Text and speech in traditional forms are intertwined with computer-mediated communication, phone calls and video-conferencing in a way that gives presence and simultaneity a new significance. Distance communication is increasing and reducing the importance of being at a certain place at a certain time. The extended access to computers and advanced technology at work has also led to an increased role for multimodality: words and visual elements are interwoven in most texts and professional talks are often given with both textual and visual support.

Every strand of workplace communication has, in one way or the other, been transformed by technology. Writing at work has been affected by technology, and new written genres and new writing processes have developed as a result of the use of fax, email and the World Wide Web.[4] The use of speech in the workplace has also been influenced by the technological advances,[5] and phone calls and video-conferencing are intertwined with computer-mediated interaction leading to new interpretations of *presence* and *simultaneity* at work.

Multimodality is not a new phenomenon,[6] but technological developments in recent decades have prompted growing interest in multimodality as a phenomenon, its function and impact on discourse. Text, speech, graphics, recorded sound and movies are interwoven in today's communication in a way which was not previously possible.[7]

The technological advances have also given rise to different types of jobs and new workplaces.[8] Call centres and help desks may function in remote parts of the world, blurring the traditional concept of workplace and organizational connection. New genres and new communicative processes have developed at these workplaces.[9]

Though these studies offer glimpses of the intertwinement of discourse and technology at work and sketch methods to enable analysis, the next step should be to analyse the consequences for the individual employees of the various changes in the conditions for work which are found in the new, global economy.

13.4.2   The individual employee in the 'new work order'

The term 'new work order' has sometimes been used to refer to the redistribution of roles, skills and knowledge in the modern global economy, (cf. Gee et al., 1996; Hull, 1997). The modern organization constantly needs to modify products and customize them in order to survive in the over-competitive global marketplace. For the modern organization, a decentralized and flexible structure with temporary and rapidly changing networks is more valuable than stability and long-lasting structures. Organizations have fewer levels, which means that there are fewer middle managers and less administrative staff, while at the same time the unskilled tasks have disappeared. In terms of division of labour, this development has meant a downward shift of responsibility to the individual employees. The organizations must find means to empower their workforces, for instance core visions and cultures should be shared by managers and workers alike. For the employees, this new situation means different and greater demands on literacy and communication skills.

Organizations competing on the global market need to be flexible and able to learn also in relation to discourse. Compared to earlier organizations, modern ones are characterized by more meetings, more documentation and also an increased need for training and advice. The 'ideal' employee is someone flexible who is continuously learning as he or she moves within the organization and between organizations, taking on new jobs and performing new tasks. Instead of unskilled workers performing routine tasks, organizations need staff who can act independently, plan their own work and take responsibility for their role in production. They should be able to communicate more or less directly with the top levels within the organization. The new work order therefore demands greater flexibility and responsibility from individual employees. Organizational structures based on workforce mobility and workplace diversity also make greater demands of the language knowledge and cultural openness of the individual workers.

13.5 Topics for future research

As has been discussed in this chapter, professional discourse has been influenced by a series of changes because of new technology and globalization. The 'new work order' has had effects on working life in general and on the working conditions for individuals employed in or networking with large or small organizations. A goal for future research is to analyse the various 'new' problem areas as well as to try to sketch how difficulties could be overcome. In this last section I dwell on a few topics which relate to the various issues discussed earlier in this chapter.

Organizations in the 'new work order' are described as having fewer levels. Hierarchies are reduced and the structural connection between organization and workplace is blurred. Nevertheless we can assume that organizations will survive as uniform entities. One topic for future research would be to explore the new roles of discourse in the construction of an 'organizational self' in the global economy and for the maintenance of a social order in blurred contextual frames. How are large organizations constructed and maintained by means of the internet and distance-communication? What role do different types of discourse play for the formation of a uniform organization?

An important set of topics relate to the employees' group affiliations in the new work order. Earlier studies have found that humour, story-telling and teasing are essential elements in the discourse of a close-knit workplace. In order to be a full member of a working group, you must, for instance, know what jokes are socially accepted and whom you can tease and in what way. A topic for future research is to analyse whether similar socializing patterns are also established in working groups held together by means of distance-communication. What roles, if any, do humour and storytelling play in distance-communication? Do these elements play a role also in distance-communication in organizations which use English – or another language – as a lingua franca? Do employees who sit at home working on their computers feel integrated into a workplace group?

251

Fewer levels and reduced hierarchies result in vagueness and tension for individual employees. The need for workforce flexibility also leads to a form of growing de-professionalization. Role relationships and identities have to be renegotiated and new ones formed over and over again. For the individual this situation is likely to create uncertainty and stress. A topic for future research would be to analyse the role of discourse in the (re)negotiation of job identities and job relationships within flat organizations.

Another topic which would be worth looking into relates to the role of discourse for bottom-up influence. The physical distance between one workplace and another is a reality in large, global organizations, which indeed means that both top-down and bottom-up communication have to be less direct. A research question is whether this physical distance hinders bottom-up influence on the organization. By what type of discourse is democracy established – and hindered – in the 'new work order'? How does the new worker get his/her voice through to the top management level? How does top management try to steer the shop floor workers? What role does language difference play for patterns of influence?

The new work order is also characterized by extended networking. Large companies merge, but there is a framework of small group collaboration in the big concerns. An interesting topic related to power and dominance would be to analyse if and how small network partners manage to influence the decisions of large organizations?

In the global economy, organizations have to strike a balance between *local* and *global concerns* as well as between *economic concerns* and *social-societal values* in order to be competitive and trustworthy. The challenge for large organizations is to find a balance in policy and practice between these various considerations. Important topics for future research would be to analyse how discourse in organizations and workplaces reflect this balance. How is diversity constructed in workplace discourse? Who is marginalized and who is made central through workplace discourse? What societal values are expressed in official documents and more informal discourse within organizations?

13.6 Conclusions

As this book has shown, professional discourse occurs in situated communicative events, where participants, who might differ in terms of domain-related knowledge, communication skills, social values and culturally derived attitudes, interact by means of text or talk for professional purposes. A central tenet elaborated throughout this book is the dual relationship between professional discourse and its contextual framework. The situated event has therefore been analysed in relation to its environmental framework – the close-knit group, the workplace, the organization, the corporation – and also to the four societal frameworks: a legal-political, an economic-technical, a socio-cultural and a linguistic. A second tenet has been the importance of a detailed and systematic analysis of linguistic data for our understanding of the dynamic and complex socio-historical reconstruction of professional discourse. A third tenet shown in the various analyses in this book is the consequences for the individual of this dual relationship between discourse and context.

I hope the theoretical framework and the analyses I have presented in this book have shed some light on the dynamic character of professional discourse and its essential role for individuals and groups in social and societal contexts. I also hope to have illustrated how and why professional discourse varies and changes and also how this awareness can enable us to influence the course developments take. But most of all I hope to have encouraged others to explore the exciting complexity of discourse in professional contexts and refine the models I have presented. Professional discourse is a relatively new field of investigation and one which is still growing. Although we have obtained answers to some of our questions, many more research issues remain unanswered.

Notes

1. Interview with a retail display designer working for IKEA (Språket, SR1, 6 September 2005).
2. A full description of this study is presented in Kankaanranta (2005b).
3. See, e.g., Holmes et al. (1999), Holmes (2000), Holmes and Stubbe (2003), Marra and Holmes (2004), Holmes (2005).
4. See, e.g., Louhiala-Salminen (1995), Bargiela-Chiappini and Nickerson (1999), Nickerson (2000), Luzon (2002), Kankaanranta (2005b).
5. See Pan et al. (2002).
6. Cf. John Swales' analysis of a university building (1998).
7. See, e.g., Lemke (1999), LeVine and Scollon (2004), Norris and Jones (2005), Karlsson (2006 and 2007).
8. Interesting analyses are found in Sarangi and Roberts, eds (1999).
9. See, e.g., Culver et al. (1997), Landqvist (2001), Kong (2002), Qvortrup (2002), Oliveira (2004), Silva et al. (2004), Wiberg (2005).

References

Adams Smith, D. E. (1990), 'Source and derived discourse', in M. A. K. Halliday, J. Giddons and H. Nicholas (eds), *Learning, keeping and using language, volume II.* Amsterdam, Philadelphia, Pennsylvania: John Benjamins, pp. 415–433.

Altenberg, B. (1998), 'Connectors and sentence openings in English and Swedish', in S. Johansson and S. Oksefjell (eds), *Corpora and cross-linguistic research: theory, method, and case studies.* Amsterdam: Rodopi, pp. 115–143.

Ammon, U., ed. (2001), *The dominance of English as a language of science. Effects on other languages and language communities.* Berlin, New York: Mouton de Gruyter.

Andersson, H. (2007), *Interkulturell kommunikation inom sjukvården. Den kommunikativa situationen för invandrare på svenska arbetsplatser 1: intervjuer.* (TeFa nr 45.) Uppsala: Uppsala University.

Andersson, H. and Nelson, M. (2005), 'Communication at work. The communicative situation of immigrants at Swedish workplaces', in B.-L. Gunnarsson (ed.), *The Immigrant and the Workplace.* (TeFa nr 41.) Uppsala: Uppsala University, pp. 27–46.

Auer, P., ed. (1998), *Code-switching in conversation: Language, interaction and identity.* London: Routledge.

Austin, J. L. (1976), *How to do things with words. The William James Lectures 1955.* Second edition. London, Oxford, New York: Oxford University Press.

Bäcklund, I. (1998), *Metatext in professional writing: A contrastive study of English, German and Swedish. Texts in European writing communities 3.* (TeFa nr 25.) Uppsala: Uppsala University.

Bargiela-Chiappini, F. and Nickerson, C., eds (1999), *Writing business: Genres, media and discourses.* New York: Longman.

Bartlett, F. C. (1932), *Remembering: A study in experimental and social psychology.* Cambridge: Cambridge University Press.

Barton, D. (1991), 'The social nature of writing', in D. Barton and R. Ivanic (eds), *Writing in the Community.* Written Communication Annual. An International Survey of Research and Theory. Volume 6. Newbury park, London, New Delhi, pp. 1–13.

Bazerman, C. (1988), *Shaping written knowledge. The genre and activity of the experimental article in science.* Madison, Wisconsin: The University of Wisconsin Press.

Bazerman, C. and Paradis, J., eds (1991), *Textual dynamics of the professions. Historical and contemporary studies of writing in professional communities.* Madison, Wisconsin: The University of Wisconsin Press.

Behtoui, A. (2006), Unequal opportunities. *The impact of social capital and recruitment methods on immigrants and their children in the Swedish labour market.* Linköping studies in art and science no. 369, Linköping.

Berkenkotter, C. and Huckin, T. N. (1995), *Genre knowledge in disciplinary communication. Cognition/culture/power.* Hillsdale, New Jersey: Lawrence Erlbaum.

Bhatia, V. K. (1993), *Analysing genre. Language use in professional settings.* London: Longman.

Boissevain, J. (1987), 'Social network', in U. Ammon, N. Dittmar and K. J. Mattheier (eds), *Sociolinguistics: An International handbook of the science of language and society.* Berlin/New York: de Gruyter, pp. 164–169.

Börestam, U. (2005), 'Culture and culture again. An inter-Nordic merger in the banking sector', in B.-L. Gunnarsson (ed.), *Communication in the Workplace.* (TeFa nr 42.) Uppsala: Uppsala University, pp. 60–77.

Boréus, K. (2006), 'Discursive discrimination: A typology', *European Journal of Social Theory*, no. 3.

Bransford, J. D. and Franks, J. J. (1971), 'The abstraction of linguistic ideas', *Cognitive Psychology*, 2, 331–350.

Bransford, J. D., Barclay, J. P. and Franks, J. J. (1972), 'Sentence memory. A constructive versus interpretative approach', *Cognitive Psychology*, 3, 193–209.

Brown, P. and Levinson, S. C. (1987), *Politeness: some universals in language usage.* Studies in interactional sociolinguistics 4. Cambridge: Cambridge University Press.

Carli, A. and Ammon, U. eds (2007), *Linguistic inequality in scientific communication today.* AILA Review, volume 20. Amsterdam/Philadelphia, Pennsylvania: John Benjamins.

Castells, M. (1999), *The information age. Economy, society and culture.* Vol. 1–3. Oxford: Blackwell Publishers.

Charrow, R. P. and Charrow, V. R. (1979), 'Making legal language understandable: A psycholinguistic study of jury instructions', *Columbia Law Review*, 79 (7), 1306–1374.

Culver, J. D., Gerr, F. and Frumkin, H. (1997), 'Medical information on the internet: A study of an electronic bulletin board', *Journal of General Internal Medicine*, 12 (8), 466–470.

Dale, W. (1977), *Legislative drafting: A new approach. A comparative study of method in France, Germany, Sweden and the United Kingdom.* London: Butterworths.

Daneš, F. (1970), 'Zur linguistischen Analyse der Textstruktur', *Folia linguistica*, 4, 72–78.

Danet, B. (1997), 'Speech, writing and performativity: an evolutionary view of the history of constitutive ritual', in B. L. Gunnarsson, P. Linell and B. Nordberg (eds), *The construction of professional discourse.* London and New York: Longman, pp. 13–41.

Dudley-Evans, T. (1986), 'Genre analysis: an investigation of the introduction and discussion sections of MSc dissertations', in M. Coulthard (ed.), *Talking about text.* Birmingham, UK: English Language Research, Birmingham University.

256

—(1989), 'An outline of the value of genre analysis in LSP work', in C. Laurén and M. Nordman (eds), *Special Language: From Humans Thinking to Thinking Machines*. Clevedon, Philadelphia, Pennsylvania: Multilingual Matters Ltd, pp. 72–79.

Duszak, A. and Urszulska, O., eds (2004), *Speaking from the margin. Global English from a European perspective*. Frankfurt am Main: Peter Lang.

Enkvist, N.-E. (1974), 'Några textlingvistiska grundfrågor', in U. Teleman and T. Hultman (eds), *Språket i bruk*. Lund: Liber läromedel, pp. 172–206.

Erickson, F. and Schultz, J. (1982), *The counselor as gatekeeper: Social interaction in interviews*. New York: Academic Press.

Faigley, L. (1985), 'Nonacademic writing: The social perspective', in L. Odell and D. Goswani (eds), *Writing in nonacademic settings*. New York, London: Guilford Press, pp. 231–248.

Fairclough, N. and Wodak, R. (1997), 'Critical discourse analysis', in T. A. van Dijk (ed.), *Discourse as social interaction. Discourse Studies: A multidisciplinary introduction*, Volume 2. London, Thousand Oaks, New Delhi: Sage Publications, pp. 258–284.

Fant, L. (1992), 'Scandinavians and Spaniards in negotiation', in A. Sjögren and L. Janson (eds), *Culture and management. In the field of ethnology and business administration*. Botkyrka, Sweden, pp. 125–153.

Fillmore, C. (1987), *Fillmore's case grammar: a reader*. R. Dirven and G. Radden (eds). (Studies in descriptive linguistics 16.) Heidelberg: Groos.

Fishman, J. A. (1970), *Sociolinguistics. A brief introduction*. Rowley, Massachusetts: Newbury House Publishers.

Fletcher, J. K. (1999), *Disappearing acts. Gender. power and relational practice at work*. Cambridge, Massachussets: MIT Press.

Flower, L. S. and Hayes, J. R. (1984), 'Images, plans, and prose: The representation of meaning in writing', *Written Communication*, 1, 120–160.

Fredrickson, K. M. (1995), *American and Swedish written legal discourse: The case of court documents*. (Ph.D. thesis. Department of Linguistics.) Ann Arbor: The University of Michigan.

Gee, J., Hull, G. and Lankshear, C. (1996), *The New Work Order*. London: Allen and Unwin.

Gibson, E. J. and Levin, H. (1975), *The Psychology of Reading*. Cambridge, Massachusetts and London: MIT Press.

Goffman, E. (1974), *Frame analysis: An essay on the organization of experience*. Cambridge, Massachusetts: Harvard University Press.

Granger, S. and Tyson, S. (1996), 'Connector usage in the English essay writing of native and non-native EFL speakers of English', *World Englishes*, 15 (1), 17–27.

Grice, P. (1975), 'Logic and Conversation', in P. Cole and J. L. Morgan (eds), *Syntax and semantics 3: Speech acts*. New York: Academic Press, pp. 41–58.

Grimes, J. E. and Glock, N. (1970), 'A Saramaccan narrative pattern', *Language*, 46, 408–425.

Grönroos, C. (1990), *Service management and marketing. Managing the moments of truth in service competition*. Massachusetts and Toronto: Lexington Books.

257

Gumperz, J. J. (1968), 'The speech community', in *International encyclopedia of the social sciences*. London, New York: Macmillan, pp. 381–186.

—(1982a), *Discourse strategies*. Cambridge: Cambridge University Press.

—(1982b), *Language and social identity*. Cambridge: Cambridge University Press.

—(1992), 'Contextualization and understanding', in A. Duranti and C. Goodwin (eds), Rethinking context: Language as an interactive phenomenon. Cambridge: Cambridge University Press, pp. 229–252.

—(1999), 'On interactional sociolinguistic method', in S. Sarangi and C. Roberts (eds), *Talk, work and institutional order: Discourse in medical, mediation and managements settings*. Berlin/New York: Mouton de Gruyter, pp. 453–471.

Gunnarsson, B.-L. (1982), *Lagtexters begriplighet. En språkfunktionell studie av medbestämmandelagen*. Lund: Liber Förlag.

—(1984), 'Functional comprehensibility of legislative texts: Experiments with a Swedish act of parliament', *Text*, 4 (1–3), 71–105.

—(1989), 'Text comprehensibility and the writing process. The case of laws and law making', *Written Communication*, 6 (1), 86–107.

—(1992a), 'Linguistic change within cognitive worlds', in G. Kellermann and M. D. Morrissey (eds), *Diachrony within Synchrony: Language History and Cognition*. Frankfurt am Main: Verlag Peter Lang, pp. 205–228.

—(1992b), *Skrivande i yrkeslivet. En sociolingvistisk studie*. Lund: Studentlitteratur.

—(1993), 'Pragmatic and macrothematic patterns in science and popular science: A diachronic study of articles from three fields', in M. Ghadessy (ed.), *Register analysis: theory and practice*. London and New York: Pinter Publishers, pp. 165–179.

—(1997a), 'On the sociohistorical construction of scientific discourse', in B.-L. Gunnarsson, P. Linell and B. Nordberg (eds), *The construction of professional discourse*. London and New York: Longman, pp. 99–126.

—(1997b), 'The writing process from a sociolinguistic viewpoint', *Written Communication*, 14 (2), 139–188.

—(1998), 'Academic discourse in changing context frames: The construction and development of a genre', in P. Evangelisti Allori (ed.), *Academic discourse in Europe. Thought processes and linguistic realisations*. Rome: Bulzoni, pp. 19–42.

—(2000), 'Discourse, organizations and national cultures', *Discourse Studies*, 2(1), 5–34.

—(2001a), 'Expressing criticism and evaluation during three centuries', *Journal of Historical Pragmatics*, 2 (1), 115–139.

—(2001b), 'Swedish, English, French or German – the language situation at Swedish universities', in U. Ammon (ed.), *The dominance of English as a language of science. Effects on other languages and language communities*. Berlin, New York: Mouton de Gruyter, pp. 229–316.

—(2001c), 'Swedish Tomorrow – A product of the linguistic dominance of English?', in S. Boyd and L. Huss (eds), *Managing multilingualism in a European nation-state. Challenges for Swedish*. Clevedon: Multilingual Matters Ltd, pp. 51–69.

—(2004a), 'The multilayered structure of enterprise discourse', *Information Design Journal + Document Design*, 12 (1), 36–48.

—(2004b), 'Orders and disorders of enterprise discourse', in C. Gouveia, C. Silvestre and L. Azuaga (eds), *Discourse, communication and the enterprise. Linguistic perspectives*. (Centre for English Studies.) Lisbon: University of Lisbon, pp. 17–39.

—(2005a), 'The organization of enterprise discourse', in A. Trosborg and P. E. Flyvholm Jørgensen (eds), *Business discourse. Texts and contexts*, Linguistic Insights no. 19. Studies in Language and Communication. Bern, Berlin, Frankfurt am Main: Peter Lang, pp. 83–109.

—(2005b), 'Medical discourse: Sociohistorical construction', in *Encyclopedia of language and linguistics*, 2nd Edition, Vol 7, eds K. Brown. Oxford: Elsevier, pp. 709–716.

—(2005c), 'The verbal construction of organizations', in B.-L. Gunnarsson (ed.), *Communication in the workplace*, (TeFa nr 42.) Uppsala: Uppsala University, pp. 78–90.

—(2005d), 'Icke-verbal representation i vetenskapliga artiklar', in B. Melander, G. Bergman-Claeson, O. Josephson, L. Larsson, B. Nordberg and C. Östman (eds), *Språk i tid*. (Skrifter utgivna av Institutionen för nordiska språk.) Uppsala: Uppsala University, pp. 303–314.

—(2006a), 'From a national to an international writing community. The case of economics in Sweden', in J. Bamford and M. Bondi (eds), *Managing interaction in professional discourse*. Intercultural and interdiscoursal perspectives. Roma: Officina Edizioni, pp. 23–45.

—(2006b), 'Swedish companies and their multilingual practices', in J. C. Palmer-Silveira, M. F. Ruiz-Garrido and I. Fortanet-Gómez (eds), *International and intercultural business communication. Theory, research and teaching*. Frankfurt: Peter Lang, pp. 243–263.

—(2008), 'Professional communication', in *Encyclopedia of language and education*, 2nd Edition, Vol 4: Second and Foreign Language Education, eds N. Van Deusen-Scholl and N. H. Hornberg. New York: Springer Science, pp. 83–95.

Gunnarsson, B.-L., Bäcklund, I. and Andersson, B. (1995), 'Texts in European writing communities', in B.-L. Gunnarsson and I. Bäcklund (eds), *Writing in academic contexts*. (TeFa nr 11.) Uppsala: Uppsala University, pp. 30–53.

Gunnarsson, B.-L. and Edling, L. (1985), *Laganvändning på kommunnivå*. (FUMS rapport nr 127.) Uppsala: Uppsala University.

Gunnarsson, B.-L. and Jämtelid, K. (1999), 'Översättning och parallellskrivning – flerspråkig textproduktion inom ett internationellt storföretag', in *Svenskans beskrivning 23*. Lund: Lund University Press, pp. 134–142.

Gunnarsson, B.-L., Linell, P. and Nordberg, B., eds (1997), *The construction of professional discourse*. London and New York: Longman.

Gunnarsson, B.-L., Melander, B. and Näslund, H. (1987), *Facktexter under 1900-talet 1. Projektpresentation och materialbeskrivning*. (FUMS rapport nr 135.) Uppsala: Uppsala University.

Gunnarsson, B.-L., Näslund, H. and Melander, B. (1994), 'LSP in a historical perspective', in M. Brekke, Ö. Andersen, T. Dahl, and J. Myking (eds),

Applications and implications of current LSP research. Volume II. Bergen: Fagbokforlaget, pp. 878–915.

Gunnarsson, B.-L. and Skolander B.- (1991), *Fackspråkens framväxt: terminologi och ordförråd i facktexter från tre sekler 1. Projektpresentation och materialbeskrivning.* (FUMS rapport nr 154.) Uppsala: Uppsala University.

Habermas, J. (1971), *Borgerlig offentlighet.* Oslo: Gyldendal.

Hayes, J. R. and Flower, L. (1980), 'Identifying the organization of writing processes', in L. W. Gregg and E. R. Steinberg (eds), *Cognitive processes in writing.* Hillsdale, New Jersey: Lawrence Erlbaum, pp. 3–30.

Hoey, M. (1983), *On the surface of discourse.* London: George Allen and Unwin.

Hofstede, G. (1994), *Cultures and organizations: Software of the mind: intercultural cooperation and its importance for survival.* London: Harper Collins.

Holmes, J. (2000), 'Politeness, power and provocation: How humour functions in the workplace', *Discourse Studies*, 2 (2), 159–185.

—(2005), 'Story-telling at work: A complex discursive resource for integrating personal, professional and social identities'. *Discourse Studies*, 7 (6), 671–700.

—(2006), *Gendered talk at work. Constructing gender identity through workplace discourse.* Malden, Massachusetts: Blackwell Publishers.

Holmes, J. and Stubbe, M. (2003), *Power and politeness in the workplace. A sociolinguistic analysis of talk at work.* London: Pearson Education.

Holmes, J., Stubbe, M. and Vine, B. (1999), 'Constructing professional identity: "doing power" in policy units', in S. Sarangi and C. Roberts (eds), *Talk, work and institutional order. Discourse in medical, mediation and management settings.* Berlin, New York: Mouton de Gruyter, pp. 351–385.

Huckin, T. (1987), 'Surprise value in scientific discourse'. Paper presented at the CCC Convention, Atlanta, Georgia, March, 1987.

Hudson, R. A. (1996), *Sociolinguistics.* Second edition. Cambridge: Cambridge University Press.

Hull, G. ed. (1997), *Changing work, changing workers: Critical perspective on language, literacy and skills.* Albany: State University of New York Press.

Hymes, D. (1974), *Foundations in sociolinguistics: An ethnographic approach.* Philadelphia: University of Pennsylvania Press.

Isaksson, M. (2005), 'Ethos and pathos representations in mission statements: Identifying virtues and emotions in an emerging business genre', in A. Trosborg and P. E. Flyvholm Jørgensen (eds), *Business discourse. Texts and contexts*, Bern, Berlin, Frankfurt am Main: Peter Lang, pp. 111–138.

Jämtelid, K. (2001), 'Multilingual text production at an international company', in F. Mayer (ed.), *Language for special purposes: Perspectives for the new millennium. Volume 2.* Tübingen: Gunter Narr Verlag, pp. 797–805.

—(2002), *Texter och skrivande i en internationaliserad affärsvärld. Flerspråkig textproduktion vid ett svenskt storföretag.* Stockholm: Almqvist and Wiksell International.

Johansson, C. (2003), *Visioner och verkligheter. Kommunikationen om företagets strategier.* (Department of Information Sciences.) Uppsala: Uppsala University.

Källgren, G. (1979), *Innehåll i text*. Stockholm: Studentlitteratur.

Kankaanranta, A. (2005a), 'English as a corporate language: Company-internal e-mail messages written by Finns and Swedes', in B.-L. Gunnarsson (ed.), *Communication in the workplace*. (TeFa nr 42.) Uppsala: Uppsala University, pp. 42–59.

—(2005b), *'Hej Seppo, could you pls comment on this!' Internal Email Communication in Lingua Franca English in a Multinational Company*. (Centre for Applied Language Studies.) Jyväskylä: University of Jyväskylä.

Karlsson, A.-M. (2006), *En arbetsdag i skriftsamhället. Ett etnografiskt perspektiv på skriftanvändning i vanliga yrken*. Stockholm: Norstedts Akademiska Förlag.

—(2007), 'Text, situation, praktik. Om ramar och resurser för tolkning av texter i arbetsrelaterade skrifthändelser', in B.-L. Gunnarsson and A.-M. Karlsson (eds), *Ett vidgat textbegrepp*. (TeFa nr 46.) Uppsala: Uppsala University, pp. 27–40.

Kaufer, D. S. and Carley, K. M. (1993), *Communication at a distance. The influence of print on sociocultural organization and change*. Hillsdale, New Jersey: Lawrence Erlbaum.

Kintsch, W. (1978), 'Comprehension and memory of text', in W. K. Estes (ed.), *Handbook of learning cognitive processes. Vol 6: Linguistic functions in cognitive processes*. Hillsdale, New Jersey: Lawrence Erlbaum.

Kintsch, W. and van Dijk, T. A. (1978), 'Toward a model of text comprehension and production', *Psychological Review*, 85, 363–394.

Knorr-Cetina, K. (1981), *The manufacture of knowledge*. Oxford: Pergamon Press.

Kong, K. C. C. (2002), 'Managing the ambiguous and conflicting identities of "upline" and "downline" in a network marketing firm'. *Discourse Studies*, 4 (1), 49–74.

Kotler, P. (1991), *Marketing Management. Analysis, planning, implementation and control*. Englewood Cliffs, New Jersey: Prentice Hall Corporation.

Kotler, P., Armstrong, G., Saunders, J. and Wong, V. (1999), *Principles of marketing*. London: Prentice Hall Europe.

Kucer, S. L. (1985), 'The making of meaning: Reading and writing as parallel processes', *Written Communication*, 3 (2), 317–336.

Labov, W. (1972), *Sociolinguistic patterns*. Philadelphia: University of Pennsylvania Press.

Labov, W. and Waletzky, J. (1967), 'Narrative analysis: Oral versions of personal experiences', in J. Helm (ed.), *Essays on the verbal and visual arts*. (Proceedings of the 1966 Annual Spring Meeting. American Ethnological Society.) Seattle and London.

Landqvist, H. (2001), *Råd och ruelse. Moral och samtalsstrategier i Giftinformations centralens telefonrådgivning*. (Skrifter utgivna av Institutionen för nordiska språk 55.) Uppsala: Uppsala University.

Latour, B. (1988), 'Drawing things together', in M. Lynch and S. Woolgar (eds), *Representation in scientific practice*. Cambridge, Massachusetts, London, England: MIT Press, pp. 19–68.

261

Latour, B. and Woolgar, S. (1986), *Laboratory life. The construction of scientific facts.* Princeton, New Jersey: Princeton University Press.

Lemke, J. L. (1999), 'Discourse and organizational dynamics: website communication and institutional change'. *Discourse and Society*, 10 (1), 21–47.

—(2002), 'Travels in hypermodality', *Visual Communication*, 3, 299–325.

Levin, A. (1997), *Kognitiva och pragmatiska mönster i professionella texter från svenska, engelska och tyska skrivmiljöer. Texter i europeiska skrivsamhällen 1.* (TeFa nr 20.) Uppsala: Uppsala University.

LeVine, P. and Scollon, R. eds (2004), *Discourse and technology: Multimodal discourse analysis.* Washington, DC: Georgetown University Press.

Levinson, S. C. (1983), *Pragmatics.* Cambridge, London etc.: Cambridge University Press.

Linde, C. (1999), 'The transformation of narrative syntax into institutional memory'. *Narrative inquiry*, 9 (1), 139–74.

Louhiala-Salminen, L. (1995) *'Drop me a fax, will you?': A study of written business communication.* (Reports from the Department of English 10.) Jyväskylä: University of Jyväskylä, pp. 1–115.

Lurija, A. R. (1976), *Basic problems of neurolinguistics.* The Hague: Mouton.

Luzon, M. M. J. (2002), 'A genre analysis of corporate home pages', *LSP and Professional Communication*, 2 (1), 41–56.

Marra, M. and Holmes, J. (2004), 'Affiliation workplace narratives and business reports: Issues of definition'. *Text*, 24 (1), 59–78.

Mauranen, A. (1993), *Cultural differences in academic rhetoric: a textlinguistic study.* Frankfurt: Peter Lang.

Melander, B. (1989), Facktexter under 1900-talet 3. Resultat från kognitiv textanalys. (FUMS rapport nr 148). Uppsala: Uppsala University.

—(1991), *Innehållsmönster i svenska facktexter.* (Skrifter utgivna av Institutionen för nordiska språk 28.) Uppsala: Uppsala University.

—(1993), *From interpretation to enumeration of facts: On a change in the textual patterns of Swedish LSP texts during the 20th century.* (TeFa nr 7.) Uppsala: Uppsala University.

Melander, B., Swales, J. and Fredrickson, K. (1997), 'Journal abstracts from three academic fields in the US and Sweden: National or disciplinary proclivities', in A. Duszak (ed.), *Culture and styles of academic discourse.* Berlin: Mouton de Gruyter, pp. 251–272.

Morris, C. W. (1938), *Foundations of the theory of signs.* Vol 1 (2). Chicago and London: The University of Chicago Press.

Myers, G. (1988), 'Every picture tells a story: Illustrations in E. O. Wilson's Sociobiology', *Human Studies*, 11, 235–269.

—(1989). 'The pragmatics of politeness in scientific articles', *Applied Linguistics*, 10 (1), 1–35.

—(1990), *Writing biology. Texts in the social construction of scientific knowledge.* Madison, Wisconsin: The University of Wisconsin Press.

Nationalencyklopedin, Femte bandet. Höganäs: Bokförlaget Bra Böcker. 1991.

Näslund, H. (1991), *Referens och koherens i svenska facktexter.* (Skrifter utgivna av Institutionen för nordiska språk 29.) Uppsala: Uppsala University.

262

Nelson, M. (2008), '"Jag kopierar andras mejl". Om andraspråkstalares skrivstrategier i yrkeslivet', in J. Granfeldt, G. Håkansson, M. Källkvist and S. Schlyter (eds), *Språkinlärning, språkdidaktik och teknologi*. (ASLA:s skriftserie 21.) Lund, pp. 163–181.

Nelson, M. and Andersson, H. (2005), 'Andraspråkstalare i arbetslivet. Data från intervjuer och fallstudier', in U. Börestam and B.-L. Gunnarsson (eds), *Språk och kultur i det multietniska Sverige*. (TeFa nr 44.) Uppsala: Uppsala University, pp. 84–97.

Nelson, M. (2007), 'Professionella och socialiserande kommunikativa aktiviteter. Andraspråkstalande kvinnor och män i arbete', in B.-L. Gunnarsson, S. Entzenberger and M. Ohlsson (eds), *Språk och kön i nutida och historiskt perspektiv*. (Skrifter utgivna av Institutionen för nordiska språk 71.) Uppsala: Uppsala University, pp. 287–298.

Nickerson, C. (2000), *Playing the corporate language game. An investigation of the genres and discourse strategies in English used by Dutch writers working in multinational corporations*. Amsterdam: Rodopi.

Norris, S. and Jones, R. H. (2005), *Discourse in action. Introducing mediated discourse analysis*. London and New York: Routledge.

Oliveira, M. C. L. (2004), 'Language, technology and modernity: A study of interaction in a call center', in C. Gouveia, C. Silvestre and L. Azuega (eds), *Discourse, Communication and the Enterprise. Linguistic Perspectives*. (Centre for English Studies.) Lisbon: University of Lisbon, pp. 65–78.

Pan, Y., Scollon, S. W. and Scollon, R. (2002), *Professional communication in international settings*. Malden, Massachusetts and Oxford, UK: Blackwell Publishers.

Peng, J. (1987), 'Organizational features in chemical engineering research articles', *ELR Journal*, 1, Birmingham, UK: University of Birmingham, pp. 79–116.

Persson, O., Stern, P. and Gunnarsson, E. (1992), 'Swedish economics on the international scene', in L. Engwall (ed.), *Economics in Sweden. An evaluation of Swedish research in economics*. London and New York: Routledge, pp. 104–126.

Peters, T. J. and Waterman, R. H. (1982), *In search of excellence: Lessons from America's best-run companies*. New York: Harper and Row.

Petersen, M. and Shaw, P. (2002), 'Language and disciplinary differences in a biliterate context', *World Englishes*, 21 (3), 357–374.

Qvortrup, L. (2002), *The hypercomplex society*. New York: P. Lang Publishing Co.

Rossipal, H. (1978), *Funktionale Textanalyse. Denotation und Konnotation als Textwirkungsmittel*. (German department.) Stockholm: Stockholm University.

Salager-Meyer, F. (1994), 'Hedges and textual communicative function in medical English written discourse', *English for Specific Purposes*, 13 (2), 149–170.

Sarangi, S. and Roberts, C., eds (1999), *Talk, work and institutional order. Discourse in medical, mediation and management settings*. Berlin and New York: Mouton de Gruyter.

Schank, R. C. and Abelson, R. P. (1977), 'Scripts, plans and knowledge', in P. N. Johnson-Laird (ed.), *Thinking. Readings in cognitive science*. Hillsdale, New Jersey: Lawrence Erlbaum, pp. 421–432.

Schiffrin. D. (1994), *Approaches to discourse*. Oxford UK, Cambridge USA: Blackwell Publishers.

Schutz, A. and Luckmann, T. (1984), *Strukturell der Lebenswelt*, Bd. 2. Frankfurt/Main: Suhrkamp.

Searle, J. R. (1969), *Speech acts. An essay in the philosophy of language*. London and New York: Cambridge University Press.

Shaw, P. (2004), 'Sentence openings in academic economics articles in English and Danish'. *Nordic Journal of English Studies*, 3 (2), 67–84.

Silva, J. R. G., Oliveira, M. C. L. and Zaltzman, C. (2004), 'Communication with customers and the quality of public services. The case of a Brazilian company', in C. Gouveia, C. Silvestre and L. Azuega (eds), *Discourse, Communication and the Enterprise. Linguistic Perspectives*. (Centre for English Studies.) Lisbon: University of Lisbon, pp. 43–63.

Sörlin, M. (2000), *Skrivande i sex europeiska företag. En studie av professionellt skrivande på banker och ingenjörsbyråer i Sverige, England och Tyskland. Texter i europeiska skrivsamhällen 4*. (TeFa nr 36.) Stockholm: Stockholm University.

Spilich, G. J., Vesonder, G. T., Chiesi, H. L. and Voss, J. F. (1979), 'Text processing of domain-related information for individuals with high and low domain knowledge', *Journal of Verbal Learning and Verbal Behavior*, 18, 275–290.

Swales, J. M. (1981), *Aspects of article introductions*. Birmingham, UK: University of Aston.

—(1990), *Genre analysis. English in academic and research settings*. Cambridge: Cambridge University Press.

—(1998), *Other floors, other voices: a textography of a small university building*. Mahwah, New Jersey: Lawrence Erlbaum.

Swales, J. M. and Rogers, P. S. (1995), 'Discourse and the projection of corporate culture: The mission statement'. *Discourse and Society*, 6 (2), 223–242.

Tannen, D. (2005), 'Interactional sociolinguistics', in U. Ammon, N. Dittmar, K. J. Mattheier and P. Trudgill (eds), *Sociolinguistics: An international handbook of the science of language and society. Second edition*. Berlin: de Gruyter, pp. 76–88.

Tarone, E. (1980), 'Communication strategies, foreigner talk and repair in interlanguage', *Language Learning*, 30 (2), 417–432.

Thorndyke, P. W. (1977), 'Cognitive structures in comprehension and memory of narrative discourse', *Cognitive Psychology*, 9, 77–110.

Valle, E. (1999), *A collective intelligence. The life sciences in the Royal Society as a scientific discourse community 1665–1965*. Anglicana Turkuensia No 17. Turku: University of Turku.

van Dijk, T. A. (1977), 'Context and cognition. Knowledge frames and speech act comprehension', *Journal of Pragmatics*, 1, 211–232.

—(1993), 'Principles of critical discourse analysis', *Discourse and Society*, 4 (2), 249–285.

van Dijk, T. A. and Kintsch, W. (1983), *Strategies of discourse comprehension*. New York: Academic Press.

Voss, J. F., Vesonder, G. T. and Spilich, G. J. (1980), 'Text generation and recall by high-knowledge and low-knowledge individuals', *Journal of Verbal Learning and Verbal Behavior*, 19, 651–667.

Waldinger, R. D. and Lichter, M. I. (2003), *How the other half works: Immigration and the social organization of labor*. Berkeley, California: University of California Press.

Wiberg, M. ed. (2005), *The interaction society. Practice, theories and supportive technologies*. Hershey, London etc: Information Science Publishing.

Wodak, R. and Meyer, M. eds (2001), *Methods of critical discourse analysis*. London: Sage.

Index